for
Dr. Ned Steele
God Bless you!

Dr. James Dantz

If It's In The Bible, It's True!

*The true story of
the love triangle of
James Oral Dorriety,
Vonzeal Davis Dorriety,
and the Lord Jesus Christ*

by Dr. James O. Dorriety

as told to Montez B. Dorriety

Personal Witness Publishing
Atlanta, Georgia
1994

Library of Congress Cataloging-in-Publication Data

This book is printed on acid-free paper which conforms to the
American National Standard Z39.48-1984 *Permanence of
Paper for Printed Library Materials*. Paper that conforms to
this standard's requirements for pH, alkaline reserve and
freedom from groundwood is anticipated to last several
hundred years without significant deterioration under
normal library use and storage conditions.

Manufactured in the United States of America
First Edition
ISBN: 0-87797-260-5
98 97 96 95 94   10 9 8 7 6 5 4 3 2 1
Cover Design by Jeffrey Gray
Distributed by
Cherokee Publishing Company
P.O. Box 1730, Marietta, GA 30061

Dedicated to Vonzeal

For Christmas 1992, she gave me little tape recorder and later she left this little message on the cassette tape.

"Jim says he's ready to start his book. He can't even show me how to turn this recorder on, so how he's going to write a book, I don't know. But he says he is and I believe him, so this afternoon will officially begin his book, the 10th of January, 1993. In just a few days we're going to check back and see how well he's done. This is his wife and loving partner and we will see how it goes."

How could we know that so very soon a single tear of joy would course down her cheek as she entered into the presence of her Lord.

For fifty years of love and companionship, I express my thanks.

Table of Contents

FOREWORD

I can't remember the first time I met Jim Dorriety. That is to his credit. He is the kind of warm, friendly person who gives every indication that you have known him always. Though I can't remember when I met him, I can recall that instantaneously I liked him.

The twinkle in his eye - the good humor - the wonderful smile - all of these things combined to draw me toward him and to let me know that I had a good, lifelong friend.

Through the years we shared our work, our mutual appreciation for humorous stories, and also have shared the joys and sorrows. Always he has done this as a man of strong faith and deep Christian commitment.

You are in for at treat as you read his book and this account of his life and ministry shared so wonderfully by his late wife, Vonzeal. The book will amuse you and serve to increase your faith as you walk with them through their pilgrimage of faith and service as servants of the Lord Jesus Christ.

Dr. James N. Griffith
Former Executive Director and
Treasurer,
Georgia Baptist Convention
Vice-President of Georgia Baptist
Medical Center

PREFACE

Jim Dorriety has been a personal friend through the years. We have worked together, preached together, witnessed together, prayed together, laughed and wept together, and of course, fished together.

It was my privilege to serve as pastor to his dear mother when the Lord called her home. I got to know other members of Jim's family at that time. I thank God for the relationship that the Shannon family has had with the Dorriety family over the years.

Reading this autobiographical account of the life, ministry, and experiences of Jim Dorriety, has been an exciting and even hilarious event! You won't be able to put it down easily. Here is the story of the Grace of God in one man's life. It is thrilling to the maximum degree. You will laugh, perhaps weep, certainly rejoice, and hopefully pray, for renewed guidance for your own life, as you seek to live constantly in the center of God's perfect Will.

Yes, "If it's in the Bible, it's true!" No where is this more graphically illustrated in a personal way than in this thrilling, first-hand story. I thank God for the life and ministry of Jim Dorriety, and encourage you not only to rejoice with us in the recording of these remarkable events, but I encourage you to share this volume with your friends. It will be a blessing to them also.

It has been my opportunity and privilege to see Jim and Vonzeal Dorriety walk through the valleys, but also to stand on the mountain tops. My life has been enriched, my ministry enhanced, and my appreciation for the remarkable, transforming power of the Grace of God greatly strengthened, as a result of these years of personal relationship with my dear friend.

Dr. Harper Shannon
Associate to Executive Secretary
and Director of Evangelism
Alabama Baptist State Convention

ACKNOWLEDGEMENTS

The writing, production and distribution of "IF IT'S IN THE BIBLE, IT'S TRUE" has not been a "one person" accomplishment. The following people have contributed from their own expertise inestimable efforts in this accomplishment.

Mrs. Charles C. Bentley, lovingly known as Jeanne, to others as Ms. B., known by me as the most outstanding and dedicated assistant for more than forty years and five churches; for her hours of proof-reading and prodding my memory for more details.

My sons, Jim and Jerry, for their dedication to their mother during her illness; their continued dedication to me after her homegoing; their individual contribution - Jerry for typesetting, layout and publishing supervision - Jim for his contribution in public relations.

Mable Harris, my cousin, who spent a portion of her life as an English teacher in high school and so lovingly assisted in preparing me for my return to college after I failed, and who so graciously took her time to proof this manuscript.

Montez Dorriety, my daughter-in-law, who took all my stories and factual information and wove them together into this written labor of love.

WITNESS UNTIL JESUS COMES

Portions of the profits from this book will go towards establishing the Vonzeal Dorriety Cooperative Program Endowment Fund for the Georgia Baptist Convention. The Cooperative Program Endowment Fund, written by Dr. Dorriety, provides an opportunity to continue to witness until Jesus comes.

If you wish to contribute a gift or if you need an application or additional information regarding this fund, please contact:

Cooperative Program Endowment Fund
Georgia Baptist Convention
2930 Flowers Road South
Atlanta, Georgia 30341

404/452-8338

INTRODUCTION

I find it an easy assignment to write a good word for a volume about my friends, Jim Dorriety, and his late wife, Vonzeal. We became friends years ago when Jim's chaplaincy ministry brought them to Atlanta and they became members of our church. They were as "at home" in the pew as they were in the pulpit, pastorium and marketplace — always exuding a sweet presence.

When I think of the Dorrietys, I envision two people in love and on a life-long honeymoon — happy, laughing, sharing and encouraging others. Jim's unusual mix of down home wit, sensitive spirit and pleasant personality, makes him an easy person to know. Whether preaching on Easter Sunday morning to a First Church congregation or entertaining a civic group with his humor — it is always person to person, which is communication at its best. He writes the same way.

Vonzeal Dorriety was the epitome of the finest God-given attributes — unexcelled in quiet dignity and a beauty which ran deep. So deep that when I was honored to give her funeral eulogy I spoke to the packed out church on "Living Life Inside Out." She was, indeed, a person whose inner relationship with God was so real, it was reflected in her daily walk and especially in her final journey through the dark valley. Her weeks of illness and consummate death was the finest commentary I have ever seen on the Apostle Paul's good word, "For me to live is Christ, and to die is gain." (Philippians 1:21)

You will have fun with this book — it is about real people. Two people who, by God's grace, knew how to live — and die! I appreciate Jim getting their story into print. Now others can travel along with Jim and Vonzeal — often laughing and sometimes weeping. But never without knowing that in real life there is a time for both.

Have a pleasant journey!

CHARLES Q. CARTER, PASTOR
FIRST BAPTIST CHURCH
JONESBORO, GEORGIA

AN OPENING WORD

My primary purpose in writing this autobiolography is to express my love to Vonzeal who gave up all her personal goals that she might dedicate herself to helping me accomplish our goals together.

So many times when she would encourage me to write my autobiography I would respond, "I would rather hear people say, 'why don't you write a book' than to write one and hear them say, "why did you write a book." She would always respond, as she did through all of our life together, "You can do it!"

It is my desire that everyone who reads this book will receive inspiration to live life to the fullest. Hopefully, my grandchildren Terri, Scott, Trae, Zack and Maggie and other young people will discover my personal formula for success - Have a goal from which to start and keep on going after you start.

Hopefully, middle aged couples will discover the joy and advantages of expressing love to each other.

Hopefully, senior adults will be encouraged to "stay alive" as they live; and to be so completely committed to the Lord Jesus Christ that their Homecoming will be as joyful and inspiring as I anticipate mine to be and as I felt Vonzeal's was.

To God be the Glory, Great things He has done!

James O. Dorriety

THE FAMILY

William Henry Dorriety
married
Nettie Stanaland
on
March 24, 1907

Their children:
Binnie Frank–1908
William Hamilton–1909
Edgar Zimmerman–1911
Allie Mae–1915
Hurlbut Lee–1916
Rena Thelma–1918
Willie Eloyce–1920
Rex Pierce–1922
James Oral–1924
Nellie Ermerlene–1925
Mary Gertrude–1928

James Oral Dorriety
married
Vonzeal Davis
on
October 3, 1942

Their children:
James Oral, Jr.
Jerry Lavon

PROLOGUE

"If it's in the Bible, it's true!"

Where does one begin the story of a lifetime? What are the words that make the foundation of a beginning paragraph? I've heard it said by writers and novelists alike that the beginning words of a book, the very first lines written, can either capture the imagination of the reader or lose his attention.

"If it's in the Bible, it's true!" Those words were spoken by my nineteen year old bride, Vonzeal, after a night of praying and weeping over the most important decision of our young lives. Those words came to mold the very foundation of our lives and indeed set us upon an irrevocable path.

It was in the early spring of 1945. We had been kneeling beside our bed until the wee hours of the morning, reading the Bible and praying for guidance. And in the simple, yet so profound, statement uttered in absolute faith in our Lord, there was a wisdom far beyond her young years.

For that's the statement that led us to dedicate our lives in the service of our Lord.

Chapter 1

1924-1938

───➤◦◄───

The fragrance of sweet warm milk blended with the aroma of fresh straw and cow waste. The morning crickets couldn't be heard over the arguing voices of two young tow-headed boys. It wasn't quite daylight yet, but I was ready to beat the daylights out of my older brother.

"That's not how you do it!"

"Is too!" I insisted, continuing to milk the meanest cow in the herd. You couldn't drive her through a forty foot gate, but she could get her foot stuck in a four pound lard bucket.

"Is not!"

"Is too, you dumb idiot!" I shouted as I jumped off my milking stool almost overturning the fresh pail of milk at my feet. Some of the warm liquid sloshed out onto my shoes. I slung my foot to remove it from the toe but only succeeded in stepping back into a deep cow pie. Mama was going to be upset; she had just finished sewing my shoes a few days ago.

Mama made our field shoes. Using a pattern for the soles, she would cut several layers of a type of hard cloth used for making heavy sacks and stitch them together until she had a very thick sole. Then she would sew the shoe top onto the sole. These shoes were used mainly for working in the fields and could be boiled and hung out on the clothes line to dry. Now this shoe would have to be washed, and it would be several days before it would be dry enough to wear again. Bare-foot again. This made me even madder, and I prepared to fight my sibling. I didn't like to lose an argument.

"You're the dumb idiot. You're just a syrup-sopping baby!" my brother taunted ignoring, my fighting stance as a steady stream of milk whooshed into his pail.

"I am not a baby. I'm eleven years old – I'm growed up! Big enough to milk this dumb old cow and big enough to whop you!" Planting my feet firmly, I let my fists cut the air threateningly around Rex's head. "Get off that stool and I'll show you who's a syrup sopping baby, you stupid—-"

"What is going on in here?" I turned and looked over my shoulder and saw my Papa standing in the doorway of the milk barn. He was only 5'8" tall, but he had a menacing look about him. He shook his head angrily. "What are you two boys fighting over now?" he roared. I assumed a somewhat meeker stance, shuffling a little and trying to look harmless. I didn't want a whipping so early in the morning. Just starts the day off wrong somehow.

"Milking," my brother answered, never missing a squirt into his milk bucket. He had long since figured out that if you're busy working, your chances of getting a licking were smaller.

"Yeah, milking," I agreed somewhat more subdued. "He don't do it right. You're supposed to turn your thumbs under when you milk. He turns his out. You get more milk faster if you turn 'em under." I argued as Papa approached the milk stall. I was already almost as tall as Papa, but he was not someone to cross even with his good-natured personality. Papa demanded respect from his kids and got it. He was a strict disciplinarian, but always fair and righteous, and lived by the Good Book.

Ignoring me, Papa righted my overturned stool and sat down at my milk pail. First he pulled an udder with his thumb turned out, then he pulled with his thumb turned in. "It don't make no difference. It still takes the same amount of time. If you boys really want to see how to milk a cow, how'd you like to hop in the truck and go over to Dothan to Hall's Dairy this morning after chores. I hear they installed brand new milking machines after the county got electricity." He finished milking my cow and stood up, slapping his hands together "Wouldn't mind seeing that myself."

"Yeah," I answered, my eyes wide, "and I'll bet you my supper's slice of pie that those electric hands got the thumbs turned under."

"Deal" my big brother sneered, just as his cow slapped him in the face with her wet tail. A delicious delight of childish vengeance flew over me as I watched Rex sputter and wipe the urine from his eyes.

Later that morning we went into the barn at Hall's Dairy and saw a man grab a suction cup and start to attach it to the first cow. My brother jabbed me in the ribs and said, "Look there, he's gonna jump start that Holstein."

"Naw," I joked, "she thinks she's about to get a permanent wave."

Papa laughed. "I guess you boys can eat your own pie tonight at suppertime."

Our last name is Irish and has many different spellings. My forefathers spelled it O'Doherty; one of them changed the spelling and dropped the O' to Americanize it. When I was born April 16, 1924, Mama named me James Oral Dorriety. By the time I came along my parents were starting to run out of names for the new babies. One day the older children came in from school and tossed their workbooks on the table. Mama noticed the Oral and Written English text book lying on top and liked the name. So I was named Oral for a grammar school textbook. It was fourteen years before I began using my first name, James.

We lived in Slocomb, a small town in the southern part of Alabama noted mostly for its lumber mill. Well, actually, we didn't live right in Slocomb – you turn right at Slocomb and go way out to the cross roads...we didn't live right at the cross roads either...you had to turn right again and go way on down the road as far as you could go. We had a big house with a breeze-way (called a dog-trot) right through the middle. We needed a big house, because there was Mama, Papa and their eleven children and, many times, my grandfather – fourteen in all. It was a really big family and I happened to be number nine and the youngest son in the family.

Mama always said she was glad she got all her children grown before germs were discovered. We didn't know what cholesterol was then either. If we'd had some, we would have fried it in lard and eaten it. And, yes, we were syrup soppers.

Papa would always tell us stories during our "fun time." One he told over and over was about when he was courting Mama. He had just reached manhood and had gotten a new horse of his own. At the turn of the century, young people anticipated getting a horse and buggy the way young people today anticipate getting their driver's license. Sunday morning he took his new horse to Church.

It was traditional courting procedure that after the sermon all the girls would go for a ride with their beaus. The young ladies were always dressed in their finest Sunday dresses with big wide hoop skirts. Modesty and necessity would require that they mount the horses from a mounting block. The boys would lead the horses up beside the block and the girls would walk up the steps of the mounting block and sit down on the horse side-saddle. Then the boy would mount his own horse and off they'd ride together.

Papa was always in a hurry, and one Sunday morning there was an unusually long line for the mounting block. All the fellows were lined up waiting to bring their horses around. But Papa wanted to get out of there fast so he came over beside Mama's horse, put his hands on the ground, lacing the fingers of both hands together and said, "Nettie, step here into my hands. Just turn your back to the horse and put your foot here into my hands and I'll lift you up." So, she did. She backed up to her horse and put one foot into his hands and he started trying to lift her – but couldn't budge her. Mama just stood there and waited until Papa finally had to ask her to step off his hands.

Years later they would laugh about how embarrassed he was to have to ask her to get off his hands. Papa was a small man, weighing about one hundred fifty-five pounds and standing only 5'8". Mama, on the other hand, was a large, beautifully shaped woman about 6' tall weighing about 185 pounds. She had a brother, Willy, who was 7'2". No wonder Papa couldn't lift her. She came from a family of giants!

Another courting story he told us during "fun time" was about his horse, Closer. Sometime soon after the mounting block incident, he got his first buggy. He hitched his new horse, Closer, to the buggy and went to pick up Mama and she bragged on his new red horse. He told her the horse's name was "Dan." He took the lines and said, "Get up, Closer," and she moved over a little bit. "Come up, Closer" and she moved a little bit more, and before they got a quarter of a mile away from her house, he had her almost sitting in his lap.

We didn't have television, so story time was a big part of our entertainment. And we'd all laugh and laugh at Papa's antics.

When I was six years old, I stole a nickel from Mama. She always kept the money for the ice man in a bowl on the kitchen table. A block of ice cost thirty-five cents for one hundred pounds. The ice man would drive up in his huge truck, bring the ice inside and take his coins from the bowl there on the table.

The rolling store, a big enclosed truck with an entire store built inside, traveled throughout the countryside twice a week. Folks could walk down to the crossroads and shop for clothes, tools, kitchen utensils and candy right there on the side of the road.

One day I sneaked into the kitchen, and when Mama was busy at the stove, I reached inside and took a nickel from the bowl containing the ice money. I stuffed it in my pocket and went on my merry way, planning to run down to the crossroads when the rolling store came and get myself some candy.

Just a few minutes later, the ice man pulled into our road. He got out, greeted me, unloaded the ice and carried it on up the porch and inside the kitchen. I followed along behind him with that little nickel burning the pocket of my overalls.

"Morning, Nettie. Got your ice here." He bent to open the icebox door. "How's that little Nellie Ermilene this morning?" He grinned at my younger sister who was playing on the floor in the kitchen.

Mama was preoccupied cooking at the stove with Mary Gertrude, the youngest (and last) addition to our family, on one hip.

"It's good to see you, Jack. With this hot spell we're having, we're all out of ice. My hands are full right now, but you know where the money is." She nodded towards the bowl on the table, and I almost died.

"Yes, ma'am." He reached into the bowl and pulled out the coins. "I'll collect the rest next week."

Mama glanced up from her pot of turnips, confused. "Isn't there enough in there to pay for the ice?"

Jack looked at the two coins in his hand, "Got a quarter and a nickel here."

"Oh, no. There's two nickels in the bowl. I put them there myself." She frowned.

My heart began to pound violently and suddenly the missing nickel in my pocket felt as heavy as a plow. Rushing outside, I threw the nickel into the dirt at the foot of the porch steps. "Mama, here it is. I found it."

Jack and Mama came out onto the porch and looked down at the nickel on the ground. Relieved she smiled, "Oh, Jack you musta dropped one."

"No, ma'am." He shook his head emphatically. "I haven't been out here since I brought the ice inside."

"Well, I'm just glad Oral found it." She gave me a knowing look.

After Jack drove off, she pulled me onto her lap. "Oral, I'm so proud of you for finding the nickel. Just think if Papa had come from the field and there wasn't any ice for his tea. You are my little hero!" She bragged and bragged on me, and the more she bragged the worse I felt. I wanted to confess and take my whipping, but didn't have the courage to do so. "I've got a peach cobbler in the oven, let's you and me go test it."

Years later, I confessed. Mama laughed, "Oral, I knew what had happened all along."

"Well, why didn't you whip me?"

"I think I did," she laughed.

And she had, because her praise stung much worse than any belt ever could have.

Cucumbers were our early spring crop and afforded Papa the funds to purchase the feed and fertilizer he needed for the coming months. There was a processing vat in Slocomb that pickled cucumbers. Rex and I, ages twelve and ten respectively, were too young to work the hard labor in the fields, so Papa entrusted us with the task of hitching our two old mules, Gray and Pet, to the big wagon and taking the cucumbers into Slocomb to sell. It was a three hour round trip.

At the pickling vats, Rex and I would stand around and watch the workers culling out the best cucumbers. Then we would collect Papa's money for the good cucumbers and load the culls back onto our wagon to feed to the hogs later. Nothing was ever wasted. Occasionally we would go to the feed store and load the wagon with fertilizer or feed for Papa.

One morning as we were returning home, Rex and I, as young boys are prone to do, became bored and began throwing the culls at the mules' ears to see if we could hit them. Some of the cucumbers were round like baseballs and were perfect for throwing. We had a great contest going when, suddenly, one of the culls hit Gray's erect little ear and stuck inside. As Gray started slinging her head and trying to reach her ear with her foot, she spooked Pet, and they began to run away. The acceleration slung us backwards in the wagon seat.

"Tarnation!" screamed Rex as he tried to control the reins.

"Do something!" I yelled at him, my teeth shattering together with each wagon bounce.

"Whoa, Gray! Whoa! Whoa Pet! I can't stop them!"

he yelled above the noise of the bouncing wagon.

"You better do something or they're gonna kill us!" I screamed. Rex was older; this was his responsibility, not mine. I was just a kid.

They tore down the road and up and over several hills, Gray still slinging her head wildly. The harness was getting tangled, and Rex and I were holding on for our lives. When mules start running away, there's no way you can stop them. Rex guided them and just barely held them in the road until we got to the bottom of a hill where there was nothing but deep sand. They began to slow. They had worn themselves out and somehow, in the process, Gray had gotten the cucumber cull out of her ear.

Rex and I looked at each other and looked at those hot, lathering mules. "We're dead. Papa's gonna kill us" Rex said, dragging out the word 'us', but I wasn't buying it. If Papa was handing out a whopping, I was looking for an older brother to blame.

"You're the one that's dead. It was your cucumber that got stuck in his ear."

"Don't matter. You're dead right along with me. Just cuz my cull stuck in his ear don't mean you're not guilty as me."

I saw the wisdom of his words and didn't argue anymore. We became consumed with figuring out a way that Papa would never know what we had done.

So we took our time the rest of the way home, stopping along the way to let the mules rest. Our two young minds went through the entire scenario. If, as soon as we got home, we quickly brushed them with the curry comb and turned them loose in the pasture, maybe Papa would never notice.

Our tactics worked because Papa, always busy with some farming concern, never knew about the runaway wagon, and we never again threw cucumbers at the mules' ears.

For years we had to shell corn by hand, but we learned if we took one cob and rubbed it against another cob we could shell the corn without too much wear and tear on our hands. A little later on, Papa got a corn sheller which was turned by hand. He put it out behind the barn.

Papa would shuck the ears, inspect them, and we boys would do the shelling. The very best was used for meal, and Papa would sack the shelled corn and throw it across the shoulders of the mule. I would take it to the mill for grinding. "Tell Mr. Kilpatrick to put half in meal and half in mush." The mush was ground fairly coarse, and Mama would cook it into what we call "grits" today. A big bowl of hot mush on a winter's morning prepared us for all the rest of the day.

Every Christmas instead of hanging stockings, we left our chairs set up around the fireplace – eleven chairs lined up for Santa Claus. Every Christmas morning we would rush to our chair to find what Santa had left us. We'd find a couple of apples, an orange, bananas and grapes – very special treats because we didn't get these fruits often during the year. Also, there in the seat of our chair, would be one special item. For the girls, this item was usually a doll.

One year all the boys got a small harmonica (you could buy one for a dime then). Another year we all got a little knife on a chain that would hook on our overalls and drop into our pockets. As Rex and I got older, we would find firecrackers in our chair. And, with the supervision of Papa and our older brothers, we'd shoot them off – usually just one at a time so as not to waste them. We especially enjoyed putting a firecracker inside a tin can, lighting it and standing back to hear and watch the loud explosion.

Cutting the tree was always a big affair with the whole horde of us tromping off into the woods to find and select the very best tree. Of course, the oldest children always had the most "say-so." Sometimes our tree was cedar, sometimes pine. But many times it was holly with the red berries already on it. We'd chop down a big holly tree and take only the top of it for our Christmas tree. Mama would use some of the rest of the holly to decorate our house.

We always had a beautiful Christmas tree and made our own decorations. During the year we would save the silver aluminum lining from cigarette packs and chewing gum. Goldtip Chewing gum came in a box about two inch square and held ten sticks of gum, each wrapped in tin foil. All during the year we saved that tin foil, and if we saw a box lying on the sidewalk, we would pick it up to carry home to Mama for safe keeping. During the Christmas holidays she would bring out the box containing the tin foil and we would carefully cut it into strips and tie them together to use as tinsel for the tree. Another use we found for the tin foil was folding the little squares around sticky sycamore tree balls and hanging them on the tree. Colored corn or Indian Corn was cut into little round circles right through the cob and wired to hang on the tree. We popped corn, and the girls threaded it into tremendous strands of popcorn. To our childlike eyes, it was the most gorgeous tree on earth.

Down in South Alabama there were great trees filled with mistletoe, and the older boys would take their rifles and shoot the upper branches off the trees and gather the clusters of green sprigs for Mama. She hung it in almost every doorway, and we younger boys would rush under each archway lest the sisters catch us and kiss us. There was always a lot of noise and activity going on in the Dorriety household.

Mama saved sugar during the year in a special five-gallon lard can to be used only at Christmas time. Every time she bought sugar, she put a couple of cups of it into the can. It was her sugar savings account. By the time the holidays arrived, she was ready to bake cakes and make candy, and she made this time of year so very special for all of her family. She was an easygoing, fun-loving mother, but I guess with so many kids, she had to be.

We had a tremendous family Bible from which Mama read to us. It measured twelve by sixteen and must have easily weighed six pounds. It had a hard black thick cover with the words Holy Bible written in scroll on the front. It was too heavy for us to hold, so Mama placed it on the floor and let us look at the beautiful pictures. There was a colored picture of Moses and many other black and white pictures. In the front of the Bible were several Bible stories for children. One of my favorites was "Our First Parents" written about the Garden of Eden.

We never knew we were poor. We had such good times, family gatherings, story time, family sings. Papa would anticipate a sing. "Boys, Uncle Acie and Aunt Bertha and their children are coming and we're going to have a family sing Saturday night when they get here. Get your voices ready." My oldest sister played our old organ, and Papa wanted us to sing "parts." Grandpa Dorriety was always there and he wanted us to sing his favorite song:

> *"This world Is not my home, I'm just a-passing thru,*
> *My treasures are all laid up, Somewhere beyond*
>   *the blue.*
> *The angels beckon me, To Heaven's open door*
> *And I can't feel at home, In this world anymore."*

Rex was nine months old when Mama became pregnant with me and being so close to the same age, we fought a lot as children. After one particularly loud argument, Mama called us both to her side and insisted we kiss one another on the lips and make up. Grudgingly, we puckered and touched each others lips ever so briefly, spitting and wiping afterwards.

Later that day out behind the barn, we had a knockdown drag-out fight. We were both disgusted because Mama had made us kiss on the lips, and Rex accused me of kissing him with too much feeling, and I insisted he was the one who kissed me with too much passion. We didn't want anyone to accuse us of being "sissy."

The first night we got rural electricity, we younguns went around with our hands over our eyes. We thought those lights were blinding us. Rightfully so for there were fifteen-watt bulbs in those sockets!

Papa permitted no grass to grow in our yard. We had no lawn. The ground was clean swept, sandy and hard. If a leaf fell or a blade of grass dared try to grow, it was pulled up and swept away. My younger sisters, Mary and Nell, loved to "play house" by drawing the outlines of houses on the ground of the yard. They would take a stick and drag it across the dirt to form the 'walls' of their houses. Inside this outline, they drew rooms. Outside there would be a road between the houses. Then they would 'go visit' each other carrying their dolls along.

They always begged me to play with them, but I refused to play house and dolls. That was for girls. However, I didn't want to be left out of the game so I devised my own game "Playing Church!" At the top end of their street, I drew out a church on the ground. I used a big block of wood from the woodpile for the pulpit and scraped the ground to form an aisle down the center. Grandpa Dorriety gave me a small red pamphlet on the Gospel of John, and I memorized most of it.

"Okay, let's play church. Who's going to join the church today?" I'd ask my little sisters.

Nell piped up, "Let Mary, she cries the best."

"Okay, everybody go home so I can come visiting." I'd order and they would scramble to their houses. I would pick up my little pamphlet and smooth down my hair and 'go out into the community.'

I stepped up to Mary's house and knocked on the imaginary door.

"Hello, Brother Oral," she greeted. "Come in."

"Hello, Sister Mary," I returned, with all the dignity an eight year old could muster. "I'm visiting the community today." I would step over the line into the house. "I do hope you and your family can come to church on Sunday."

"Oh, yes. We'll be there."

"Good, well – see you then." I'd wave goodbye and go across the 'road' to the next house and knock.

"Hello, Sister Nell. How's the little one today?" I'd lean over and pat her doll on the head.

"Just fine, Brother Oral. Want some tea?"

"No, I must be going. I've got lots of folks to see today. I'll see you at church on Sunday." I'd walk pompously out the door, one arm holding the pamphlet close to my chest.

"Thanks for coming. Bye-bye." Nell waved from her doorway.

Sometimes the neighbor's children would join us in play, and I would have several families to visit. After all the visitation was complete, I'd walk up to the end of the street and into my 'church.'

Soon the 'congregation' would arrive, and I would step up onto my pulpit and begin to preach the Gospel of John from my little red pamphlet.

"In the beginning was the Word, and the Word was

with God and the Word was God." I would shout in my little voice.

"Amen!" shouted five year old Nell.

"Hallelujah!" shouted four year old Mary.

"The same was in the beginning with God. All things were made by Him," I continued. "There was a name sent from God whose name was John the Baptist!"

"Hallelujah!" shouted Nell.

"Amen!" shouted Mary.

"Let's sing 'Just As I Am'," I'd say. We always sang that particular song because it was the only one we knew all the words to.

> *"Just as I am without one plea*
> *but that thy blood was shed for me. . ."*

Our little voices would get louder and louder.

> *"And that thou bidd'st me come to Thee,*
> *O Lamb of God I Come. I Come."*

Mary, who could cry real tears, would slowly come down the 'aisle' to join the church. And she would start to cry and fall down on the floor.

"Praise the Lord!" Nell would shout and raise her hands up to the sky, her little doll dangling limply in the air.

"Let's pray. God, thank you for bringing Sister Mary to us today to be saved. Amen." I'd finish; then we'd all go congratulate Mary. Then I'd run to the church door and shake hands as everyone went back home.

This game would consume us for hours, and we played it again and again – singing, praying and playing church. For a couple of years it was our favorite game.

Papa was a sharecropper and we never owned any land of our own. But he was a good farmer who never raped the land but instead improved it constantly. He kept the fence jams cleaned out and built new terraces to protect the land from erosion, and every winter he would clear and take in a few new acres of farmland which provided new fields of the richest soil, requiring little or no fertilizer. He owned his mule teams, plow tools and cattle. This allowed him to rent his land outright (a term called standing rent) instead of renting "on halves." The landowner provided all the mules and fertilizer but split the profits. Industrious and ambitious, he negotiated a yearly flat rate for the rental of the land.

Our best crops were corn, cucumbers, cotton, soybeans and, oh yes, sugar cane. We had a cane mill where we extracted the juice from the stalks. There were big rollers which sat on a pedestal and a huge lever that went across the top, higher on one end, so we could hitch a mule to it. The mule would walk round and round turning the cogs all day long.

On the inside of the track, we placed a big pile of cane and then poked the stalks between the rollers. This process squeezed out the juice. From there the juice would run and into a barrel. I'd stand there and feed four or five stalks of cane in, and as the rollers turned, the juice squirted onto my face and clothes. In the process of a day's work my clothes would get completely saturated with the juice and stiffen as they dried. My face would be covered with cane juice; I could lick my lips and taste that sweet sticky sap.

From the sugar cane, Papa made syrup so thick and heavy that on a cold morning it would fold on a plate like a blanket. He'd fire up the pans because the longer it cooked the thicker it got. As it cooked, the impurities would come to the top and we'd skim off the foam. The honey bees loved to swarm around the vats, and sometimes they'd get so excited they'd just drop into the large boiler and we'd skim them out of the vat, too.

Later on we were able to afford an evaporation pan with partitions in it. As the juice would cook through the divisions, we could cut off each partition and skim off the impurities, then open the gap and let the liquid run into the next partition.

My mama made heavy biscuits; you know the cat-head type biscuit – the large biscuits, the kind you could lay on the opposite side of a plate full of thick syrup and pull all the way through and have it hold on. Papa always referred to Mama as his "dough beater." Honestly, her biscuits could wipe a clean place right through the center of the syrup. Now you try to do that with these modern biscuits today, the kind you beat over the side of the counter to get out, and see what happens.

We had a bad habit of sopping the plates off the table and breaking them. You get thick syrup and tough biscuits, and you can break a lot of plates. To solve the problem of broken plates, Papa threatened to nail tin plates to our table with twenty penny nails. But we just laughed and said we could sop the heads off those nails too.

Sometimes today I am introduced by what is now my official title – *"The Syrup Sopping Servant From Slocomb."*

There were three black families living on the farm who helped Papa with the farming. One of those families, the Hatleys, became dear friends of mine when I was about nine years old. John Hatley had the largest biceps I'd ever seen, and he was easy-going and always cutting up with me. I always wanted to be around John because he was always funning and I was just a little cut-up myself, always looking for mischief.

Mary, John's wife, helped Mama with the washing and cooking. In the fall when we'd pick the cotton, there would be about fifty field hands to feed at the noon meal. Mama would go out in the yard with an apron full of corn and begin scattering it for the chickens. As they gathered around her feet to eat, she would reach down and grab one, sling his head off, toss him over her shoulder and pick out the next victim. After they stopped flopping, she scalded the feathers off and got the chickens ready to cook. Sometimes we had five or six hens cooking in the big black iron pot outside. Then she and Mary would roll hundreds of dumplings. The meal consisted of chicken and dumplings, turnips, cornbread and sliced tomatoes. Mama had a number two washtub which she used only for making iced tea for these large meals.

John and Mary had two children, and I was vaguely aware that she was expecting another child, but at nine years old, I didn't give it a lot of thought. That is I didn't until the morning John came to the house very early, and asked Papa if he could borrow Papa's truck. "The baby was born last night, but didn't live long. Can I borrow the truck to carry the body to the cemetery? I already made the pine casket and everything's ready."

Papa assured him that he could borrow the truck, and I asked Papa if I could go with him. John turned his sorrowful eyes to Papa, "Sure, it's okay by me. He can help me dig the grave." So I went with John to his house. Mary was crying, but it didn't bother me much because I really didn't understand what was going on. John and I took the box and put it on the seat between us in the truck and drove out to the cemetery. We had two shovels, and together we dug the grave in silence until John got it just like he wanted. Then he went to the truck and got the box which contained the body of the baby and, while I knelt on the opposite side of the grave, he gently lowered the box into the hole with his giant arms and huge muscles. Lovingly and cautiously he placed the casket in the bottom of that hole; then as he brought his arms up out of the hole, they continued to go up and he lifted them up to the sky. Offering his baby to the Lord, his eyes, like pools of water, burst into tears; huge tears rolling down his black face. He never said anything, just continued to kneel there with arms lifted to the heavens. Then he bowed his head for a moment as if to pray. We got up and shoveled the dirt back into that small hole. Nothing was said.

That image of burying that infant has always stayed with me.

I visited John Hatley in 1985 and invited Norman Alexander, a deacon at First Baptist Church of Blakely, Georgia and clerk of the Superior court, to go with me. Mary had died and John was just a shadow of his original self with hair as white as snow. We had such a wonderful reunion, visiting and weeping together. As I drove away from this visit, I looked back in the rear view mirror and saw him standing in the road with his arms once again lifted up to the heavens. John was a witness to me, and I have used the memory of his simple, pure faith many time to witness to others.

One day my older brothers, Frank, Edgar and W.H., were heading into town with the wagon. I wanted to go with them and began running behind the wagon with my arms stuck up in the air, screaming, "Let me go, too! Let me go, too!"

Papa cried out to them "Take that boy with you!"

Frank, my oldest brother, reached over as he stood up in the moving wagon, grabbed my arms and picked me up to bring me over the top of the wagon. He raised me to about his shoulder height ready to heave me into the wagon, but the perspiration on my hands from the exertion of running created an unhealthy environment between our clasped hands. I started to slip from his grasp. He dropped me and I fell, hitting flat on my stomach. It knocked the breath out of me, and by the time I revived my family was all around me thinking I had been killed. That evening I got special attention at the supper table and I milked the situation for all it was worth.

In 1931 we had a Model T Ford, in addition to a surrey, wagon and buggy. There were too many of us to go in the car and on trips we divided up. Some of us went on one trip, some the next. Mama always prepared a big picnic meal of fried chicken, ham, biscuits, syrup and syrup lids for sopping syrup. We always had plenty of food, and tied it onto the outside of the car. Sometimes we covered sixty-five or seventy miles in a day. Usually when we'd stop to eat, we would have a real picnic time beside a creek somewhere.

The gasoline in the Model T was gravity fed into the motor from the tank which sat in front of the windshield. When the gas got too low, it wouldn't fall into the carburetor and sometimes we would have to turn around and back up a hill, turn around at the top, drive into the valley, turn and back up the next hill. That was just a little flaw that Mr. Ford finally corrected.

During the time I was growing up, my older brother, Edgar, was usually the official driver. He always put me inside the car to manage the spark and gasoline, two levers, one on either side beneath the steering wheel. He gave me instructions to hold the gasoline lever at one position and the spark lever at another position while he got out and, with the front end of the crank, turned the motor to start it. At that moment, I was to give it more gas and less spark. Of course, being a seven year old boy, I felt that I knew something about automobiles since I had helped him crank it on many occasions. On one such occasion, I gave it too much spark and not enough gas. As he twisted the crank with his right hand locked over the handle, the motor backfired which reversed the flow of the crank, causing it to hit his wrist. He came around from the front of the automobile with his right hand stretched out – the back of his hand lying back upon his arm with his palm sticking straight up. He said, "Look!"

I thought that was so interesting and said, "How in the world did ya do that?"

"It's broken!" he shrieked through clenched teeth, pure terror in his face. "Run get Mama and Papa."

I scrambled from behind the steering column and hustled across the road shouting, "Edgar's hand's laying back up over his arm. Come look!"

Mama ran over and, with the older brothers holding him, grabbed Edgar's arm.

"Son, I know this is going to hurt, but I've got to straighten this arm out." She took both of her strong hands and yanked his wrist right back into place while Edgar screamed at the top of his lungs. She ordered the older boys to run to the clay bank and dig a bucket of clay, and, swiftly and expertly, she began to sift and knead the clay like dough, adding turpentine and molding a cast onto his arm. She then sat with a kerosene lamp and held Edgar's arm over the chimney of the lamp, drying the clay cast until it was completely hard. He was never taken to the doctor, but his arm came out just fine except for a knot on the side of his wrist.

He called it his Mama Knot.

Mama Knot – Mama not only was our doctor, our barber, our cook, our shoemaker, our seamstress – whatever the needs – she was always there to take care of us.

We were an energetic bunch of kids always busy with some sort of fun activity. One of the boys' favorite sports was bull-riding which usually took place on Sunday afternoons. Papa never worried about our being around the animals, and he didn't mind if we broke a bull for riding – that was all right with him. We had one bull we were having a particularly hard time breaking, so a crowd of neighbor boys came from church one Sunday afternoon with the express purpose of breaking this bull. In our efforts to catch the wild animal, we hemmed him up and got him into a corner of the lot where there was a storage shed. The shed held all the plow tools, and, of course, all the plows had hard hickory handles on them.

This bull was so wild and scared, he panicked and made a lunge to escape us, but one of the sharp ends of the plow handle hit him in the side behind his ribs and punctured his hide all the way through to his stomach. Papa came out and investigated, then sent for some of the neighbors to help him slaughter this bull. There were no professional slaughter houses to butcher the dead animal, but we didn't want to waste the beef. I remember Papa and the neighbors saying, "yes, it's all right to do this on Sunday," because the Bible says in Luke 14:1-6, "It came to pass as He came into the house of one of the chief Pharisees on the Sabbath day that they watched Him. And, behold, there was a certain man before Him that had the dropsy. Jesus answering spake unto the lawyers and Pharisees, saying, 'Is it lawful to heal on the Sabbath day?' And they held their peace. And He took him, and healed him and let him go; and answered them saying, 'Which of you shall have an ass or an ox fallen into a pit and will not straightway pull him out on the Sabbath day?' And they could not answer Him again to these things."

There was no refrigeration to keep the meat so it had to be used all at one time. The beef was divided among all the neighbors, and for several days the whole community had beef to eat.

We cured our hams in a salt box. Papa had a giant wooden box where, in the fall, he poured a layer of salt on the bottom, topped with a layer of ham, another layer of salt, a layer of sides (the bacon part) and finish with a top layer of salt. For six weeks the salt would purify the meat, removing the juice. We could check on the progress by looking at the "salt line" as the meat began to shrink. After the six weeks period, the meat was removed and hung in the smoke house. We filled that little house with hickory smoke from coals from a fire outside. For days we'd keep that little building filled with hickory smoke. When all the juices were gone, we had country cured ham.

Then bad things began to happen to the economy back in the late twenties and early thirties – something known as the "days of the depression." Something called a "stock market" crashed, and at first I thought the men on the radio were talking about cattle. Times were really rough for us country folks because all we had to eat was country ham, red-eye gravy, thick syrup and hot biscuits with cow butter. We didn't have pop-tarts or frosted flakes. We didn't have the finer things of life like light-bread.

Unfortunately, as the economic depression deepened, factories began to close; farm prices sank and finally the banks began to fail. The times were really hard for most, and it got pretty rough at our house. Papa's health had begun to fail, and the doctor bills wrecked our already strained economy. In 1932, Franklin Roosevelt was elected President and immediately after his inauguration he initiated the program known as "the New Deal." But it was still several years before the fear of starvation subsided for many.

When I was nine, almost ten, I mischievously found myself under the bed in the front room when my sixteen year old sister's boyfriend proposed to her. The front room was similar to a living room with table and flowers and rocking chairs, but no couch. Mama would never permit a couch in the front room because the boys and girls courting were required to sit in individual chairs. There was, however, a bed in that room (a paradox, yes, but with eleven children we needed a bed in every room), and I "happened" to be under that bed the day Willie Dee proposed to my sister, Rena. I tried not to snicker as I eavesdropped on the plans for their wedding. He was planning to go to Geneva, Alabama to purchase the marriage license since he was going in that direction anyway.

Rena said, "Are you sure we shouldn't wait on the license? What if I back out before time for us to be married?"

He immediately answered, "You're not supposed to back out!"

About the time that Rena had Willie D. really sweating over the possibility that she might not marry him after all, I found what I thought was a perfect opportunity to make my escape. This was juicy gossip, and I couldn't wait to announce it to the world. I scooted out from under the bed in one quick agile movement and made a dash for the door. Caught off guard by the unexpected sight of me, Willie D. still managed to lunge, trapping me before I could escape from the room.

"Just what do you think you're doing, brat?" he asked, grabbing me up with both legs kicking. "Where'd you come from?"

"Spying on us as usual," Rena sighed.

"I'm going to tell, I'm going to tell," I taunted furiously trying to squirm away from him.

Rena said, "Ssh...Oral. Listen to me. Don't tell Mama and Papa. We're not ready for anybody to know."

In a little sing-song voice, I sang, "Rena loves Willie Dee-e."

Willie D. placed my feet back on the floor, and Rena knelt to reason with me. "Oral, please don't tell. If you promise not to tell Mama, I'll be extra good to you. Please." They bribed me into keeping the secret, and from then until the date of their marriage, they were very good to me and I played it to the hilt. Rena had to do a lot of extra work for me, including sweeping the yard and doing my other chores.

This was about the same time that Rex and I decided to go chicken-fishing. We'd been down on the creek with our cane poles catching blue gills. We thought we were the world's best fishermen. We strutted back into our yard with our little cane poles over our shoulders, and Rex said, "Hey, I'll bet we could even catch catfish next time."

Never at a loss for words no matter how dumb, I spouted off "Or even that old cat over there." I pointed in the general direction of the sleeping tom cat in a corner of the yard.

About that time a chicken walked across our path. We looked at each other and cried, "Or a chicken!"

"Let's go chicken-fishing," Rex suggested.

"Yeah-boy. Let's do," I agreed.

We got out on the porch with some corn and our poles with the hooks on them and decided we'd do some chicken-fishing. We baited the hooks with the corn and sat back on the porch and dangled the fishing poles out over the edge of the porch waiting for some of the chickens strutting by to become enticed by the corn. Hardly a moment passed before we each simultaneously caught a chicken. Of course, we had not really expected to catch one, nor had we anticipated what would happen if we caught one, much less two. Immediately, the most horrible screaming you've ever heard came from the chickens. Feathers started flying. We glanced at each other in fright; we could not pull them up and, we could not let them go.

"What do we do now?" I screeched excitedly over the squawking.

"Oh! Oh! Oh!" was all Rex could yell. His chicken was dancing on the end of his line, and he was clutching his pole in a death grip.

"Should I turn him loose?" I asked, beginning to laugh at the hilarity of the situation.

Finally, there was so much noise that Mama and Papa came running into the yard. Papa summed up the situation in a flash and began trying to catch the line of my pole and work his way down to the chicken. Mama tried to grab the other chicken on Rex's pole but couldn't catch the frantic fowl.

Finally Papa was able to lay hands on my prancing poultry and took its head clean off. Ditto for Rex's catch of the day. My wide grin dissolved when I saw the thunderous look on Papa's face as he turned towards us boys. "I oughta wring your necks, too!" was all he said before stomping back into the house, leaving the two headless chickens flopping around for Mama to dress.

Those who were home for dinner that night, not including Rex and me, had fried chicken. We were exiled to our room, but we could hear our older brothers and sisters cackling with laughter around the kitchen table.

We never ever wanted to go chicken-fishing again.

In the spring of 1935, one of my older brothers, Hurlbut, turned eighteen years old. Broad in the shoulders and tall, Hurlbut had thick brown hair worn a little long and slicked-back. His blue eyes crinkled when he laughed, which he did a lot and I thought he looked just like a movie star. He was my hero and I admired him, emulating everything he did. It even appeared he might become a minister, for even at his young age, he studied the Bible and taught a portion of the men's Bible class at church.

Papa asked Hurlbut to take me to the field with him and teach me how to break in fresh mules. Since I was too small to handle a plow, Papa put extra lines on the mules and instructed me to walk beside Hurlbut and the plow. When my brother said, "GEE," I snatched the right line, and when he said, "HAW," I snatched the left line. This was the training process for the mules until they learned the vocal signals. It was also a training process for me.

One afternoon we were plowing with a heavy steel-beam plow, breaking up fairly new ground in a young field. In the process of plowing, the plow point hit a root under the ground, snagging it and forcing the plow handle sideways and catching Hurlbut in his right side. It was a tremendous blow, and he doubled to the ground writhing in pain.

"WHOA!!!" I screamed at the two old mules. Dropping the lines, I rushed back to my brother's side.

"Hurlbut! Are you all right?" I tried to help him to his feet, but he pushed me away, clutching his right side as he gasped for breath. "Want me to go get Mama?" I suggested almost hysterically. "Hurlbut, answer me!"

"—Nooo—" he whispered, barely able to get the word out of his mouth. His face was contorted in pain, and as I felt the panic rise, I thought he must really be hurt. The only thing I knew to do was go get help, but he didn't act as though he wanted that. I shielded my eyes with my hand from the bright sunlight and looked back across the field, searching for a family member, but no one was in sight. Helplessly I stood in the big clods of dirt, arms and legs akimbo, wanting so desperately to help my big brother but not knowing what to do.

For what seemed like hours, I watched him writhe in pain, but in reality it was probably no more than ten minutes. Finally the pain lessened a bit, and he said, "I'll be okay. I just need to wait until the pain goes away." His breathing was very shallow and his face was very pale.

"Hurlbut, I think I should go get Papa now, don't you?" I begged.

"No, it's not serious. That plow handle just caught me in the side. I'm feeling better already. See if you can help me up."

He grimaced as I leaned over to support him as he rose to his feet. When he was finally able to stand straight, he said, "Let's just get a couple more rows plowed and quit for the day."

"Okay." I brightened. That sounded great to me. I'd go fishing.

"Oral, don't tell Mama about this," he cautioned as he slowly took his place once again behind the plow as I picked up the mules' reins.

"Why not?" It didn't seem so bad anymore. I didn't see that it needed to be a secret. It was just an accident.

"Cause if we tell her, she'll get alarmed and won't let me go to the country party tonight, that's why," he reasoned. "GET UP!" he yelled to the mules. A country party was an opportunity for young adolescents to get together and have candy pullings, cake walks, box suppers, dancing and music. And, of course, to see their sweethearts.

"Hurlbut, are you sure you're okay?" As an alert eleven year old with ten brothers and sisters, I had learned that if we were keeping something from Mama, there was always a reason. This didn't seem like a big deal anymore – not now that he was up and feeling fine again. So why did he want to keep it from Mama?

"Just don't tell her and then she won't have any reason not to let me go to the party."

"HAW!" he yelled at the mules, and I yanked the left rein.

"But what if she finds out we lied to her?"

"We're not lying to her. We're just not telling her something."

"If something happens and you get sick again, won't I get into trouble? You know . . . cause I knew about it . . . you know . . ." I fumbled for the right words.

Hurlbut chuckled, "You mean guilty by association?"

I gaped at him, "Guilty by a-whatseeation?"

"Association."

Hurlbut was the smart one in the family. He had a high school education, read his Bible daily and occasionally taught the men's class at church. He was my idol. I worshiped him and loved to talk to him. He always taught me something new.

"See, " he continued, "guilty by association means that you look guilty, whether you really are or not, just because you were with somebody who really is guilty. If you go around with thieves, everybody will think you're a thief, too."

"Oh!" That made perfect sense to me.

"GEE!"

I adjusted the mules reins to the right. "Guilty by association," I mused almost to myself. "Does it say that in the Bible, Hurlbut?"

He thought for a moment. "Well, I can't think of a passage that says just that, but remember, Oral, you are judged by the company you keep."

So, true to my word to Hurlbut, I didn't mention the accident to anybody, and Hurlbut went to his party that evening. The next day he was very sore and came in from the field early because his stomach was hurting. Mama put him to bed and gave him a purgative. The following day his temperature was extremely high, and by early afternoon he was delirious.

Mama and Papa were scared, and being unwilling to leave his bedside, sent the older boys in our '31 Chevrolet over to Dothan to get a doctor immediately. After the doctor finally arrived and examined him, he insisted we take him to the hospital without delay. We laid him in the back seat of the doctor's car and tried to make him comfortable. I was crying and distraught so Mama agreed to let me ride with Hurlbut in the doctor's car while Papa and Mama followed in the Chevrolet. The older kids stayed at home to take care of the farm work.

On the way to the hospital I tried to talk to my brother. "Hurlbut, you're going to be okay. We're on our way now to Dothan Hospital." But he didn't hear anything I said. He just moaned. I started crying again. "Doctor, is he going to be all right?"

"Well, we don't know what's wrong with him yet. We certainly hope so."

"What do you think it is?" I insisted. After all he was a doctor; surely he had an idea of what the problem might be.

"It's hard to say, son. But we'll do the best we can for him, I promise."

"Have you ever seen anything like this before?"

"Worrying is not gonna change anything, son." He gave me a glance of compassion. He was driving pretty fast, and his knuckles gripping the steering wheel were white. "Maybe you oughta say a prayer." He said gently.

I screwed my eyes shut and prayed all the way to the hospital.

Hurlbut was taken into surgery on a rolling bed. At about four o'clock that afternoon the doctor came into the waiting room. "I'm very sorry, but your son is in critical condition. His appendix appears to have been ruptured for a couple of days, and the poison has spread all through his system. He may not make it. I'm very sorry, folks, we did everything we could." Mama began to cry as the impact of his words registered.

My young heart stopped. Hurlbut couldn't die. Then I remembered the plow handle. I tugged on Papa's sleeve. "The plow handle gouged him the other day out in that new south field. Right here," I grabbed my own side to demonstrate. "He hurt pretty bad for a few minutes. Did that do it?"

The doctor nodded. "Could very well be. He's being brought into a room; you can go visit him now."

Later they let me go into the hospital room to see him, and he was writhing in agony, but still delirious. Before daylight Hurlbut died. His death was one of the biggest blows that ever befell our family.

The night after we buried him, I said my prayers, "God, I want to grow up to be just like Hurlbut. Take care of him 'cause I loved him."

On my pillow I closed my eyes and remembered him. . . I saw his hair blowing in the wind, his sun-browned face laughing, his arms and legs pumping furiously in a downhill race with Edgar in our Model T Ford. Edgar had promised Hurlbut if he could keep up with the car, he'd let him drive it. Hurlbut flew like a gazelle down that slope, racing side-by-side with the automobile, while I leaned out of the window shouting encouragement to him over the honk of the horn.

With that memory, I cried myself to sleep that night, as did others in the household.

Papa's eyes that had always sparkled with warmth and mischief were now dull and gaunt looking. Mama was melancholy and rarely smiled anymore.

We never had any snow in Slocomb, and the first time I actually remember seeing snow was after we moved to Banks, Alabama. The railroad came right through the town from Montgomery and Birmingham, and during the winter months, the news would spread that there was snow on the trains coming south. We'd hear a train whistle in the distance and race to the tracks to see snow on top of the boxcars.

The older kids were growing up and scattering, and soon I was the only boy left at home with two younger sisters. Papa's health had begun to deteriorate, and he was in terrible condition. The lining of his stomach was gone and he wore a wide belt to help hold in his abdomen. It finally became apparent that he was no longer able to continue farming. So, to help the family, I dropped out of school and started contributing to the family upkeep. I had just finished sixth grade, and that was the end of my formal education at the time.

Outside of Banks, Alabama, where my family lived in 1937, there was a huge gorge deep in the woods behind our farm. The edge was like a giant ditch sixty feet across and forty feet deep. My buddies, Dick Barr, Jr., Stump Smith, Gary Darrell, Billy Hudson and I were fascinated by the sheer size of this canyon and enjoyed climbing the edge of the bluffs up one side and down the other like mountain goats. One of our favorite games was Fox and Dogs, and we spent hours chasing one another up and down the gorge and through the woods.

"Let's build a bridge across," Dick suggested during a particularly vigorous game of Fox and Dogs. "Then we could just walk across instead of climbing up and down all the time."

The five of us stood there and stared at the gorge, our brains beginning to work on the problem, using all of the brainpower we had amassed in our thirteen years of living. "That's gonna take an awful lot of lumber."

"Well, maybe a rope across. We could tie it to those two trees on either side," said Gary.

"What? And climb hand-over-hand?" asked Billy.

"Well, do you have a better idea?" I asked.

We sat down and began engineering the problem adding, up all the supplies we had access to. "What about that old roll of cable that's out behind our barn? We could tie it to those trees."

"Yeah, but how are we gonna get across?"

"We've got an old tickle (wheel) we could use. If we stretch the cable across and put the tickle on it, we could pull ourselves across with a rope."

"But don't we need something to hold us up?"

"Well, if we tied a straight chair underneath the tickle, we could sit in it as we rolled across!" That was it. That was the answer. We scattered – one to get the cable, one to get the rope, one to get the straight chair, and one to get the tickle. And, oddly enough, our plans seemed to work out just fine. We tied the cable to each tree on either side of the gorge, but because the cable wasn't long enough to reach all the way across, we had to splice it in the center with baling wire, being careful not to leave a knot which might snag the straight chair as it rolled by.

We got our bridge constructed and ready for a test ride. Stump Smith and I began to argue loudly over who would have the privilege of the first trip across the gorge. The arguing turned into a big fight which I lost because Stump was bigger than I.

He boarded his transportation while two boys ran down and up the other side of the gorge to handle the rope and pulley. They began to pull the straight chair across.

The wheel was rolling across the cable and working

fine until it got to the spliced area right over the middle of the gorge. Stump was having trouble getting the tickle to roll across that part of the cable. In his efforts, he jerked himself up out of the seat to take a bit of weight off the tickle; the splice separated leaving him sitting in mid-air.

I watched in horror as Stump, both arms spread like wings, fell to the bottom of the gorge in his straight chair. I don't believe I've ever been so frightened in my entire life. As we looked into the gorge, we saw a pile of broken bones and wood that once was Stump and the straight chair. We raced to the bottom of the gorge, knowing he must be dead. When we got there, we heard moaning and groaning; he wasn't dead, but he was severely injured.

The four of us dragged him out of the gorge and to the house as carefully as we could. He was, of course, taken directly to the hospital where surgery was performed, but he always walked with a limp after the accident.

Many years later I returned to Banks, Alabama to preach a revival at Banks Baptist Church, and Stump and his wife invited me to stay with them. He owned a very successful tractor company and raised palomino horses on his huge farm. Good natured, he joked and laughed with me about how he won the fight, but lost the war.

Two noteworthy things happened when I was fourteen years old. One, I worked a thirty acre farm all by myself and rode a mule four miles to the fields every day. The farm was owned by Mr. Dick Barr. We rented the farm for halves: Mr. Barr furnished everything – land, fertilizer, seed – and I did all the work for one-half of the profits. Mama put my meat and biscuit and syrup in a bucket, and I'd carry it with me to the fields.

I plowed and worked a full year in Banks Alabama. At the end of that year we gathered up everything we had and sold it all. I paid what we owed at the store and had $22.75 profit left for the whole year's work.

The second noteworthy thing I remember when I was fourteen years old was my salvation experience. Barefooted and wearing an old pair of overalls, I was the only person saved during the Bank's Baptist Church's revival. On the last day of that meeting, when old Brother Glover gave the invitation, I left my seat in that church house and went forward to accept the Lord. I was embarrassed that I wasn't better dressed. Brother Glover asked some of the men if they would prepare the banks of the Richland Creek for the baptismal service during the afternoon.

One of the deacons responded by saying, "Brother Glover, there's a big cloud building in the southwest, and it looks like its going to be a stormy afternoon. Since we only have one boy to baptise, suppose we postpone it until you come back again."

Brother Glover immediately replied, "Oh, no! It will be three months before I come back, so we need to go ahead and have the service this afternoon and let the Lord take care of the weather." This proved to be a very wise decision because before Brother Glover returned in three months for our quarterly worship service, I had left home and perhaps would not ever have been baptised had it not been done that afternoon.

In the weeks following my baptism, Papa and Mama moved into an apartment in Dothan, Alabama where Papa was able to find work doing a little light sanding and clerking at Ragsdale Furniture, a used-furniture store. The weekend we moved my family to Dothan, I set off on my own.

I walked the twenty miles from Dothan to Slocomb and hired out to Mr. Jess Hundley , my sister's father-in-law, as a plow hand for fifty cents a day, plus board. I thought I was going to make a fortune and "live it up." That mule and I began to really plow that black dirt out in the searing Alabama sunshine. All day long I walked behind that mule and did a lot of dusty day-dreaming. After the back band was set right, the old plow just sort of took care of itself.

Almost in a daze, I'd follow along behind that mule and think and dream. Finally, one warm day in January, I came to a brilliant conclusion, "Man, this is rough work. Do I want to do this the rest of my life . . . look at the south end of a north bound mule for the rest of my life?"

So at fourteen years of age, I made up my mind that I wouldn't say "get up" to another mule if he were to sit down in my lap. I'd just let him sit there.

That was the year, 1938, the crops failed.

Chapter 2

1939

━━►•◄━━

ith all the confidence and ignorance of an adoles-
cent, I said, "Mister Hundley, if you'll pay me my
money, I've got some places to go." He gave me my
money and I left all but fifty cents with Mama and hit
the road hitch-hiking. I did an awful lot of hiking, not
much hitching.

My parents thought I was going to visit my brother
in Columbus; my brother thought I was still safely at
home with Mama and Papa. On my own, I struck out
into the world.

Hungry and broke, I found myself in Columbus,
Georgia. The bus station was my hotel the first and
second nights. On the second day I stood in line with
all the hundreds of hopefuls at Bibb Manufacturing,
but we were told there were no jobs.

On the third day, still wearing my dirty coveralls,
old shoes and dirty fingernails, I went back to Bibb
before daylight to be the first in line when the employ-

ment office opened. As I sat there, alone and hungry, a nicely dressed man, arrived to unlock the front door. He glanced my way before entering the building. "Son, we don't have any jobs today."

With nowhere else to go, I continued to just sit there on the curb. After the secretary arrived, I entered the employment office and stubbornly asked again for a job. The secretary reconfirmed that there were no new jobs available at this time. As I stood there, the gentleman from the early morning stuck his head around the corner of his door. "My name is J. R. Jolly. Weren't you the lad I saw outside this morning before daylight?"

"Yes, sir." Hard-boiled little kid that I was, I took this as an invitation to walk right into his office. This tall, thin man had a kind-looking face and a soft-hearted look about him.

"I told you we don't have any jobs."

"Mr. Jolly, I've got to have a job."

"Where are you staying?"

"At the bus station." I mumbled.

He looked at me, and I saw sympathy in his eyes as he asked, "Have you had any breakfast, son?"

I said, "Breakfast? I haven't had breakfast, dinner, supper or anything."

Already knowing what my answer would be, he asked, "Aren't you hungry?"

"I'm starving!" And I was.

He got up from his desk, saying, "Let's go across the street to the restaurant." I didn't argue with him. At the diner, I ordered sausage and eggs with biscuits and gravy. The waitress brought the hot biscuits and I broke one open, hungrily watching the steam rise from the center. Quickly I speared a pat of butter with the tip of my knife and threw it in there. Nothing, not even Mama's biscuits, had ever tasted that good. Mr. Jolly sipped a cup of coffee and watched me eat that biscuit, silently observing my dirty fingernails. Making fast work of my breakfast, I tossed the final crumbs in my mouth. Finally, he said, "Son, I want you to run over to the barber shop and take a shower there in the back. It's just about four doors down the street; you'll find it. Here's twenty cents. Then meet me at M.J. Dunaway's store next door."

Obediently, I did as he instructed, paying with the change he'd given me. After my hair was clean and my fingernails scrubbed , Mr. Jolly bought me some clothes on his credit at Dunaway's, with the understanding that I would pay him fifty cents per week until the bill was all repaid. That was when I was sure I had a job. Next, he took me over to the Smith's house on Hemlock Drive and introduced me to Mrs. Smith who ran a boarding house. I was given a room to share with another boy about my age.

Having settled all of this, we went back to the Bibb Manufacturing office and filled out my employment application. This was when I learned that my official name was James O. Dorriety, not Oral Dorriety. From that day on I became James or Jim.

Mr. Jolly put me to work in the cotton mill that very night on the 11:00p.m. shift. This was the same cotton mill where there were no jobs available earlier in the day. This understanding man had just made a place for me. I couldn't thank him enough. In fact, every chance I had, I'd pop in to see him, say hello and thank him again for his kindness. Looking back on the experience, I think Mr. Jolly must have been a Christian. His kindness was a witness to me.

My job consisted of pushing a hand truck loaded with drums of cotton roping, up and down those big alleys of the weave shed, setting them off and picking up the empties. But, I didn't just push that single axle hand truck; I ran it – literally. It held about twenty small barrels, and I found that if I pushed the hand truck fast enough I could jump on the back and steer it down the aisles using my body weight. I was having a ball.

At the time, of course, I never realized that I was developing a philosophy of always doing more than I was asked to do. I was just trying to keep my job by making myself indispensable. If the boss had to let somebody go, chances are he'd keep the one working the hardest. Because I was strong, young and healthy, I'd run all night long – doing my job, the other fellow's job, anything that needed to be done – just working because I was making $12.87 a week. My room and board cost five bucks a week. Fifty cents went to M. J. Dunaway for my clothes; I sent Mama five bucks a week, and I still had more money than I'd ever had in my life.

Of course, I'd never shaved, never needed to. The superintendent of the mill, Mr. Turner, came through one night and stopped and looked at me real hard.

"Son, how old are you?"

I didn't know who he was, so I glibly replied, "Oh, different ages, how old are you?" After working there for several months I thought I was already grown.

Soon afterwards, I was informed why the superintendent had been so interested in my age. The Fair Labor Standards Act, which included the child labor law had been enacted requiring a person to be at least sixteen years of age to work full-time in a factory. It also set a limit of eighteen years minimum for all occupations that were particularly hazardous. The foreman of the factory said "You've got to quit."

Surprised, I said, "Why?" I was working hard and earning my pay.

The foreman walked me into his office and sat me

down. "I've never had a boy work as hard as you've worked, and I really hate to do this," he said. I could see the pity in his eyes.

I pleaded, "Please don't make me quit now. Surely you can figure out a way to let me work."

But after a few months, Bibb Manufacturing had to let me go. It was the law.

With the realization that I had to get another job immediately, I went to the local grocery store, Jacobs' Grocery, and asked Mr. Jacobs, the owner, for a job. He said he didn't need anyone, but I just hung around anyway – waiting and watching. I didn't have anything else to do.

The telephone rang, and I heard him say, "No, I'm really sorry. I don't have anybody to send with your groceries. If I had someone, I'd be happy to have them delivered."

I went up, tapped him on the arm and said, "I can deliver them."

"Hold on a minute," he said to the receiver. "Do you know where Hemlock Drive is?" he asked me.

"Yes, I live on Hemlock."

"Ok," he said back into the phone, "give me your order. I can have them delivered."

Immediately upon hanging up, he gathered the groceries, while instructing me how to deliver them. He placed them in the giant basket of an old-fashioned bicycle with a very small wheel on the front and a normal wheel on the back. I had never in my life ridden a bicycle, but I didn't tell him that. I left the store pushing the bicycle across the street, a normal procedure anyway, but continued to push it all the way to the lady's house on Hemlock. As I delivered the groceries, the lady's neighbor was visiting, and she exclaimed, "Oh, I wish I had known you were ordering something from the store; I would have ordered some things, too."

Immediately I said, "Why don't you tell me what you want, and I'll go to the store and get them for you." So I took an order for groceries.

I left that house extremely happy, jumped on the bicycle, tried to ride it, fell off, got back on, tried and continued to try until I learned to ride the bicycle on the way back to the store.

When I got to the store, I rushed in to tell Mr. Jacobs about my order for the groceries. He pulled the order, and I set off back down the street peddling as hard as I could. After delivering them, I came back and began to help him stock the shelves. When we closed that afternoon he said, "See you at seven o'clock tomorrow morning."

"Yessir."

I continued to work there all week, and on Saturday evening he gave me ten dollars for the week's work. For several months I continued to help Mr. Jacobs' at his grocery store.

Just as I turned sixteen, I decided to join the army. I went out to Fort Benning, Georgia, lied and told the recruiting officer I was eighteen years old.

"Are you sure you're eighteen, son?"

"Absolutely, Sir. I won't have any problem getting a signature from my parents verifying it." He signed me up with the understanding that I would remain in the barracks waiting for my paperwork to be approved.

I went right out and forged my parents' signatures, and waited long enough to make the army think I'd mailed the papers home and then returned them, swearing all was correct.

I was having a great time lying around on a cot in the barracks all day, eating three square meals, chatting with the soldiers and waiting for my papers to come.

Then they found out my real age and kicked me out without letting me join the army.

Nothing was going right for me, and by 1940 I had gotten the idea that everybody was against me. The whole world was against me. I was really dejected. People couldn't get jobs. Unemployment levels were at unprecedented heights.

Returning from Fort Benning to Columbus, Georgia, I stopped at a large restaurant, Firm Roberts Cafe, went in, found Mr. Roberts and told him I desperately needed a job.

Mr. Roberts was a great big fatherly-looking man, pear shaped and bald headed, and he listened with compassion.

Then he asked me, "Where do you live, son?"

"I don't have a place to live. I've been staying out at Fort Benning," and I told him my story. "Don't worry about me having a place to stay. Can't I just sleep in the restaurant at night?"

He gave me a job hopping cars in the tremendous parking lot of this restaurant. He took me home and let me sleep in his garage on a cot until I could find a boarding room. His garage was totally enclosed and far more luxurious than the farm houses we had lived in. I ate my meals at the restaurant.

That's when my downfall really started. Beer and other drinks were served in this popular restaurant where many of the officers from Ft. Benning brought their lady friends to eat and drink.

Every morning the teller gave each of us car-hops five dollars in change. Then when a customer placed an order, we turned in the order to the kitchen, paid for the food out of that five dollars, then collected for the food. At the end of the day, we'd return the five dollars back to the teller, and whatever was left over in our aprons was our tips for the day.

Then I got another brilliant idea. "Well look, I think I can do better than this."

One day a customer drove up for curb service and ordered a couple of beers and a sandwich and handed me a five dollar bill. I gave him change for one dollar. I already had a dollar bill in my hand ready to show him that's what he had given me.

He challenged me and said, "Son, I gave you a five,"

"No, Sir," I retorted, "you gave me a one."

He insisted, "I know I gave you a five."

I bluffed, "Friend, you gave me this one." I waved the substituted dollar bill at him. "If you say that one more time, I'll drag you out of that car."

He said, "Oh, I'm sorry," excused himself and drove off.

Surprised, I thought, "That's pretty good. I'll try that on the next guy, too." And I did and I guarantee you that soon I was almost making more money than the owner of that restaurant. I gypped almost everyone who came in there. I'd keep his change and just cheat him out of it.

Then I got in cahoots with the cook. I'd go inside the kitchen and help him make sandwiches, and we'd pass the food through the window so I wouldn't have to go by the counter to pay for the food. One hundred percent profits, plus tips. I had already made up my mind that the world was against me; everybody was against me. If I was going to get anything or go anywhere, I was going to have to fight for it. To me it was a matter of survival – a boy without any supervision. For thirteen months, I worked seven days a week, then partied almost all night long in the sin city of Phoenix City, Alabama. My friends and I walked into Phoenix City where it seemed everything was legal, even for boys. We went to bars, started gambling, shooting pool and, of course, drinking.

But my salvation had never left me. I always felt guilty doing these things, but finally my dishonesty began to get on my nerves and eat at my insides. One evening I was particularly tired as I kicked off my boots and lay down on my bed in the boarding house. It was well after midnight and my clothes and hair smelled like kitchen grease, but I was too tired to clean up. The ceiling above me looked none too steady, and then I felt my cot shake as I began to weep. Exhausted, I finally cried myself to sleep.

This became a pattern of remorse. I wept nights, knowing that what I was doing was wrong, feeling so dirty and filthy spiritually. But I was alone and had no supervision or direction in my life, and the instinct for survival was stronger than my guilt.

It finally dawned on me that something wonderful had happened to me when I was fourteen years old. The foundation was there. I just needed a way to come back to it. So I decided that I'd better stop stealing before I got into real trouble. There was no other direction in my life at that time. I just knew that I had to remove myself from temptation.

I quit that job and got another one in the Cash Drugstore, owned by the pharmacist Dr. Malcolm Forte, a Methodist Steward and one of the greatest guys I believe I've ever known. I started working for him, and he liked me. He trusted me to drive his automobile, let me drive his children to their music classes and let me drive his wife shopping. He entrusted me with his bill collecting, and I would drive his automobile on my collection route.

The movie theater was right next door and there was a hole in the wall between the soda fountain and the theater where and we sold sodas to the theater patrons, passing them through the little cubbyhole. I became an outstanding soda jerk. I prided myself in keeping the stainless steel counters sparkling clean. I used my fingers and baking soda to scrub until they glittered. We always got one hundred percent on our inspection rating.

There was a branch post office inside the drug store, and I was authorized to help out so I obtained a little postal experience in the process.

But, in the meantime, I continued my bad habits. I started buying a half pint of whiskey and hiding it in the soda fountain. I mixed the whiskey in a Coca-Cola and nipped on it during the day, sometimes finishing that whole half pint before I got off work.

If that weren't bad enough, at night, I'd continue partying with my buddies. We'd really have a good time, going from one night club and bar to the other. Never once did I get drunk, but I'd just sip all day and all night long. I wanted to drink enough to feel good and to find a way to escape from the harsh realities of life.

But one day at the drugstore, Dr. Malcolm Forte came in and bellowed, "Oral," (he called me Oral and still does today) "Oral, get back in my office; I want to see you for a minute. Let Sammy take the counter for you."

I went back and, as soon as he came in, I knew there was something bad wrong. The next thing I heard was the slamming of the door to his office. I turned and looked at that big guy, and he was trembling all over. I could almost count his teeth through his lips, his lips were so tight. He said, "You're nothing but a smart-alec kid. Just to think I trusted you to drive my children and wife, with you drinking all this time. Off from home, nobody to tell you what to do, you really think you're something." Well, he was fixing to work my plow over. I knew that I was in for it.

And strangely enough, I guess I would have permitted him to do it. But I talked him out of it. I just literally talked him out of it. I promised him, and I meant it, that if he'd just give me another chance, I'd never drink another drop. I'd just leave it alone. And being the kind-hearted fellow that he was, he gave me another chance.

Chapter 3

1941-1942

———⟫•◦•⟪———

Then I met another marvelous man. His name was Sam Clark, and he was the owner of Clark's Grocery down the street. He began to take a personal interest in me and to beg me to come to his church. He was a Deacon at Porter Memorial Baptist Church.

"I want you to come to church. How about coming to church Sunday." he pleaded again and again. Every time he came into the drugstore, he'd see me over behind the counter, joking and cutting up with every-body, and he'd lean over that counter and say, "Please come to church with me Sunday." Never ever did he walk away from the soda fountain without saying, "Come to church; there's a lot of young people I'd like you to meet."

Then he'd leave, and I'd get on with my foolish histrionics, laughing with the customers and flirting with the women.

I got so aggravated with him because he worried

and nagged me to death. Every time I'd see him, "Why don't you come to church?"

If I could see him coming in time, I'd get out of his way so he couldn't ask me. One Saturday afternoon, I rounded the street corner, and there stood Sam Clark and he said, "How about coming to church Sunday?"

Suddenly, I had had quite enough of him. I wanted to tell him to get off my back. But when I turned to really give him a piece of my mind, I saw tears in his eyes and it totally disarmed me. He put his arm around my shoulder and said, "Son, I'm interested in you. I really want you to come to church. If you'll come, I'll wait outside for you and we can sit together."

I thought, "Well, hell! I guess I can go one time and maybe that'll satisfy him." Besides, I had just bought my first sport coat, a navy blue plaid sport coat, and my very first tie. Those clothes had been hanging in the back of my closet just waiting for a good place to wear them. "Boy," I thought, "that's the place for me to wear my new sport coat."

And that is the only reason I agreed to go.

I said, "Okay, I'll be there tomorrow morning."

That Sunday morning, I was up early, shaved the fuzz off my upper lip, and got dressed up in my new clothes. I was so excited. First time I'd ever been in a city church in my life. I had only attended services in the little country churches of Banks, Alabama and Union Baptist Church and a few other country churches around Slocomb .

Sure enough, good to his word, Sam was standing right by the front door, waiting for me. He bragged on my appearance, shook my hand and made me feel so good and welcome. We entered the church and sat down together towards the back. I was scared completely to death right up to the moment that the "magic" happened.

I spotted a beautiful young girl about fourteen years of age coming down the aisle with her mother. She caught my eye. I stared at her as she passed by and continued to watch the back of her head. She had on gloves and a little round straw hat with a turned up brim that perched on the back of her head. Underneath that hat was the most beautiful long brown hair. Her face was radiant. She was perfect.

It was love at first sight for me. First and only time I'd ever felt that way.

She sat down a few aisles in front of me and, stunned, I just sat there and watched her throughout the entire service. My insides quivered all through the service. Every nerve ending in my body was twitching. I don't even know whether they had preaching that day or not. I didn't hear a word the preacher said. I was fixated on that beautiful girl.

As soon as everybody got up and started out, I clawed my way to the aisle to see if I could get acquainted with her. But I didn't. I'd missed her.

During the afternoon I couldn't get the image of that girl off my mind. I called all my friends and described her to them, but no one knew her. I was tormented by the vision of the back of her head. I had to find out who she was. Then I had another of my brilliant thoughts, "Dummy, if you go back tonight you may see her again."

That evening me and my sport coat went back to church and sure enough there she was. After the service there was a youth fellowship, and guests were invited to attend. I was so excited. I went up to her but just stood staring, disarmed by her beauty. Before I could get my tongue to move, she looked at me and tilted her head slightly and all that thick luxurious hair shifted around on her shoulders.

"Hello," she said, "my name is Vonzeal Davis. Are

you new?"

My brain was a whirlwind. Her name is Vonzeal Davis. Vonzeal. Unusual. I rolled the name around in my head locking it in place.

I loved her name. Plus, she had the most elegant white hands and rich hair I'd ever seen. She looked at me, waiting. "Hello, I'm Jim Dorriety," I finally managed to stammer, and she rewarded me with a beautiful shy smile. I determined at that moment that I didn't care what I had to do to make it happen, Vonzeal was going to be my girl. I had a goal in life. My very first real goal.

During those few moments we talked together, I learned everything I could about her. She attended Jordan High School and walked to the corner of 38th and Second Avenue to catch the school bus. My heart began to pound because that was the exact corner where I worked at Cash Drugstore. How could I have missed her? I invited her to come by the drugstore on her way home from school.

She told me her telephone number was Fairfax 3-7695. I'll never forget that number. I left church that evening a new man. My entire life and every thought now centered around Vonzeal Davis.

One afternoon that week, she and three of her girlfriends came into the drug store, and I made them all sodas. Soon she began to come by regularly. Dr. Forte didn't know (but will when he reads this book) that he bought Vonzeal so many sodas and extra dips of ice cream.

And, of course, I found that I could go back to church the next Sunday and see her again. I began to court her in a very limited, careful way, and we became sweethearts and began to fall in love. Well, actually she began to fall in love with me. I'd been in love with her from the first moment I'd laid eyes on her.

Every Sunday I to and froed Vonzeal and her mother, Miss Elsie, to church and back, strutting down the street so proud to be seen with them. I began to worry a lot about my appearance and personal grooming. I wanted to look just as good as she did, so she would be proud of me.

This period of time was a marvelous experience as I continued to become more involved in the church and more active for the Lord. Other problems began to fade away, and from that time on I don't guess you'd find anyone as happy as I was . Always happy, always laughing.

Of course, there was one little problem. That nickel I'd stolen from Mama when I was six had long since been resolved, but now I had to face myself and Mr. Roberts at the Firm Roberts Cafe.

Terrified, I went back to him with the idea that if he would help me determine how much I'd stolen from him, I'd start paying it back. I admitted how I'd stolen from people on the lot, how I'd stolen food out the window.

It was apparent to me that there was a good possibility that he might even call the law and have me arrested, but I knew that I had to come clean. "Whatever you say it is, I'll start paying on it, and if it takes the rest of my life I'll pay it all back."

With tears in his eyes he said, "Young man, you have just paid me. Your willingness to come back and look me in the eye and tell me this convinces me that you mean what you're saying."

He didn't know how much he was preaching to me. Looking back, I have no idea if Mr. Roberts was a Christian or if he was a member of a church. He wouldn't accept anything from me except my confession.

That's when I began to feel totally clean spiritually

and began to follow where I thought the Lord was leading me. I came back to the altar of the church to get things clear with the Lord and rededicated my life. There had never been any doubt on my part of my salvation at age fourteen, and even though I did everything, and more, that any unsupervised boy would do—fighting, drinking, lying, cheating, gambling, stealing— in my heart I knew I was saved.

Many years later I found 1 John 1:9, "If we confess our sins, He is faithful and just to forgive us our sins and to cleanse us from all unrighteousness."[1]

But back then at seventeen, all I knew was that I had to get right with the Lord. I'd had nothing to do with my birth – I did not start it, I could not stop it – I was conceived and born into the Dorriety family through my mother's womb.

The next birth I experienced was my spiritual birth. John 3:3 begins, "Jesus answered and said unto Nicodemus, 'Verily, verily, I say unto thee, Except a man be born again, he cannot see the kingdom of God' Nicodemus saith unto him, 'How can a man be born when he is old? can he enter the second time into his mother's womb, and be born?' Jesus answered, 'Verily, verily, I say unto thee, except a man be born of water and of the Spirit, he cannot enter into the kingdom of God. That which is born of the flesh is flesh; and that which is born of the Spirit is spirit. Marvel not that I said unto thee, Ye must be born again.'"

The new birth experience is identical to the first physical birth experience in that it happens and has longevity. If it's impossible to get unborn physically, then it's impossible to get unborn spiritually.

There were only three men who ever showed any interest in me back during those five years from ages

---

[1] The scripture passages herein are taken from the King James version from which I have always taught.

thirteen to eighteen. One man showed interest in my morals, Malcolm Forte; and one man showed interest in my spiritual life, Sam Clark. And, of course, Mr. Firm Roberts forgave me and taught me a valuable lesson.

Since I didn't own a Bible, Vonzeal gave me one of hers, the one she had won for perfect attendance in Sunday School. I loved that Bible. It had a zipper around it, and I could smell her sweet perfume on its cover. I would even sleep with that Bible and began to read it in a stammering way. My lack of education didn't allow me to read very much.

This Bible is one of six Bibles I have retired because of their condition. After fifty-two years of use, this is the one Bible I love above all the others.

As I continued to court Vonzeal, I'd look for ways to make myself attractive to her. One day during the Brill Cream days of slicked-back hair, I pulled a lock of hair down and curled it onto my forehead, then went over to see her. I thought I looked so sexy and stylish. She moved real close to me, reached up and pushed that lock of hair back in place. The touch of her cool soft hand on my forehead really set me on fire. In fact, I pulled that lock right back down the next time I went over to see her, hoping she'd touch me again.

One Sunday evening during the service, I reached and took Vonzeal's hand in my own and squeezed lightly. She squeezed back, and I knew at that moment that she was my girl. The little hand squeeze became our signal of "I love you" and remained so until the end.

Needing to make more money, I went to work at Tom Houston Peanut Company filling the hopper with peanut butter. The round crackers moved down on a conveyor belt, under a machine which squirted a tiny amount of peanut butter onto the cracker, exited on the other side where hundreds of girls sat placing the tops on the peanut butter and crackers.

This was the time when I first learned about sexual harassment – from the boy's point of view. There were eight of us boys working with about three hundred girls and women. They teased us unmercifully with sexual innuendoes. I received a good lesson in how to side-step a proposition. I was in love with Vonzeal; she was the only one.

I brought her a little bouquet of flowers, and when I gave them to her, she reached over and put her cheek next to mine, not to kiss me, but just to say "thank you." I literally turned to run. "Where are you going?" she asked, astonished at my actions.

"I'm going to get you some more flowers!"

When the Japanese attacked Pearl Harbor on Sunday, December 7 of 1941, I didn't think much about my entering the service at that time. My older brother Rex enlisted in the Marine Corps, was accepted and left that afternoon for Paris Island, South Carolina to begin his training. From there he went to the Pacific.

Monday, everyone brought their radios to work and listened to the news as President Roosevelt declared war. Many of the men listening with me knew they would be leaving soon to serve their country. It was an emotional time, and several went immediately and joined up. But I was still young and deeply in love and wanted to stay at home and be with Vonzeal.

During this period of time, my life became so beautiful and wonderful and sweet. We began planning for our marriage. We walked down to Skinner Furniture Store and picked out a beautiful bedroom set, complete with a vanity holding a huge round mirror and a high poster bed. In addition, we bought a three-burner kerosene oil stove and a white metal table with two chairs. We put it all on lay-away and decided when it was all paid in full, we'd get married. During the following weeks, I had never been more frugal. I wanted that furniture paid off quickly!

Three months later, we spoke to Brother Wilson about marrying us, and set our wedding date for Friday night, October 3rd. He informed us that that was the evening of a revival, but we could be married after the service if we wanted. "I know a family in Phoenix City," he told us, "the Kenny Family of the Kenny Trio, outstanding gospel singers. They have a gorgeous home, and we could have your marriage ceremony there in that beautiful home, if you'd like."

It was easier to get married in Phoenix City, Alabama than in Georgia since Alabama had no mandatory waiting period after application for the marriage license. With Vonzeal's mother's signature, we obtained our marriage license and planned to marry the following Friday evening.

With our furniture paid off, we had it delivered to our little apartment. Actually it was just one large room, but we placed a free-standing partition in the middle and formed a bedroom on one side and a seating and cooking area, complete with our three-burner stove, on the other. Next to this one large room was a small, yet complete, bathroom. We had our apartment furnished and ready.

Right before our marriage in October, I received a notice to report for examination for the service by the latter part of November. I thought it ironic that I couldn't get into the army when I had wanted to, but now that my life with Vonzeal was beginning, Uncle Sam remembered and wanted me.

The evening came for us to be married. Ms. Elsie had made plans for a midnight wedding supper at her house. Brother Wilson drove us to the Kenny home in

Phoenix City. Jack Kenny, who later served as business manager for the city of Phoenix City, sang a solo "I Love You Truly," while his sister played the piano. As he was singing, a big beautiful cat on the porch outside climbed up into the transom window above the door and perched, watching us. Brother Wilson couldn't see the animal, but we could, and we stood there, squeezing each other's hand, giggling and watching that cat while Jack was singing. It was a beautiful moment which stayed with us right on through our life together as we remembered that marvelous moment when that cat caught our attention and joined our wedding party.

Vonzeal and I were married very young – six days after her sixteenth birthday, and I had just turned eighteen. We both loved the Lord and loved each other with undying passion and were planning a wonderful life together. Even though we were very young, in so many ways we were mature. The Lord was leading us. First of all, we loved the Lord individually. I loved the Lord and had rededicated and reconsecrated myself. Vonzeal loved the Lord, had been saved and baptised and dedicated herself to Him. When we began to examine our love for one another, we decided we simply could not live apart, but we were mature enough to feel that if we each loved the Lord individually; and we loved each other; we had a love triangle that would last forever and forever. No evil force in the world could ever break through. On the basis of that foundation, we put our lives together.

The Lord had given me my companion.

Later that evening we joined our families at Miss Elsie's and enjoyed a marvelous midnight supper. But I couldn't eat that meal fast enough.

My bride was pure, virginal and unknowing in the ways of husbands and wives. She had just turned sixteen without the benefit of any of today's educational advantages. But we were so in love and delighted in each others presence that our happiness overcame everything. And I was a young stud of eighteen, almost as pure as she. Well, I had grown up on a farm and knew the ways of animals. That counted for something.

And, of course, nature, as it always does, took care of everything.

Vonzeal dropped out of high school and began learning the ways of being a good wife. She kept our tiny apartment immaculate, and my clothes were always clean and heavily starched. She learned to cook and delighted in pleasing me. I felt I was the luckiest man alive. We enjoyed one another's company and giggled and gossiped like the best friends we were. Our entertainment consisted of long hand-holding walks, swinging in an old porch swing and just sitting and reading. We read our Bibles and prayed together daily. It was a healthy marriage.

And because it was "healthy" we had our little disagreements. But we vowed from the very beginning never to go to sleep mad at one another. There were some nights when we thought we'd never get to sleep.

Her posture and demeanor were almost impeccable. She held herself erect, not with pride, but with poise and grace. She always displayed such dignity. I couldn't believe my good fortune.

Well, she wasn't a saint, but I sure was in love with her. In all the fifty years we were together, she never embarrassed me in public – she had style.

Our love transcended everything. Everything, that is, except our love for the Lord. Our faith was growing and maturing as we enjoyed the fellowship of our church.

Vonzeal immediately worked up a five-item budget for us in tiny white envelopes.

Envelope #1 was designated "The Lord's Money:" Malachi 3:10, "Bring ye all the tithes into the store-house, that there may be meat in mine house, and prove me now herewith, saith the Lord of hosts, if I will not open you the windows of heaven, and pour you out a blessing, that there *shall* not be *room* enough to *receive* it." Vonzeal always placed our tithe into Envelope #1 before she divided the remaining portions into:

#2 groceries and household money,
#3 clothing,
#4 medical,
#5 recreation.

She allocated our cash the moment we got it and apportioned it into those envelopes. We spent our money accordingly until there was no more, and we did without. We didn't even realize the wisdom of what we were doing. We were just kids trying to find a practical way of doing things. When, from one week to the next, we'd have a few coins left over in an envelope, the budget would be readjusted accordingly. Less would be allocated to one envelope; a little more to another. All except the envelope marked "The Lord's money" – we never had anything left over in it. We went to church every Sunday and tithed our ten percent.

If we had a little bit left over, sometimes we'd go out to eat. Sprayberry's was one of our favorite places to go because they served chili dogs and milk shakes. Or we would hop a bus and go to Dinglewood Pharmacy, "the home of the scrambled dog." They served a wiener in a bun, cross-cut into small bites and topped with chili, onions and tomatoes. (It is still a very popular place to eat today and still serves the scrambled dog).

Our little five-envelope system was the way we got our education in managing our household money. When two people work at it like that, they're going to succeed.

The very first meal Vonzeal cooked for me was

boiled wieners, mashed potatoes, green beans and upside down cake. She made the cake by placing pineapple and cherries on the bottom of an iron skillet, adding the batter and cooking it. Then when she turned it out, all the beautiful topping was on the top of the cake. It has remained my favorite cake all through the years.

Then, just two months after we were married, it was determined by somebody up there in the Pentagon, that I needed to go and help Uncle Sam. I was in one of the first groups of eighteen year old boys from Columbus to be drafted into the service.

When I showed up for my physical in November of 1942, I was 6'2", weighing in at one hundred twenty-nine pounds. Solid man. I haven't been able to figure out to this day why they called me "Slim."

They shipped me to Ft. McPherson for examination to see if I was a fit subject for the military. They got about one thousand of us out there, took our clothes from us and put us out there buck-naked at Ft. McPherson. You can't imagine what a horrible looking sight that is. There's nothing beautiful about a thousand naked men.

We finally marched through this hall and came out on the other side, and they stamped a piece of paper, handed it to me and said "Approved!"

And I said, "Approved for what?"

"You pass, Slim, keep marching!"

And I said, "I pass for what?"

And he said "You're in the army."

"Man, hasn't anybody examined me!"

"Slim, the only things that could happen to you would be a skin disease or a broken bone. We can just look at you and examine you."

I received my instructions to report for active duty in January, 1943.

Chapter 4

1943

———>•◦•<———

 $\boxed{\text{M}}$ y brother-in-law, Claude Henry McCoy, had been
in the military so he gave me some advice. "Now, Jim,
whatever you do – keep your mouth shut and stay
away from headquarters. Don't volunteer for anything.
Don't say anything unless they call your name. Don't
do anything unless they tell you to do it. If they tell you
to do something, do it. And you'll get along all right."

Well, I was trying to follow his instructions – the
only instructions I had. And so the first morning we fell
out before daylight and stood in line for roll call. But
nobody called my name, so I went back to the barracks
and went to bed.

Honestly, I lay around until the troops came in at
lunch. I got up, went to the mess hall with them, ate
everything in sight, they went back to the field, I went
back to bed.

The next day . . . same thing. They called the roll;
nobody called my name, so I went back to bed.

I did that again on the third day. Then I got to

thinking, "You know, I could come up with bed sores staying inside like this." So I decided to check up on the problem. I went down to the orderly room, knocked on the door and the old first sergeant hollered "Come in." I walked in, just a giant of a man, and stood there in front of him. I just stood there...didn't know how to salute.

"What do you want, Slim?" He roared. "What's your name, Slim?"

"Dorriety, Sir."

He inclined his head and gave me a hard look that scared me slam to death. I stood a moment in silence contemplating the situation. "Sergeant," I said gingerly, "I've been here three days and everybody else's got something to do. I don't have anything to do." The bomb had been dropped; I waited for the explosion.

He narrowed his eyes and continued to stare at me. The look he gave me could only be described as scathing. The moment seemed to stretch into an eternity, and my insides began to tremble. Maybe, just maybe, I was in a lot of trouble.

Then he reached for his roll book, licked his fingers and began to flip through the pages. When he came down to my name, he shouted at me "Haven't you heard me call Do-rid-i-ty out there?"

He began to curse! He said some things that wouldn't be proper to repeat here. Words I'd never even heard before. He expanded my vocabulary and increased my street smarts while I waited for his tirade to end.

Finally, in a normal voice, he asked, "Where you from, Slim?"

"Slocomb, Sir." I managed to gulp out.

"Slocomb, New York?" He asked in sarcastically.

"Is there a Slocomb, New York?" I was so excited to think there might be another Slocomb, I temporarily forgot the trouble I was in. He glared at me, amazed at my stupidity. "I'm from Slocomb, Alabama, sir." I clarified meekly.

"Well, get on back to the barracks, and when the troops come in we'll do something about this." I backed out of his office.

On my official record, I'm marked AWOL for three days because I didn't answer to the mispronunciation of my name. My stupidity was probably the only thing that saved me from the stockade.

I learned quickly that when the army shipped out a group, someone in that group was going to be designated the "leader," and I started working towards that position. There were seven of us who were put together in a group after all the others had shipped out. In talking among ourselves, we realized that all of us had only one thing in common, we each had had some postal experience.

So I started getting myself positioned in the eyes of the sergeant. If we were doing KP, I was number one KP. When we were told to do something, I'd get there first and be the last to leave. I channeled all of my energy into becoming the leader.

When we were called to ship out, sure enough, I was selected as the group leader. The first sergeant and commanding officer brought me into the office and put a black arm band with corporal stripes on it and made me "acting corporal" group leader for the boys that were shipping out. The commanding officer handed me the secret orders and no one but me was supposed to know where we were going.

"Private, it's your responsibility to see that everyone is dressed correctly in his army overcoat with his gas mask at his side in its holster. Muster them out to the train station at 0400 hours."

Only after the train left Atlanta could I tell those young soldiers where we were headed. They were all looking to me for information and, of course, I played it to the hilt, squeezing as much importance from it as I could.

We traveled during the night, and about daylight we could see some snow flurries on the sides of the hills. When we got to Little Rock, we thought we were in a foreign country. The ground was white with snow. It was the first snow I'd ever seen on the ground. This two and one-half ton army truck carried us out to the camp and, of course, we almost froze to death in the back of that truck. When we got to the camp, we learned we were staying in tents and were assigned into platoons.

So here I was inducted into the service, and they sent me way out there to Little Rock, Arkansas. It was the furthest I'd ever been away from Slocomb. And I thought I was gone forever – way out there at Camp Joseph T. Robinson.

During the evenings, I spent my time trying to stay warm on my cot and writing long love letters to Vonzeal. The first Sunday that I was permitted to leave base, I found a Baptist Church. A lovely motherly and fatherly couple, the Smiths, invited me, just a recruit fresh out of basic training, for Sunday lunch. I was lonely out there all by myself, missing Vonzeal, and I gladly accepted their invitation. Just one soldier in a crowd there in that church, but they invited me to go home with them, and Mrs. Smith served the most wonderful meal. We talked and talked. They were interested in my family and the military, but all I wanted to do was talk about Vonzeal, and I did. They insisted that I call her at their expense from their home phone. They got acquainted with her on the phone. Later that afternoon, they asked if Vonzeal and I would like to come live with them there in their extra bedroom.

You see, Mr. and Mrs. Smith had two sons of their own in the service, and they were hoping somebody was taking care of their boys.

Vonzeal and I were excited about the possibility of being together again, so we worked it out that she would come, but her mother, Miss Elsie, wouldn't let her travel alone since she was still only sixteen years old.

We talked and worked out all the details for Vonzeal and Miss Elsie to come. They bought two tickets on the Greyhound Bus from Columbus, Georgia to Little Rock, Arkansas. We planned that I would meet them at the bus station at a certain time and take them out to the Smith's house.

As luck would have it, the base got the news that President Franklin Roosevelt was coming to visit the base the very day that Vonzeal and Miss Elsie were due to arrive in Little Rock. Everything had to be cleaned and shined, and duties assigned in proportion to our rating inspection.

I polished my boots and rifle until they glowed and was selected to be the personal escort for President Roosevelt to the Chapel. Some of the boys were given road duty to stand at attention beside the road as he rode by. I was to escort him from the car door up to the chapel door, stand there at parade rest until he came out, then walk three steps behind him as he returned to his car in his wheel chair.

That day I was proud to be his personal escort. After his visit to the chapel, when he stood up from the wheel chair to get back into the car, he turned around and looked me right in the eye. I presented arms. He reached over and hit me on the arm and said, "Good job, Soldier," and turned around and sat down in the car. It thrilled me to my toes; he was my hero.

Roosevelt was said to have a way of personal communication that made everyone seem like a personal friend. He believed in four freedoms: Freedom of speech, Freedom of worship, Freedom from want, Freedom from fear, and these became the battle cry around the world.[2]

Unfortunately for me, the entire base had been restricted, and Vonzeal and her mother had left Columbus on their way before we received the orders for the restriction. Nobody could enter or leave the base. She had no idea where she was coming except Little Rock, Arkansas because I had assured her I would meet her at the station and take her to the Smiths. Now, due to orders, there would be no one to meet her, and she and Miss Elsie would be stranded at the bus station alone and confused wondering where I was.

I was frantic with worry and decided I was going to go over the fence and meet her at the bus station regardless of the consequences. There wasn't enough army to keep me from doing that. But common sense told me to go to the first sergeant in my company, and, even though he was taking a chance, he gave me special permission to leave. He helped slip me out with a pass in case I got caught by the MPs. A taxi met me at the front gate of the base. I slipped inside that taxi, drove straight to the bus station and sat there until I saw the bus pull in. Only then did I step outside that car. I met them, put them in the taxi, delivered them to the Smith's home, kissed them and said goodbye, got back into the taxi and returned to the front gate of the base. No one ever found out.

All in all I was stationed at Little Rock about three months in field cadre, a course for teaching basic training. I went through the NCO school to prepare. At the end of that training, my troop was selected to go to a

---

[2]When Roosevelt died of a cerebral hemorrhage in April 1945, it was on the eve of complete military victory in Europe and within months of victory in the Pacific.

brand new base, Camp Fanning, Texas, to open that facility and get it ready to receive the first troops. It was an Infantry Replacement Training Center. We were in the thick of World War II and the infantry was losing more men than any other part of the army. The center was giving them eight weeks basic training and shipping them straight overseas to combat.

That first weekend in Tyler, Texas I was left in charge of quarters CQ because I didn't want to go into town and party. I was a happily married man. This was the first weekend on a brand new base with no other troops except our unit.

Lying on my army bunk writing a letter home to Vonzeal, I began to have a pain in my right side. I lifted my leg for relief, then lifted a littler higher, but the pain kept intensifying. Then I realized I couldn't put my leg down because the pain was so severe.

Finally, I somehow managed to get off the bunk to seek help, but I didn't have anybody to leave in charge. I was there all alone. Fortunately, there was a jeep outside, and I knew there was a little army field hospital on base, so I drove myself over there.

That was the youngest doctor I'd ever seen in my life, just an intern. But I had acute appendicitis. That young lieutenant and two male nurses, gave me a spinal injection and performed surgery right then and there. And I talked to them while they operated. I talked about Hurlbut and how the plow handle had ruptured his appendix causing his death. I talked about how so many of my brothers and sisters had had their appendixes removed. "Do you think it's something we ate, Doc? Do you think it's all those blackberry seeds we ate?"

He chuckled. He knew I was talking just to try to act brave; after all this was the first surgery I'd ever had. He said, "Soldier, the muscles in your stomach are so hard and defined, I'm going to be able to remove your appendix without cutting through a muscle. I'll just cut between them."

The fourth day after my surgery, I went back to the company area. The eleventh day I was allowed a ten-day leave to go home. I rode a Greyhound from Tyler, Texas to Columbus, Georgia, on a bus that was so packed there were people standing in the aisles. In my crisp uniform and polished boots, I felt so sophisticated that I got up and gave a lady my seat and rode part of the way standing, my stomach incision barely healed.

During this time, I also began developing arthritis in my knees and feet. This physical problem finally became so pronounced that two of my toes began to draw up and swell. I couldn't even wear shoes. I was informed that I would need surgery to correct the problem at a later date.

Therefore, I was given an honorable discharge from the army in 1944. I went home to Columbus where Vonzeal and I fervently got back into our church work together.

Chapter 5

1944-1945

———⇒》・0・⟨⟨———

As a young couple, we were having a great time working with the intermediates. I didn't know it at the time, but I had begun to preach to those intermediates, and we met with them almost every night.

After my discharge I returned to work at Tom Houston Peanut Company where I worked as assistant warehouse superintendent, overseeing the recycling of the crates and boxes.

I'd call Vonzeal during the day and say, "Honey, let's get some hot dogs ready, call all the kids and tell them to meet us as soon as I get home. We're going out into the community." I couldn't wait to get off work so I could get home and get with those intermediates and go out and do the Lord's work. That to me was the greatest work in the world.

Vonzeal and I attended "singing school" together to learn how to read "shaped note Gospel singing," taught by Mr. Snyder, a popular music teacher in Columbus.

We enjoyed singing duets and were always available to perform when asked. We had a great friend, B. F. Pugh who was music director at the North Highland Assembly of God. This church held a thirty minute Sunday Night radio program beginning at 10:30p.m. from the church auditorium. Mr. Pugh invited us to sing duets and to sing with the choir. We usually left Porter Memorial each Sunday evening, had refreshments at some restaurant and then joined the North Highland Choir for their radio program.

We never got tired of being in the Lord's work. Our happiest times were at church with our young intermediates or at community revival meetings.

And then, of course, I began to feel God's pulling me into the ministry.

Finally, one night our pastor, Brother E. R. Broadwell, began to preach on the subject, "And he saith unto them, Follow me, and I will make you fishers of men. And they straightway left their nets, and followed him," from Matthew 4 :19 and 20.

And Brother Broadwell dwelt on the word *make*.

"You follow me," the Lord said, "And I'll *make* you what I want you to be."

At the end of the service that night, I was asked to lead in prayer. That was the first time I'd ever been asked to pray in public, and I was so frightened that I couldn't find words to say. Vonzeal thought that I hadn't heard the preacher, so she squeezed my arm and when she looked up at me, she saw I was weeping. She held on to me real tight, and as I began to pray, I began weeping out loud and praying. Weeping uncontrollably. The presence of the Holy Spirit had touched me. When I finished, Vonzeal and everyone around us was weeping.

People began asking, "Has God called you to preach?"

"You should be a preacher!"

Something like that had already entered my mind, and I'd begun having little discussions with myself saying, "No, I can't preach – with only a sixth grade education – that's impossible. No." But a voice inside me would argue, "Come on – preach!" Again, I'd shake my head and say "No, I can't." But I kept feeling the urge, so strong and passionate.

Vonzeal and I went home that evening and read the Bible and prayed together. I shared with her my feelings of inadequacies. When we finally went to bed, we still couldn't sleep. We got up and read the Bible together again, got on our knees and prayed some more. This indecision continued on through the night until about 3:00a.m. when we found this verse of scripture:

Matthew 6: 31-33, "Therefore take no thought, saying, What shall we eat? or, What shall we drink? or, Wherewithal shall we be clothed? (For after all these things do the Gentiles seek:) For your heavenly Father knoweth that ye have need of all these things. But seek ye first the kingdom of God, and his righteousness; and all these things shall be added unto you," and Matthew 10:16-20, "Behold, I send you forth as sheep in the midst of wolves: be ye therefore wise as serpents, and harmless as doves. But beware of men: for they will deliver you up to the councils, and they will scourge you in their synagogues; And ye shall be brought before governors and kings for my sake, for a testimony against them and the Gentiles. But when they deliver you up, take no thought how or what ye shall speak: for it shall be given you in that same hour what ye shall speak. For it is not ye that speak, but the Spirit of your Father which speaketh in you."

Vonzeal was lying across the bed, listening to me read this passage, and I asked, "Honey, do you really think this means what it says?"

"Is it in the Bible?" she asked.

"Yes, I just read it to you, didn't I?"

She raised up from the bed and stated, "Well, if it's in the Bible, it's true!"

And the Lord moved our hearts. We didn't need anything else. "If it's in the Bible, it's true." The Bible is eternal, it is divine and it is the inspired Word of God. At that time, I knew nothing of those concepts. All I knew was what she said, "If it's in the Bible, it's true!" That meant that I didn't have to worry about my life, what I'll wear, or what I'll say, because the Bible said that these things would be given to me in the hour of my need. God will tell me what to do.

And we began our walk with God.

On that night in March, 1945, we went down on our knees again by the bed and committed what we had to the Lord. We didn't have much; we didn't have anything really. Just ourselves. That was all we had to commit to the Lord. Together we committed ourselves totally to the Lord.

And then we got excited about it. We got up, dressed and walked (we didn't have any transportation) down the street and woke our preacher and got him up out of bed to share with him what had happened.

We walked over and woke Vonzeal's parents, then my parents to tell them the news. Afterwards we began visiting everybody in the community, telling them what had happened. I went to work that day and had a great day. I told everybody at the Peanut Company what we had experienced. That morning at my desk I snuck a few free minutes to read the entire book of John. When I got to chapter 14, "Let not your heart be troubled; ye believe in God, believe also in me. In my Father's house are many mansions: if it were not so, I would have told you. I go to prepare a place for you."

I was inspired to write down these words:

THE GREAT HOMECOMING
I'm thinking of a home on the other shore
where sorrow and pain will come no more.
Instead there will be peace and joy and love
in that beautiful home that's waiting above.

I'm praying that there on that judgment day,
I can hear my blessed saviour say,
Come ye faithful servant true
And receive the rewards I have prepared for you.

Oh how happy I'll be
to think of the loved ones that I'll see.
To live forever and forever more
in that beautiful home on the other shore.

I'm praying that you, somehow, some way,
Will think of that coming judgment day.
Think of that saviour so kind, true and brave
That rose victorious over sin, hell and grave

Trust Him to the extent that he'll save your soul,
And come journey with me to that blessed home.

I used words in this poem that I didn't even know how to spell. But they were in my heart, engraved there, and they have never left me.

The following Sunday I went forward during the invitation to make the announcement that God had called me to preach, and I had surrendered to the ministry. This announcement was made to the church, and the church voted to license (or liberate) me to exercise that gift. This is the normal procedure in the Southern Baptist Church. When one feels called to preach and has demonstrated his sincerity to the church, and the church feels he has the commitment and has been divinely called, they will license him (sometimes called liberate him) to exercise the gift of preaching. Sometimes he is referred to as a licensed preacher and sometimes a liberated preacher. This simply means that no church has called him as a pastor. He will not be ordained as a pastor until a church is impressed enough with his preaching to call him as their pastor. A licensed preacher is authorized to preach and to exercise the other gifts with the exception of the ordinances of the church. As far as the Southern Baptists are concerned, a licensed preacher is not authorized to baptise, to administer the Lord's Supper or to perform wedding ceremonies. All of the other functions of a preacher, he is at liberty to do, but primarily he is to preach and demonstrate his skills so that some church will eventually call him as pastor. When that happens, the interested church requests his home church to ordain him to the gospel ministry so that he might serve as their pastor. This is a very high moment in the life of any young preacher.

After he has made his commitment personally, followed by his public announcement to his home church in a regular worship service, the church will vote and place in the minutes of the church that they have liberated or licensed this young man to be involved in ministry.

Our pastor, Brother Broadwell said, "Jim, you're going to preach two weeks from now."

"Two weeks! Oh, I don't know if I'm ready..."

"I've got to be out of town that week, and it will be a perfect opportunity for you to fill in for me – without having me looking over your shoulder. Don't you think?"

So I agreed to preach my first sermon two weeks before Easter, 1945.

I thought I could probably just preach forever, and I prepared about an hour's worth of sermon on The Great Commission, Mark 16:15, "Go ye into all the world, and preach the gospel to every creature."

I developed my sermon on "Who is to go?" I am to go, you are to go, we are all to go. Go *where*? Into the world, everywhere. And tell *what*? The Gospel. Jesus died and rose again. *Why* are we going to do this? Because the world's lost.

I got my *"who,"* I got my *"where,"* *"what"* we're going to tell and *"why."* I didn't know enough to write the thoughts down.

Coming home from work Friday evening before I was to deliver my very first sermon, I was sitting on a city bus, and heard one of the two ladies sitting in the seat in front of me talking.

One said to the other, "Are you going to church Sunday?"

The other lady answered immediately, "Oh, yes! I'm going to Porter Memorial. I understand there's a young boy who's going to preach his first sermon, and I've never heard anybody preach his first sermon."

I was mortified. I pulled my cap down over my face and slid down into my seat. It frightened me, and I prayed and prayed all the way to my bus stop. Someone was making a special trip to hear me preach!

Vonzeal listened to my sermon over and over, and we discussed it and prayed about it. She continued to console and reassure me.

That Sunday morning came, and Vonzeal made sure my shirt was starched and ironed to perfection. I wore my Sunday suit – the only suit I owned. Everything was ready for that first sermon. We were excited, yet so very nervous.

We got there and I was, of course, going to sit on the platform with the Deacon and the Minister of Music. Vonzeal and I were separated for the first time.

When we came out on the platform in that *giant* church,[3] all I saw were eyes. Every eye on me, every direction I looked from the balcony to the floor. I was never more frightened in my whole life.

I searched for Vonzeal, but I couldn't locate her in the auditorium and all during the song service, I scanned the auditorium for her. She wasn't sitting where we usually sat. I trembled inside and thought, "I'll never be able to preach if I can't find her."

Finally, I saw the top of her head; she was looking down and as I spotted her, as though it were magic, she raised her face and our eyes met. Tears were streaming from her eyes and tears began to flow from mine. All the fear vanished then because she winked at me through her tears. I knew I could do this.

So I stood to preach when the time came and finished my whole sermon in ten minutes. My *Who, What, Where,* and *Why* was almost stated in that fashion. My whole sermon was over, and I'd just started. Here I was – finished. And terrified. I still needed forty more minutes of material.

So I just simply began telling the congregation what had happened to me two weeks earlier when Brother Broadwell had preached his sermon, "I'll make you to become fishers of men." I described in detail how the Lord had called me and shared with the congregation the testimony of our decision.

That turned out to be the sermon that I needed to tell. Everybody watched, listened and wept. It was a wonderful, terrible sermon.

When I gave the invitation, two people came for-

[3]The church where I'm currently pastor has a vestibule bigger than Porter Memorial's whole building.

ward to be saved. One of those was Phillip Clark, the son of the man who had persuaded me to come to church, Mr. Sam Clark. The other was Gladys Miller who continues to be a dear friend until this day.

After my first sermon and my announcement to the church, Porter Memorial Baptist Church, during their business meeting, licensed me to exercise the gift of preaching.

Our revival meeting started the following Sunday with Brother Jim McRay. During the week of revival meeting, thirty-six of our intermediates were saved.

Vonzeal and I were shouting and having a glorious experience.

One night, Jim McRay said to me, "Jim, you should come to Mercer and go to school."

"Mercer University," I thought. "I don't even know how to spell it." And I couldn't tell Mac that I was only educated through the sixth grade. I was too embarrassed to tell him that. But every time we'd see him at Church, he'd repeat his plea, "Come to Mercer."

The week wore on, and I told Vonzeal "Let's get Brother Mac to come over here and get him all by himself and let me tell him why I can't go to Mercer."

Vonzeal went to her mother and borrowed silverware, dishes and everything we would need for our dinner guest. With her mother's help, she prepared the meal. On Friday evening he came over, and I confessed to him, in a very reserved way, the fact that I only had a sixth grade education. "Mac, I can't go to college. I have too far to go."

Brother Mac exclaimed "But wait, don't be so sure. There's a provision at Mercer. We have special students there who take remedial courses."

I didn't know what the word remedial meant.

"Come on, Jim, you can start to Mercer, and later you can take a test and get your high-school diploma.

You'll be all right. How about coming up Thursday of next week and let me introduce you to Dr. Dowell?"

"Who's he?"

"The President of Mercer. And while you're there you can meet some of the other preacher boys."

With much trepidation, I agreed. Perhaps more out of curiosity than anything.

Early the next Thursday morning I got up and caught the 3:00a.m. bus into Macon, Georgia, then walked all the way from downtown to Tattnal Square on Mercer University's campus. There I sat on a bench, looking at that gorgeous school until daylight – laughing at myself.

"What a fool you are, Jim Dorriety. You don't even know what you're going to say when he introduces you to Dr. Dowell. What makes you think you can go to school here?"

I sat there nervous, scared, feeling lost and out of my element, until finally the sun peeked over the buildings. At daylight I walked over to Brother McRay's house and knocked on his door. He and his wife, Sybil, were waiting for me, and I had breakfast with them.

After our meal, he walked me up to Dr. Dowell's office and introduced me. Before the day was over, I was enrolled in Mercer University as a special student.

Chapter 6

1945

———⟫•⟪———

I caught the bus back home, and Vonzeal and I packed and moved into an apartment right on poverty row at Mercer University. We sold our 1936 Oldsmobile for three hundred fifty dollars. I told her, "That's enough, that'll be enough money."

"But what are we going to do for a living?"

My belief was so strong, I said, "Well, honey, we don't have to worry about that. God will take care of us. We have enough money. We've got three hundred dollars to get us through college. Besides, remember what God said in Matthew 6:31 "Therefore take no thought about what we'll eat, drink or wear."

We paid fifty-five dollars for a man to move us to Macon. I paid my tuition fee, our utility bill and housing for a full quarter. We didn't have any debt. Plus, we had a little bit of money left over.

So I started college in Macon, Georgia, and Vonzeal and I moved our church membership to Tabernacle

Baptist Church where Dr. A. C. Baker was the pastor. This was the church many young ministerial students from Mercer attended.

My first quarter at Mercer University, like an idiot, I signed up for General Biology, Modern History, Christianity and Physical Education.

The only problem was . . . I had a little academic problem, they told me. Well, one glorious thing about my ignorance – I didn't know what I had. I thought, "well if you don't know what you've got, it'll probably go away. No need to take anything for it. It'll work out. Just go by faith."

My very first college class was Biology. The word biology was not in my vocabulary, so I didn't have an idea what the course was about. But I was extremely excited as I sat there on the front row of the classroom. I'm a college student!

The professor, Dr. Carver, entered the room and laid his book on the most cluttered desk you can imagine. Standing in front of the students he asked, "What is life?"

My hand shot straight up. He turned and looked directly at me, and suddenly I realized that I wasn't quite sure where I should go with the answer. "Life is living?" I swallowed, embarrassed.

"Okay. What's living?"

"Living is breathing, walking..."

He nodded. "What does that mean?"

"Relationships, talking..." My resources were exhausted. I shrugged that I had no more answer. Suddenly I wished I'd kept my hand down.

"All those answers are correct," he said to the class. Biology is the study of life from its beginning to its end, and perhaps we will never know all there is to know about life. But biology is an effort to learn everything we can about life." This was the foundation he gave us to begin this class.

I leaned proudly back in my seat. I knew this subject. This was going to be easy.

About three weeks after we arrived at Mercer, of course, our money was gone. Vonzeal got a job at Bibb Manufacturing Company's home office in Macon working as a clerk in the finance office while I attended school.

Before Vonzeal received her first check, we ran out of food. The only thing we had in our pantry was a big bag of dried black-eyed peas, a box of powdered milk and three boxes of corn flakes. For breakfast we'd eat corn flakes with the mixed-up powdered milk. For supper, we'd have fried cornbread and black-eyed peas. We ate two meals a day, every day for two weeks, still praying and thanking God for everything we had.

Sitting at our dinette table one night studying my textbook, I heard Vonzeal, who was reading the newspaper, exclaim, "Oh, that's so pretty!"

"What?" I asked. She showed me a picture of a blouse in the paper, and when I looked at it, I became upset because I had no money to buy her that blouse. Suddenly, I realized that here was something my wife wanted that I couldn't provide.

"Well, I don't have any money, but I'll tell you what I can do," I was angry. "I can quit school and go get a job and make money!"

"I didn't mean that I wanted it. I just thought it was pretty," she consoled.

But that didn't satisfy me, "Well, let me put these books down, and I'll go make us a living!"

The more she consoled me, the madder I got, mainly because I was enjoying the consoling. "I'll quit school!" I insisted.

One of the many gems of wisdom that Vonzeal gave me was this. "Jim, let me tell you something. I'd rather continue to eat black-eyed peas and cornbread and drink water and know that we are in the direct center of God's will than to have this blouse or any other thing in the world. We're in the center of God's will, and He will take care of the other things later."[4]

Then just as we were beginning to feel desperate, a wonderful thing happened.

Dr. Hansford Johnson, the head of the Christianity department, came to my apartment on Saturday and said, "Jim, there's a church over in Eastman, Georgia that needs somebody to preach, and I wonder if you'd go."

Later I learned out that the only reason he'd asked me was because there was no one else available. All the other ministerial students were busy.

Without hesitation I said, "Yes, Dr. Johnson, I'll go. What's the name of the Church."

"New Daniels Baptist."

"I'll take it, I'll go."

"Oh, by the way, they want you to be there tonight."

"That's fine, I'll be there tonight."

After he left, Vonzeal asked how were we going to get there. We had no transportation. I answered, "I don't know, but get dressed first."

Vonzeal had drawn her first check from the mill – twenty-five dollars for working that week. I went downtown to Dunlap Chevrolet, found Mr. Dunlap and told him my predicament. I said, "We just need some transportation, and if my wife and I can't find any other way we're going to hitch-hike."

In addition to his dealership, Mr. Dunlap had a car rental business, and he brought out a brand new,

---

[4] Years later when I was able to hand hera $100 bill and tell her to go buy something for herself, I'd remember the sacrifices that she had made so we could continue in the Lord's work.

black Chevrolet, filled it with gas and said, "Preacher, you go on."

Oh, it felt so good to be called Preacher. I never had been called Reverend or Pastor before.

So we drove to Eastman, Georgia where Dr. Johnson had given me directions to a store and told me to ask for a Mr. Law. "He'll take care of you and get you to the church."

We found Mr. Law, and he took us out to his house. Brother Law said, "Now Preacher do you and Vonzeal want to eat before or after church?"

"Oh, let's eat before church," we piped up. We were so hungry, and I hoped we could get something else again after church. So we ate before church and I preached that Saturday night, then stayed over and preached Sunday morning and again Sunday night.

Sunday evening several people came by to say, "Preacher, I put a little package in your car; I hope you enjoy it." And the church paid me twenty-five dollars for my services.

When we got in the rental car after Sunday evening service, the back seat was *filled* with groceries. We drove out of town until we were safely away from the community and pulled off to the side of the road. Vonzeal and I climbed into the back seat to see what we'd gotten. It was better than Christmas!

There was a whole country ham, and eggs buried in meal, sweet potatoes, canned pork chops and canned sausage. We had a real prayer meeting right there beside the road. Then we drove on home and unloaded the groceries and had prayer again. We got all that food out on the counter and admired it before we put it away in the pantry.

Then I drove downtown and asked the night clerk at the Chevrolet rental company how much I owed him for the automobile. He figured it up, and the bill came to twenty-four dollars. I used the twenty-five dollars I had received from New Daniels to pay him and happily walked back to our apartment at Mercer. We had a pantry full of groceries, and that was good because I was hungry again. Plus, we still had Vonzeal's pay check.

The following Sunday was a fifth Sunday, and we decided to get on a bus and go to Columbus to visit our families. I immediately went to see Dr. Forte.[5] He still had the drug store, and he was busy filling prescriptions when I got there. Falling right back into my old routine, I started waiting on customers while I told him about school and my church.

"Last Sunday I preached at New Daniels Church."

"Well, how'd you get there?" he inquired, counting out two dozen or so red pills.

"We rented a car with Vonzeal's paycheck and got paid just the right amount to come out even." I was so proud. "But that's just fine, because those church members gave us a lot of groceries. We're eating high on the hog!"

In another hour or so, he said, "Come on, I want you to make a trip with me." We got into his car and drove down to Second Avenue to Ray Dowling's filling station and used car lot. I knew Mr. Dowling because he was a member of Porter Memorial Church.

I milled around while Dr. Forte and Mr. Dowling went outside to talk. These were grown men, and I was still just a young man and didn't want to interfere with their business. I saw them come back in, and Dr. Forte wrote a check to Mr. Dowling, transacting some business.

When he came out, he had the keys to a blue 1938 Ford dangling from his fingers. "I just bought myself a new car. Do you mind driving it back to the drugstore for me?" So I followed him in this clean, beautiful Ford

[5] I still, to this day, try to see him every time I'm in Columbus.

and brought the keys back to him.

"What a sweet driving little car. It's just squeaky clean." I complimented him on his selection.

He turned around and, instead of taking the keys, he said, "Just put them in your pocket. I bought it for you. You've got to have a proper way to get to your church."

I broke down. "You can't do that. I can't afford to pay you for that car!"

"Well, I know that. But, if you ever can, do, but if you can't, it's all right."

Vonzeal and I were overwhelmed. We drove home in that car. I sat behind that steering wheel like a king, and every time I'd look over at Vonzeal, she'd be giggling.

In 1968 I went back to Columbus and visited with Dr. Forte. When I got there, he was teary eyed. When I asked why he was weeping, he said, "I've just received the greatest blessing I think I've ever had. Your sixteen year old son, Jerry, came by a little while ago. He asked to see me privately, and I took him back to my office. Jerry said to me, "Dr. Forte, I want to thank you for what you did for my Dad when you bought that Ford for him. I've heard him tell that story so many times, and I just want to thank you personally for what you did for my family."

New Daniels Baptist Church asked me to return and preach again, so Vonzeal and I drove over in our new Ford. After the service during a conference that Sunday, they called us to their pastorate. With a copy of their minutes in hand, I returned to Macon and delivered that request to Dr. A. C. Baker at Tabernacle Baptist Church, with a request from New Daniels that I be ordained into the ministry so that I might serve as their pastor. Dr. Baker began to make arrangements for that ordination. All pastors have their own personal plans and procedures. Dr. Baker first got the church to approve the ordination; then a service was scheduled for that particular ordination, usually one of the regular worship services. He then took the responsibility of calling together a presbytery examining council, which would examine me theologically. Dr. Baker, of course, did this many times since many students at Mercer were members at Tabernacle.

One of Dr. Baker's personal requirements was that the one to be ordained have lunch with him and spend most of the day with him preceding the night of his examination. This was a period of time which Dr. Baker felt he could use to instruct a young pastor and let him know what was to occur during the examination. The experienced pastor could put the novice at ease and help with any advance questions he might need to have answered.

It just so happened that Dr. Baker had asked Dr. Hansford Johnson, head of the the Christianity department at Mercer University, to serve on that ordaining council. The others were Brother L. B. Sauls, pastor of Second Baptist Church, Dr. Osterly, pastor of Tabernacle Baptist Church and Dr. A. C. Baker, himself.

In the day which I spent with Dr. Baker preceding the examination, we spent a couple of hours talking before, during and in a session after lunch. Then I was released to go home and get prepared to return early to meet with the ordaining counsel. He began to talk to me about things which I might encounter as a pastor. In fact, I was tremendously impressed with his sharing with me the responsibilities which I would have, the type of personality which I would need to maintain, the type of personal relationships which I would need with people. I was being set aside to represent the Lord and

Christianity, but also the Southern Baptist Convention. I was to represent all others who were involved in the ministry. All preachers are judged by one and my involvements would be a reflection not only on me, but also on all other preachers.

However, I was shocked and embarrassed when he said, "Brother Jim, you must be very careful in your relationship with the female members in your church." I was shocked, because I could not believe anyone who confessed to being a Christian, let alone a minister, would ever be involved, or even tempted to be involved, in an immoral way with someone. I could not believe what he was saying. He shared with me experiences of some ministers who had been totally destroyed because of their impropriety in their relationship with a female member of their church. This was embarrassing to me as a young preacher. I tried to assure Dr. Baler that there would never be this sort of problem with me. But he continued to warn, "You must listen . . . and I want you to hear and heed my words. I witnessed the destruction of one young preacher who, during a counseling session with a young lady from his church, was accused of attempted rape after her efforts of enticement were rebuffed. She ripped her blouse open and ran from his office calling for help and falsely accused him."

When I got home, I talked to Vonzeal about the admonitions Dr. Baker had given me. I was distraught and said, "I'm really concerned about Dr. Baker. He must have a dirty mind!" It just seemed to be a total impossibility that this type of situation could ever occur.

Vonzeal reacted very positively in favor of Dr. Baker. "We must listen to what he says and prepare ourselves in the event that anything like this happens to you. I'm sure Dr. Baker's intentions are pure, and we will just have to work this out for ourselves."

"Well, how would I handle something like that?" I asked her.

"Jim, if a female member of the church approaches you, and you become uncomfortable, let's just sit down and talk about it. We'll decide how to handle each situation as it arises – together."

So we decided that should I ever feel that a female member of the church was making suggestive comments or actions, I would let Vonzeal know who it was and what type of enticement it was. We didn't know the wisdom of this at the time, but we used our tactic all through our ministry. In any particular type of situation where I felt that there was someone with whom I was uncomfortable, based on their words or actions, I would immediately share it with Vonzeal, and together we would pray and commit that person to the Lord. Vonzeal would also help watch that I never got in a precarious position with that particular individual. Our being forewarned proved to be a very positive thing all through our ministry. And we were wrong occasionally. Sometimes I was mistaken, when I just thought someone was making advances, and they were not. Vonzeal and I felt that this was the proper procedure for us to follow together, and we were never faced with any embarrassing immoral situations. When I visited female members in their homes, Vonzeal, or one of the deacons, accompanied me.

One of my most embarrassing moments happened during a visit with a lady in the hospital. Hers was not a private room, and there was a lady in the next bed who said, "Brother Dorriety, don't you remember me?" I looked at her lying on the other bed in the hospital room, but I was not sure if I knew her, so I answered, "I don't recognize you."

"Well, you should," she emphatically replied. "I'm a member of your church." She told me her name.

Without thinking, I blurted out, "Oh, you'll have to forgive me. This is the first time I've seen you in a nightgown lying on your back." Then I realized what I had just said and became so befuddled and embarrassed. I had only meant that I had always seen her at church all dressed up, but my words had come out all wrong.

The ladies enjoyed a big laugh at my expense, and later when I shared the story with Vonzeal, she laughed too.

During the ordination examination, the evening after my day spent with Dr. Baker, I was extremely frightened. Dr. Hansford Johnson, head of the Christianity department at Mercer and one of the professors whose course I was flunking, was on the counsel. I knew that he could ask me questions I could never answer . . . he'd already done so on examinations at school. Then Dr. A. C. Baker asked Dr. L. B. Sauls to serve as secretary and asked Dr. Hansford Johnson to lead all of the questions since he knew that Dr. Johnson would know the fields which needed to be covered, such as my call to the ministry and my knowledge of doctrine. This frightened me! The ground rules were that after Dr. Johnson asked me a question, any other member of the counsel could follow up with any other question in that particular line of thought. When they were satisfied, Dr. Johnson moved to the next area.

We all sat together in the counsel, and the meeting opened with prayer. Dr. Johnson very formally asked me my first question. "Mr. Dorriety, let me ask you first of all . . . who is God?"

My mouth was dry and my heart was racing. I thought, "Oh me, I've already missed the first question." I stalled for time. "Dr. Johnson, God is . . ." I paused and started again with my mind racing through scriptures, trying to find an answer. "God is . . . uh, God is . . ." About the third time I said "God is . . .," I remembered that there is a verse that says, "God is love." I was so thrilled when that thought came to my mind and I blurted out, "God is love!"

He nodded his approval, but waited for more.

My mind continued to race with my heart racing right along with it. I continued again. "God is . . ." Then I remembered that God had created the world, and I said, "God is the Creator!"

He again nodded his approval, but continued to wait for more.

So for the third time, I tried to determine who God is. I was stammering, "God is . . ., God is . . ., God is Eternal!"

He nodded his approval again, but still continued to wait for more.

In my desperation, I felt that I might possibly faint because I thought I was totally failing the very first question. Finally I blurted out, "God is a Spirit!"

At this point, Dr. A. C. Baker came to my rescue and said, "Dr. Johnson, I really feel this young man has answered as well as any of us could."

Dr. Johnson agreed, "He sure has." Then to me he said, "Mr. Dorriety, I didn't ask you this question to embarrass you, but I wanted to teach you something. That is that man's mind will never be able to comprehend God in His entirety. God is above all things, and there is no way that we, as finite human beings, can ever reach a level where we know . . . for His ways are higher than our ways and His thoughts are higher than our thoughts."

Dr. Johnson's tremendous lesson continues to linger with me to this day.

Then he moved on into other areas, and I began to feel comfortable in my examination and was ordained by the counsel the following Sunday, November 21, 1945.

It was not long after that, a year or so later, when I was studying the Bible passage where God had asked Moses to go and deliver the children of Israel from Egyptian bondage. Exodus 3:13, "And Moses said unto God, Behold, when I come unto the children of Israel, and shall say unto them, The God of your fathers hath sent me unto you; and they shall say to me, What is his name? What shall I say unto them?"

Immediately I thought of that ordaining moment when Dr. Johnson had asked me "Who is God?" Here is Moses saying, "Who are you?" I thought, "Oh, boy, I'm going to find out now who He really is."

Exodus 3:14, "And God said unto Moses, I AM THAT I AM: and He said, thus shalt thou say unto the children of Israel, I AM hath sent me unto you."

I paused for a moment and reflected upon my ordaining examination. I began to understand what He meant, "I am that I am." "I am whatever I need to be. I am whoever I need to be. I am that I am. I am capable of being whatever I need to be at the moment."

As I sat there, I realized that I had answered Dr. Johnson correctly in the first two words I had uttered. If God says of Himself, "I am . . .," there is nothing more I can say except, "God is!"

On the Sunday following my ordination, we were called to preach part-time in Byron, Georgia at a country church – Tharpe Memorial Baptist Church. Tharpe Memorial asked me to preach on the first and third Sundays. Each church was paying me twenty-five dollars a week, so now I was making seventy-five dollars per month. The next Sunday Harrison Baptist Church, south of Atlanta, called me to preach on the third Sunday. I had three churches and was making one hundred dollars per month.

From those two weeks that we ate black-eyed peas and cornbread and prayed and thanked God for what we had, Vonzeal and I have never wanted for anything. We had everything we needed, and most of the things we wanted.

But, we have always kept a bag of dried black-eyed peas and powdered milk in our pantry. To this day you'll find those two items in my house.

Of course, I struggled through that first quarter at Mercer. You know the grades I made at the end of that first quarter?

Three F's, and a "C" in Physical Education.

Three big fat F's.

One of those F's was, of course, biology. But I had learned more in that classroom studying under Dr. Carver, than I had ever known about biology. Receiving that F was not a negative; it was just a little set back. I knew when I returned the next quarter, I would pass biology. Yes, I got an F, but I now had knowledge about a subject I had known nothing about four months ago.

So I decided I'd start the second quarter. I figured I was just a slow starter. My philosophy had always been to decide what I wanted to do and just keep doing it until it was finished.

I signed up for English and I always flunked English. Today if I had to take it, I'd flunk it. I don't know a split infinitive from a dangling participle . The words sound like profanity to me. They tell me they are not, and I hope they aren't.

I signed up for algebra, even though I didn't know one algebraic sign from another. When they started talking about logarithms, the closest thing I knew was log rollings. My other courses were guidance, physical education and hymnology, taught by Dr. Arthur Rich.

And, of course, I retook biology.

At the end of that quarter I went down and got my credits. I was thrilled because I made only three F's.

I made an A in hymnology, obtained a B in physical education, and finally passed biology – with a C.

My transcript is the most unusual transcript of any student who has ever attended Mercer University, and that's a matter of record. I have six F's and minus fifteen honor points in only two quarters of school. I was going in the wrong direction.

But, of course, I registered for the second year of college. When I got there, the registrar had a note attached to my registration form which read, "Send Mr. Dorriety to see Dr. Dowell." So I went to see Dr. Dowell. I couldn't understand what could be wrong.

He was a tiny, little man, very formal, but possessing a great spirit. "Dr. Dowell," I said, "I went to register a while ago and they won't let me go to school."

He was kind and talked for a while, trying to calm me down, and said in his very formal way, "Mr. Dorriety, we need to talk about it a little bit. I want you to sit down and let's talk." So I sat and we talked.

Anxiously I asked "Why won't they let me go to school?"

And finally he admitted, "Well, you're having academic problems."

I answered, "No, I haven't had any academic problems that I know of; I have a headache once in a while, but I take aspirin and it gets all right."

But I couldn't tease him or talk him out of it. He told me the institution's reputation was at stake. "We're going to just have to ask you to leave school."

I answered, "Well they tell me in order to become a preacher, I've got to get an education. And I've just now gotten started; I've just passed my first course. Now you want to throw me out. Please let me stay; I'll make it -just give me a little more time," I pleaded. "What does it matter if it takes me ten years, if you'll just let me stay?" I leaned over and clasped the edge of his desk so hard, my knuckles turned white. I didn't want to leave school. I didn't want to admit failure or defeat.

"Son," he answered, "Please go back and get some foundation. If you'll do that, I'll personally see that you have no problem getting back into Mercer."

They didn't let me stay. I had to leave.

Chapter 7

1946-1950

Broken-hearted and embarrassed, we left that beautiful campus not knowing where to turn next. "Well, that's it," I thought, "the end of my career." But I knew God had called me to preach, and I just had to preach.

When I came home from Dr. Dowell's office and faced Vonzeal with my failure, I saw what she was really made of. For the very first time, I saw who Vonzeal was. She straightened her spine and set her face. "Jim, it's just not meant to be right now. We must just continue to trust the Lord. Don't feel bad; you have done all any man could do; so you must believe that there is a plan in all this. Let's just go on and see where He leads us."

"I've let you down!" I sobbed. I'd always been a fighter, and the thought of failure was unbearable to me. The thought that I was less than I should be in Vonzeal's eyes was destroying me. I was the man of the house. She should not have the worries that she was forced to face. I loved her and wanted our life together to be as perfect as I could make it.

"No, you haven't let me down," she insisted. "God is in control of us. Let's get control of ourselves."

The following Sunday was a fifth Sunday, our only Sunday off from our three part-time churches. We decided a change of scenery would do us good, so we drove to Dothan, Alabama to visit Vonzeal's loving aunt. With the humiliation and defeat still so acute, we weren't ready to face our parents.

Vonzeal's cousin worked at a shoe store in Dothan, so we went over to visit with her that Saturday afternoon. While there, we were introduced to another lady who worked there. She was from Cottonwood, Alabama.

"Oh, you're a preacher? Where do you preach? Are you preaching anywhere this Sunday? Can you preach for us at Cottonwood tomorrow?" The questions flew at us.

"Where's Cottonwood?"

"About twelve miles from here. We don't have a pastor right now, and the guest pastor canceled. Would you please preach for us tomorrow?"

Vonzeal caught my eye, winked, and I said, "Yes, I reckon so."

That morning we got dressed and drove down to Cottonwood, Alabama. No one knew us. No one knew we'd flunked out of Mercer University. No one knew the heartache we felt. I stood and preached that morning and that afternoon the pulpit committee called me as their full-time pastor. With almost no reservations, we accepted, and then I preached the Sunday evening service.

After that evening service, the principal of the Cottonwood High School came over and introduced himself. "Brother Dorriety, can you deliver the Baccalaureate Sermon at graduation three weeks from now?"

I had no idea what a Baccalaureate Sermon was, but I answered, "Sure, I'll be glad to."

On the way home that night Vonzeal said, "Jim, isn't that an important sermon to students graduating from high school?"

"I don't know, but I'll figure out what it is. That's three weeks from now. There's plenty of time to prepare. We've got a dictionary; I'll look it up, if I can figure out how to spell it."

On the way back to Columbus to prepare for our move to Cottonwood, I stopped by to see Brother Broadwell. I told him about the Baccalaureate Sermon. He explained not only Baccalaureate, but also Commencement, and gave me one of his outlines.

So I gratefully accepted his outline and, with this as a guide, I developed my own sermon entitled "Building A Life," which was inspired from my own experiences as a weaver in the weave shed at Bibb Manufacturing Company.

As cotton threads come off the spools and pass into the fingers of the upper and lower warps, they reverse through the shuttle One would be down and the other up, then reverse while a constant thread passed between them, weaving a solid sheet of cloth.

Building a life is like weaving cloth. The outer life, such as actions and appearances, are the upper threads. The inner life, which represents one's hopes and aspirations, desires and dreams is like the lower threads. As the fingers of time pass between the threads, reversing aspirations to actions and dreams to realizations (and, if you keep your threads straight, strong and pure) you will weave a beautiful, sturdy fabric for life.

Well, they told me it was the greatest Baccalaureate Sermon they had ever heard. And I still couldn't spell it.

Vonzeal was expecting our first child, and I knew we had no money to pay for his birth. We decided that we could get along without our car, the Ford that Dr. Forte had purchased for us. We would just walk everywhere we needed to go. Cottonwood was a small town, and we lived within walking distance of the church, grocery and bank. We sold the car and put the money in the bank for our child's birth. Then a family in the church, whose son had left for college, loaned me his bicycle to use.

Of course, I never could keep up with the bicycle when was visiting and running from one store to the other. Someone would call and say, "Preacher, you left your bicycle down here outside my store. Thought you'd want to know where it is."

It worked just fine, pastoring a church and driving a bicycle, except when you were leading a funeral procession. Looked kind of funny.

But the Lord always provided. A wonderful elderly couple next door, Mr. and Mrs. Kelley, always brought the keys to their car over to us every evening, just in case Vonzeal's time came during the night.

Finally, just after midnight one night, Vonzeal woke me and said, "Get up, Jim and let's pray. It's time to go to the hospital." We got on our knees beside the bed and prayed two prayers. First, we prayed for her safety during the birth of our child. Second, we prayed for our child's salvation when he became of age.

We drove the Kelley's car to the hospital and waited all that night, all the next day and on into the second night before Jimmy was finally born. And we had the money to pay all the hospital bills.

Dr. Forte never really realized the value of that one gift he gave to us. He made it possible for us to have transportation not only to our churches, but also to Dothan where we encountered the lady who invited me to preach and become pastor of Cottonwood Baptist Church. Then finally to sell that car and have the money to pay for the birth of our first son was an added bonus.

In 1946, God, very dramatically, brought the problem of families affected by the tragedy of divorce to my attention while I was still a very young preacher here in my very first full-time church. Two young couples in town had eloped after their high school graduation. Neither of their marriages worked out and both couples went through the tragedy of divorce. A man and a woman from each marriage, returned to our little town, met and began dating.

They became active in the local church, and I became their pastor. The entire church knew that they were sweethearts, and the time came when they wanted to be married, and the young man came to me and asked if I would perform their ceremony.

I remembered what Brother Wilson, one of my fathers in the Faith, had said to me, "Don't ever marry anyone who's been divorced." On that basis, I politely declined.

Of course, that did not stop their marriage, but it stopped their worship in our church. To show my naivete, I went back to them to find out why they were no longer attending church. This young man, a little older than me, looked me in the eye but didn't invite me inside their home. He stood on the porch and angrily said, "You mean you would have nothing to do with our marriage, and now that we are married you want us to come to your church? As far as I'm concerned, you and the church can go to hell!"

My heart was broken. I turned from that experience and went on my way back into that little town. The only other minister there was a retired Methodist minister. With tears in my eyes, I went straight to his home and rang his doorbell. After I shared with him what had happened, he invited me inside to study the Bible and pray with him. For weeks afterward I sought guidance from my Bible and prayer and, based on what I thought the Living Word of God said, I changed my mind. From that time on I met to counsel with the couples, but I still married them.

The most dramatic thing I realized was that God did not hold me responsible for what happened to people prior to my getting acquainted with them, but, from the moment I encountered them, God held me responsible for my ministry towards them.

There are a great number of families who have, in some way or another, either personally or through a family member, experienced a divorce. And it is a tragedy. But remember this – Jesus loves you. He really loves you. If you have experienced the tragedy of divorce, you can still be a first class Christian, for God forgives all manner of sin, including divorce. There is only one unpardonable sin, and it is not divorce. It is to "blaspheme against the Holy Ghost." No theologian would argue with that. Only one unpardonable sin. Mark 3:28-29, "Verily I say unto you, All sins shall be forgiven unto the sons of men, and blasphemies wherewith soever they shall blaspheme: But he that shall blaspheme against the Holy Ghost hath never forgiveness, but is in danger of eternal damnation:"

Find a church that will love you, accept you and allow you to be a full first-class Christian. Find that church and get active in it.

I was scorned by so many of my fellow Baptist preachers when the news spread that Jim Dorriety would perform a ceremony for those who had experienced the tragedy of divorce.

Little did I know that one day, later on down the years, I would experience this tragedy in my own family with both of my sons.

While attending an associational pastors' conference, we decided to have a county-wide crusade. My friend, Dr. Henry A. Parker, pastor of First Baptist Church, Dothan, made a motion. "I nominate my young friend, Jim Dorriety, to be chairman of the Crusade Committee."

I almost fainted and tugged on his arm, "No, no, no. I can't do it."

He leaned over and whispered to me, "Don't worry, I'll help you."

They elected me Chairman, but Dr. Parker did most of the work. He wrote letter after letter for my signature. I told him what I wanted to say, he composed the most magnificent letters, and I signed them as if they were mine. Dr. Parker unselfishly served in the background with me. We invited Dr. Jess Henley[6] from Atlanta, Georgia as the Crusade Evangelist. During the crusade, in the city auditorium at Dothan, we had many professions of faith, a couple of whom later became outstanding preachers themselves.

To be the Chairman of that Crusade Committee felt great. Leading the group was the first big thing I had ever done. And it was all because of the unselfishness of Dr. Henry A. Parker, who took me by the hand and led me through that project.

During that year, my hometown church in Slocomb, Alabama invited me to preach their revival, and then they called me as their pastor. I declined, but they kept insisting.

"I need to go to school" I told them, "and I really

---

[6]Dr. Jess Henley has been my friend since then and I have invited him to almost every church I've ever been for revival meetings. In one of the greatest revivals we ever had, I baptised 115 people for the week. At another revival we had 141 additions to the church!

want to go to school. If you deacons will let me go to school, I'll be your pastor."

"You mean to college?" they asked.

"No, I mean back to high school." Embarrassed and humiliated, I opened my heart and told them that I had flunked out of Mercer University. "I want to be a regular high school student, play football and do everything a regular student does."

The deacons and the principal of the high school, J. B. Davidson, met for a discussion, but decided that it would not look right for the pastor of the First Baptist Church to be a regular high school student.

As an alternative, they had a suggestion; "Instead of sitting in class as a student, let's treat you as a teacher. In the meantime, we'll get tutors to tutor you. That will help you maintain the proper image as pastor of our church."

I agreed and, as a result, they called us to the pastorate of the Baptist Church in Slocomb. I became a substitute teacher at the high school even as I was earning my own high school diploma.[7]

I had two tutors – Annie Laurie Stutts and Mable Dorriety (later Harris). Mable helped me tremendously with my sermons, enunciation, pronunciation, English and diction.

Then at twenty-four years of age, while still in high school, I enrolled at Chipola Junior College and began earning credits. One of the professors, Dr. Nobel Bell was teaching a course on the Life of Christ from a textbook he had written called "An Exegetical Analysis of the Life of Christ."

---

[7]While there I began a choral program. One of the boys in the choir, Earl Tew, went on to graduate from Samford University with a high grade point average, then went to seminary and later became Vice-President of the Alabama Baptist Convention. Today, he introduces me as his high school teacher.

Dr. Bell died during that term, and his wife completed teaching the course.

One day after class Mrs. Bell motioned me to her desk, "Jim, Nobel was about your size. Would you be offended if I offered you some of his clothes?"

"I'd be honored." Young preachers don't turn down many offers.

We found that his suits, his shirts, even his shoes were an absolutely perfect fit. She must have given me ten to twelve suits, a dozen dress shirts and several pairs of shoes and socks.

Therefore, for several years, without two nickels to rub together, I was one of the best dressed preachers in Alabama, wearing the clothes of Dr. Nobel Bell.

Two years later, I graduated from high school with the class that I had been teaching for two years. My loyal, patient wife, Vonzeal, and my son, Jimmy, were there to watch me graduate from high school. I was twenty-five years old.

But, do you know what I did? As soon as I graduated from high school, I took my transcript of credits and my framed diploma and went straight back to Mercer University.

I put my diploma and my transcript on Dr. Dowell's desk and said, "Here I am, and I'm ready to go to school."

A small fellow, he got up and came around to where I stood, and, of course, by this time I had really put on some weight. He embraced me; his arms barely reaching around me. We just stood there and wept for a moment. Then he composed himself, broke away and readmitted me to Mercer.

The morning that my resignation was considered by Slocomb Baptist Church, there were a lot of tears in the congregation and in our eyes. Our son was now approaching three years of age and we were well entrenched in our ministry with their loving and generous fellowship.

Even after I presented my resignation, no one would make a motion that it be accepted. There was a lot of sniffing out in the congregation. Finally, after a long, poignant pause, the chairman of the deacons, and one of the eldest deacons there, Earnest Harris, stood and said, "I can understand that none of us wants to make the motion to accept our young pastor's resignation, so let me offer a substitute motion. Let's give Brother Jim and his family a 'leave of absence' to go back to Mercer University and complete his education."

The congregation voted on that motion, and I returned to school, anxious to complete my education.[8]

I went to the administrative office at Mercer and said, "Okay, I'm back. Let's just destroy my old transcript because it's got so many F's on it, and that's an embarrassment to me."

"I beg your pardon?" the administrator replied, raising her eyebrows. "Destroy your transcript?"

"That's right. I'm starting all over – brand new. I don't need that old transcript anymore." I was positive there shouldn't be any problem doing this.

"Mr. Dorriety, we can't do that!"

"Oh, sure you can," I insisted. "I want to just ignore everything I've done up to this point and start all over."

"Mr. Dorriety, that is *not* how the system works," I was informed icily. "Your transcript stands as is!"

I was angry to think that I would have to keep all those F's on my transcript. However, years later, I realized that I could turn that stumbling block into a blessing. I began to share my experience with high school and college students. The number of places I have

---

[8] That motion has never been removed from the minutes and we're still on leave of absence from the First Baptist Church of Slocomb, Alabama.

shared this story has been inspiring to many young people. I remember being introduced by a young pastor in Indiana, and in the middle of the introduction he broke down and wept. When he got his composure he said, "Dr. Dorriety doesn't know this, but he came to speak at our state convention and shared his difficult education experiences with us. He didn't know that I'd been fighting the same battle – that it was impossible for me to be a preacher because I did not have the education. After hearing him speak, I was inspired to start back to school. And, it's such a joy for me to be here now and introduce him to you as our guest evangelist at our revival meeting."

From then on, I didn't have any academic trouble at Mercer. I took the comprehensive exam, and (I was just a C student so forgive me if this sounds like I'm bragging, but I am), made four hundred and eighty out of a possible five hundred on the general education index. I was thrilled.

We enjoyed every moment as I went back through Mercer the second time around. My supportive companion Vonzeal was always there for me, reading every textbook I studied. Although she never graduated from high school, she loved to read and obtained her own education by studying all of my textbooks along with me. She was very artistic and studied piano lessons as a young adult and played, as well as sang, during many of our services. Her other past-times included ceramics, sewing, millinery, tailoring and painting.

I was a college student when Bill Bright first organized Campus Crusade. I heard about the four spiritual laws from other college students who were involved. Wondering if this guy was what he seemed to be, I decided to travel from Alabama to North Carolina to sit in on his conference and hear him first hand.

When I got to the auditorium, the usher handed me a blank piece of paper and a pencil as I sat down. The first part of the service ended, and Dr. Bright stood and said, "All of you have been given a blank sheet of paper, and I want you to write down your sins. We're going to take a spiritual bath." And then he said, "At the bottom of the page, I want you to copy 1 John 1:9, that says 'If we confess our sins, he is faithful and just to forgive us our sins, and to cleanse us from all unrighteousness.' Write those words down and confess your sins. You can then destroy that paper because He has forgiven you and your sins are gone. You will have taken a spiritual bath."

At that moment, I determined that I didn't have any sins and did not need to perform that particular exercise. I left the auditorium and stepped out to check on my automobile . I found where I had parked and decided to get in and listen to the radio for a while before going back for another session. As I sat there in the car, a sudden spotlight began to glow on the white sheet of paper I was still holding in my hand. In fact, the image frightened me . . . until I thought of one sin. But I was instantly relieved to realize the street light was shining down through the windshield and onto that piece of paper. But then I thought, "Well, since I've remembered that sin, I may as well write it down."

Before I finished writing that one, I thought of another one and wrote it down. Then I almost ran out of paper. Completing the exercise, I copied 1 John 1:9 and sat there in my automobile and literally took a spiritual bath. I was revived.

It was a marvelous exercise . . . and I learned that Bill Bright was real, and I know that Campus Crusade has done a great work across the years.

Vonzeal and Jimmy didn't move back to campus

right away. We rented a small apartment in Columbus and attended a little mission called Kendrick Memorial Baptist Church in Columbus. When Kendrick asked me to become their very first pastor, they were worshiping in a big barracks which had been moved from Ft. Benning. During the eleven months we were there we had one hundred and eleven additions to the church.

Every Monday morning, I commuted the one hundred miles to school in our blue 1946 Ford Club Coupe, returning to Columbus Wednesday for Prayer Meeting at Kendrick, going back to Mercer Thursday morning and returning again on Friday afternoon. On Monday, Tuesday and Thursday nights I remained on campus and stayed in the old Sherwood Hall. After about nine months of the constant commuting, coupled with all the responsibilities of church, family and school; the strain began to wear on me physically.

During this time, I had surgery on my toes to correct the problem which had developed in the service.

There was a pretty town called Lizella about twelve miles from the Mercer Campus. Every time I'd drive through this little community I would always think, "Boy, if I only had twelve miles to commute, what a joy it would be. Surely, there must be a Baptist Church in this city." Finally, on one particular Monday morning , I decided to find that church. Off the main road, in the little town, I found the beautiful Baptist Church of Lizella, Georgia. Right beside it sat the Methodist Church, and behind both churches was a large cemetery.

I drove my little coupe up into the church yard and looked it over, bowed my head and prayed. My prayer was simply this: "Lord, this would be so much better.

Only twelve miles from campus. When they need another pastor, I could be available. I have three more years at Mercer and this would be an ideal place for us to spend it. If it is at all possible, please make it so. Amen."

Then I drove on my way.

Imagine my surprise when a few weeks later, the school registrar, Frank Clark, called me into his office and said, "I had a call from Lizella Baptist Church wanting to know if you would come and preach. They're without a pastor, and they're looking for someone. They've heard of someone by the name of Dorriety whom they want to try out."

My heart was thrilled, and I immediately said, "Yes, I'll go this Sunday."

We found the most loving people; the congregation was so excited, and we had a marvelous morning service. We met in the afternoon, and they offered me two Sundays a month. There was no pastorium for us, but they assured us they would do anything they could to help us.

So I agreed to become the part-time pastor of Lizella Baptist Church.

But where were we going to live? I immediately went to Dr. Dowell and told him my housing predicament. He called Mr. Hattrick, the business manager, and asked him to find us an apartment on campus. And the Lord took care of the rest.

A month passed and we were so happy. Then a unique thing happened. I met another man on campus by the name of Daughtery, pronounced the same as Dorriety. When I related this information to the people at Lizella, I heard that he was actually the one they had learned about and wanted to come preach the trial sermon.

They had called the wrong pastor. But they loved us and kept us anyway. The Lord had heard and answered my simple prayer. Matthew 7:7, "Ask, and it shall be given you; seek, and ye shall find; knock, and it shall be opened unto you: For every one that asketh receiveth; and he that seeketh findeth; and to him that knocketh it shall be opened." In simple faith, I asked for that church, I knocked on that door; I waited and received an answer.

If it's in the Bible, it's true!

Jenkinsburg Baptist Church called us to preach part-time also. Now I had two churches, Lizella and Jenkinsburg .

Our family budget still operated on the original five envelope system. One – the Lord's money, two – groceries and household, three – clothing, four – medical and five – recreation. We had continued to follow this principle over the years together.

Jenkinsburg was paying thirty-five dollars per Sunday, and one Sunday Vonzeal had put the three dollars and fifty cents tithe into the envelope, but that was all we had to our name. Period. We had been invited after the service to have lunch with a family from the church. They enjoyed riding around every Sunday afternoon and buying ice cream. I thought, "If I put this money in, we won't have one penny this afternoon. And if we do stop to get ice cream, I'll be embarrassed because I can't even offer to pay for Jimmy's and Vonzeal's ice cream." So I decided I'd keep the Lord's money in my pocket until the evening service; therefore, if I had to use some of it, I could.

But that afternoon, the family paid for our ice cream, so I still had the three dollars and fifty cents in my pocket in the envelope.

That night during the song service the devil started talking to me. There were some things I would have loved to buy my wife and I thought, "I think I'll just keep it, and when they pay me my thirty-five dollars tonight, I'll have thirty-eight fifty, and maybe I can buy Vonzeal something special."

During the final song, I opened my Bible and began looking for my sermon. And I couldn't find it. And I began to look and flip. You don't know what misery is until you've got to preach and you've got no preach. That is misery. And suddenly, I realized I had the Lord's money in my pocket, and I turned to Willy J. Sanders and said, "Willy J., sing one more song." I was hoping they'd sing *"Rescue the Perishing."*

Willy didn't know why, but he announced another hymn. As the congregation began singing, I stepped off the platform, walked to the Lord's table and took that envelope out of my pocket. Placing it there in the offering plate, I made a vow, "Lord, if you'll just let me preach tonight, I won't ever be guilty of doing this again."

When I walked back up on the platform, I opened my Bible and found my passage of Scripture. I preached that night and heard what all young pastors love to hear. "Brother Jim, that was the greatest sermon you have ever preached."

After several months, I began going out to Lizella on Wednesday nights and conducting prayer meetings. One Sunday the pulpit committee asked me if I would possibly consider giving up the Jenkinsburg Church to go full time with Lizella. Since Lizella had been my answered prayer, I reluctantly resigned from Jenkinsburg Baptist Church just as they were planning their "Homecoming." Jenkinsburg determined this would be the ideal Sunday for me to preach my last sermon at that church.

While I stood in the pulpit and resigned, in a beautiful gesture of love and understanding, Jenkinsburg decided to invite the entire Lizella church congregation to come and be their guest at their Homecoming celebration. The combined services would afford them the opportunity to *send us to Lizella*, giving me a chance to preach to both of my congregations at one time.

We began to plan for the "Homecoming" celebration. Standing in the pulpit, I asked, "What should we serve? How should we handle the meal?"

Mr. Patrick, an elderly man in the church, raised his hand. "I have plenty of hogs, and I will be delighted to give as many as necessary to feed everyone. But we'll need to get someone to slaughter and barbecue them."

Immediately, I piped up, "I'll barbecue those hogs!" The congregation was shocked to hear their young pastor volunteering to slaughter hogs, but I convinced them I knew what to do, old farm-boy that I was. "But I'll need some help."

Harry Ridgeway, a personal friend, was there, so I asked him and Huey Hooten (who just happened to have a pick-up truck) to go out to Mr. Patrick's farm with me to help kill and dress the hogs.

The Saturday morning came for us to go out to Mr. Patrick's and get our three 280 pound hogs. We had the barbecue pits dug and ready with all the hickory wood. The barrels were ready to scald the hogs. The church ladies were working on the vegetables and other plans. We were all so excited. In order to get the meat ready for Sunday lunch, we planned to begin cooking Saturday afternoon and continue through the night.

We stayed up late Friday night planning. Step one: Kill the hogs. Step two: Bleed the hogs. Step three: etc. etc. Everything was planned to go like clockwork.

Old Mr. Patrick had suffered a stroke a few years back and was unable to get around very well. He walked with difficulty and used a cane. Therefore, he simply told us to come on out to the farm, and he described where these hogs were penned.

Huey, Harry and I jumped in the pick-up and headed out to Mr. Patrick's farm with a twenty-two rifle and knives. A young pastor and two young men were taking on a big responsibility.

As we passed the yard to go to the barn, we looked back towards the house and saw Mr. Patrick standing on his back porch, holding on to the post and waving his walking cane in the air. We thought he was waving at us; we waved back and moved on towards the lot where the hogs were penned.

The first pen we came to had a lot of hogs, not just three. All of them looked the same size, so we decided he must just want us to pick the hogs we wanted. We glanced back towards the house and he was still standing there waving his cane in the air. We waved back.

"Harry, let's catch this one." The three of us wrestled that hog into the back of the truck; I grabbed the rifle and shot the hog right between the eyes. We grabbed the second one and then the third one. In just a matter of minutes, we had all three hogs slaughtered, bled and ready for the scalding water.

We glanced back towards the house as we drove away. Mr. Patrick was still waving his cane in the air. We waved at him again and drove away. We didn't know until later that Mr. Patrick was yelling, "Stop, that's the wrong pen. Those are my registered Durocs. The pen with your hogs is further on down. Stop!"

But we had some of the finest barbecued pork anyone could ever eat. Fortunately, Mr. Patrick was good-natured and forgave us and even laughed with us.

The following Sunday we began our full-time ministry at Lizella Baptist Church which, as I have already mentioned, sat beside the Lizella Methodist Church and shared the cemetery. Since the beginning, the two churches had shared fellowships, attended one another's revivals and had enjoyed a general feeling of goodwill and cooperation.

But a few years previous, they had become estranged when a visiting Baptist evangelist had said some rather harsh things about the Methodist's belief of sprinkling. In fact, the two congregations had become completely alienated because of his remarks.

When I became their full-time pastor, I learned that the Methodist pastor was also a student at Mercer University. He and I met and decided that we'd try to correct this problem which had existed for years. We began going into the community together and visiting every home in that little town. We went door to door, introducing ourselves and inviting people to come to either church they chose. The word began to spread in the community. The Methodist and the Baptist ministers are visiting together; they are cooperating.

On the first fifth Sunday, we planned a joint worship service between the Methodists and the Baptists. I suggested we hold it in the Methodist Church because I felt we needed to go the extra mile since the Baptist evangelist had caused the problem. The other pastor agreed provided I would do the preaching. No mention of the problem was made to either of our congregations; we just planned the meeting.

And it worked. We were amazed that the two congregations began to worship together again in sweet fellowship. They continued their union services on the fifth Sunday until 1992.

The members of the congregation were so generous with me and my family. After prayer meeting Wednesday night, we'd always find a couple of dozen eggs, or a fryer chicken in the back seat of our car brought by the Scott Long family who owned a chicken farm.

Richard and Ida Ivey, the dairy owners, always

brought sweet milk, buttermilk and cream. Whatever they had, they shared with us.

But our financial problems were far from over. The church salary was very small and our family was growing. Plus, tuition and books had to be purchased.

One morning we found ourselves, once again, totally out of money. I made the statement, "I think it's time for me to quit school, get a job and work awhile."

Vonzeal, as she always did, said, "Oh, no! No, we cannot do that. You go on to school and forget about it. Who knows. The Lord may send us some money in the mail today." She hurried me out the door and disgruntled I went on across campus to my classes.

At noontime, I came home for lunch, and she met me at the door both laughing and crying as she threw her arms around me. It frightened me because I'd never seen her with that kind of expression.

"Honey, what's wrong?" I was so confused.

She pulled her arms from around me and showed me an envelope in her hand, containing a check for twenty-five dollars. "This came in the mail today!" There was no note nor explanation, and we had no idea who this check was from. We didn't recognize the signature, and the check was drawn on a bank in Atlanta. The money was a miracle. We cashed the check and came home rejoicing in the Lord.

We later learned that the check was from a man whose wife's funeral I had preached three months prior in Jenkinsburg while I was still pastor there. The man had finally located us and the check just happened to arrive the day Vonzeal had said, "Who knows. We may get some money in the mail today."

We never thought of the events as coincidental. We thanked the Lord for it and received it with gratitude. Philippians 4:19, "But my God shall supply all your needs according to his riches in glory by Christ Jesus."

If it's in the Bible – it's true!

The professor of church history at Mercer, Dr. Harold McManus, and I loved gardening together. Vonzeal and his wife, Louise, had become good friends, and our children Harold, Jr. and Jim, Jr. loved to play together. Sometimes Harold and I kept the boys, and the wives went shopping or to the movies together.

Jimmy had asked his mom why she kept a moth ball in the pockets of our clothes during the summer. "To keep bugs off the clothes," she had explained.

One Saturday afternoon, Harold and I worked in the garden while Vonzeal and Louise went to a movie. The two boys were out playing. Harold and I were talking and laughing and keeping a loose eye on the boys.

The next morning I went out to the garden and found a moth ball at the base of every plant in the garden. I called Harold, "Come look at this."

Harold picked one up and sniffed it. "These are moth balls; where did they come from?" He asked incredulously.

About then Vonzeal stuck her head out the back door and asked, "Jim, what happened to all my moth balls? They were in the dresser drawer yesterday, and now I can't find them."

Our sons, Harold, Jr. and Jim, Jr., had taken the moth balls. Knowing that they would keep bugs off our clothing, and after hearing their dads talk about keeping the bugs off the vegetables, they had put two and two together and had solved the gardening problem by placing a moth ball at the base of every plant in that little garden.

Mercer University had a requirement that all tuition fees be paid in full before a student could take the final exams. I got to the end of the quarter, lacking fifty dollars of tuition. Thinking I could borrow the money, I walked to a bank in downtown Macon with nothing but my signature for collateral. The banker stood up from his desk and said, "I'm sorry, we can't loan money to a ministerial student on a signature only" and walked away from me. The tears began to flow from my eyes, and I quickly rushed outside to the sidewalk where I stood consumed with self pity, desperation and embarrassment. Humiliated, I rubbed my eyes brusquely to remove the mist.

Walking down the street towards me was a blind couple, husband and wife; he with his guitar and she with her small accordion, arms linked together, a tin cup on the end of his guitar, she leading with her cane. They were singing, "Farther along, we'll know all about it. Farther along, we'll understand why."

The words of that song seemed to minister to me and I reached in my pocket and took out all I had left, a few dimes and nickels. After dropping all my money into his cup, I window-shopped on down the street, following them and listening to their songs. "Cheer up, my brother. Live in the sunshine. We'll understand it all by and by."

Back at Mercer campus, I went straight to Dr. Dowell's office and announced, "I'm going to have to drop out of school. I lack fifty dollars having my tuition paid; I've tried to borrow it and cannot. My exams begin tomorrow so I'm just going to have to wait and work for a while."

He immediately stood up, reached for his wallet and said, "No, you aren't!" He pulled out five ten dollar bills and said, "Get across the hall and give this to Lucille Johnson, pay your tuition fee and get on home and start studying."

"I didn't ask you for a loan," I stammered when he put the bills into my hand.

"I know you didn't; now get out of here and start

studying."

And I did.

After the sermon the following Sunday at Lizella Church, I became aware that the Deacons were having an impromptu meeting around the piano, while I greeted the departing congregation. In a few minutes, after most everyone was gone, Willy J. Sanders, the chairman of the Deacons, and the other five deacons walked up beside me.

"Pastor, we just had a Deacons' meeting, and we decided to do something for you. Scott Long suggested that we all give you a ten dollar bill. Here's six ten dollar bills, one from each of us." They each stuffed a bill into my pocket.

At that moment, I was sure that they had learned what had happened to me during the previous week, but I discovered later that they had never heard a word about our problems. They knew nothing about the bank's turning me down or about Dr. Dowell's loan of fifty dollars.

God provided five ten dollar bills to return to Dr. Dowell and ten dollars for me and my family. You can imagine the thrill in my heart.

Monday morning I marched right into Dr. Dowell's office and returned his fifty dollars. "I didn't expect you to pay this back," he said. And I shared with him the events of the preceding day.

He laughed and said, "It appears to me that you just need to let the Lord know and he'll take care of your needs." Luke 6:38, "Give, and it shall be given unto you; good measure, pressed down, and shaken together, and running over, shall men give into your bosom. For with the same measure that ye mete withal it shall be measured to you again."

I was asked to preach a revival in Skirum, Alabama

on top of Sand Mountain, Alabama. We were driving an old '41 Plymouth which had once been on a taxi line in Macon and had a hole in the roof. It didn't have a heater so, in the winter, I'd take a quilt and hang it in the door, roll up in it and fall in like a mummy. I carried my harmonica along so I could have music. Driving up the gravel road on top of the mountain, I wasn't sure if I was on the right road or not. I spotted a man leading a mule along and thought, "Well, he ought to know if this is the road to Skirum." I applied the mechanical brakes, but they locked and the car skidded on the gravel sending dust flying everywhere. The old man's mule became frightened and began to rear up while the man tried to settle him. I let my window down and pointed to the road ahead, "Is that the way to Skirum?"

He answered, "If that don't, I don't know what will!" Honest, he really said that. Of course, as I drove off, I figured if I'd lived all my life around a place called Skirum, I'd probably have a handful of retorts for strangers too.

I found Skirum and preached several days. On Wednesday, I said to the Pastor, Brother Carl Johnson, "Let's allow the people to do some preaching and testifying."

He nodded his approval, and different ones in the congregation began to rise from their seats to give testimony.

After several minutes, a lady on my right stood up holding an infant in her arms. She was looking up at the pulpit and began, "Brother Dorriety . . . ;" then she looked down at her infant and never said another word. She just stood there and cradled that infant. A few moments passed, it seemed like an hour, and the tears began to fall from her eyes and she sobbed aloud.

I knew I was in trouble. I was a young preacher and

didn't really know how to handle a situation like this. I looked over at Brother Carl for help, but he had his face buried in his handkerchief, his shoulders shaking with sobs. Then I heard others weeping. Then, without understanding, I, too, began weeping with big tears rolling from my eyes. I didn't know what else to do so I just stood there waiting and weeping.

Then I heard a man's voice in the back of the building break into sobs. He stood and moved into the aisle and started down. As he passed the lady with the infant, she rushed towards him. He ran and fell at the altar, and she followed him down. She laid the sleeping infant at my feet at the altar and embraced her husband. And he was saved. Several others were saved in that morning service, and I never even opened my Bible to preach. John 6:44, "No man can come to me, except the Father which hath sent me draw him: and I will raise him up at the last day."

Our son, Jimmy, was a very active, open and talkative three year old. One Sunday we were eating lunch with Mr. and Mrs. Clyde Jordan, when Mrs. Jordan noticed that Jimmy had already finished his lunch ahead of everyone else. She asked, "Jimmy, I have vanilla ice cream for dessert. Would you like some now?"

He answered immediately, "No ma'am, but if you will put it in a sack, I will take it home with me to eat later." He was a true preacher's son!

One Sunday morning, while the offering was being received, Jimmy asked his mother for some money for the collection plate. Vonzeal opened her purse and found she had nothing but the one silver dollar she had carried for many years. This coin had been a gift from her brother and held sentimental value. However, in order to eliminate the possibility of disappointing her son, she reluctantly handed the cherished silver dollar to Jimmy for the offering. He dropped it in proudly, then proceeded to lay his head on her lap and go to sleep.

After the service as everyone was leaving, Vonzeal was approached by Willie J. Sanders. "Mrs. Dorriety," he said, "I have always made it a policy to replace every silver dollar in the offering plate with a dollar of my own and give that silver dollar to our pastor's wife."

Vonzeal's face registered surprise and she replied, "Mr. Sanders, when the Lord impressed upon you to practice this, He probably already knew there would be a time when a silver dollar would be given with reluctance only to keep a child from crying, so, He has not only met my needs, but blessed you in helping Him to fulfill it."

Could it be because of Vonzeal's faith that God gave back her silver dollar? Psalms 37:5, "Commit thy way unto the Lord; trust also in him; and he shall bring it to pass."

During this time, I learned that if I signed up for ROTC, I could later go into the reserves and earn thirty dollars per month. Plus, in the meantime, I would have a uniform to wear, and, since I was a veteran, I could advance faster in the military. So I signed up and soon advanced to Cadet Major. Later the entire unit elected me as their Chaplain.

Through ROTC, I developed leadership skills and made some of my best grades at Mercer. The very prestigious fraternity, Scabbard and Blade, elected and pledged me. And finally I reached my commission as a regular army officer, which meant I could start earning thirty dollars per month in reserves. In order to receive my commission, I signed a waiver. The waiver simply stated that I could not use my ministerial status as an exemption should there be another war and/or the Secretary of Defense deemed it advisable for me to serve in the military. World War II was over, and that was the war to end all wars, so I wasn't worried. I gladly signed the waiver.

Guess what? In the late forties and early fifties, the conflict began developing in Korea. I knew there was a possibility of my being called, but since I was still a student, only months away from graduation, and this was such a small war, I felt very secure.

In 1951, during the final quarter of my education at Mercer, only three months away from my Bachelor of Arts degree, Uncle Sam pointed his finger at me and said, "Sorry, soldier. I WANT YOU!"

"Again!"

I wrote back, "I regret that I won't be able to attend . . ."

Chapter 8

1951-1952

—————⇒•◦•⇐—————

M y graduation from Mercer was put on hold, and I was forced to resign from my beloved Lizella Church. They had a great celebration for us and then, with Vonzeal and five year old Jimmy in tow, I reported for active duty at Fort Lee, Virginia.

I checked in to Fort Lee two hundred twelve pounds of fat Baptist preacher.

Since I was a Second Lieutenant, I was permitted to live off base. We found a little furnished garage apartment and moved in. My three month assignment included taking a Quarter Master Training course before I would be assigned a permanent base.

Monumental Baptist Church was located in that community, so we went to Prayer Meeting on Wednesday night and met some wonderful new friends and began attending services there. The pastor had recently suffered a heart attack and was unable to continue with his full-time ministry, so he asked if I would take the Sunday evening services. So I began sharing the preaching duties with this pastor.

Very soon after, it became apparent that Vonzeal was expecting our second child.

During this period of time, Monumental Baptist Church asked me to preach their revival meeting, and the additional love offerings and honorariums helped take care of most of our financial problems.

After serving the three months at Fort Lee, Virginia, we decided it was time to get Vonzeal, who was now almost seven months pregnant, back to Columbus to her mother's home to await the birth of our second child. We left at night in our little Nash Statesman Super automobile, carrying a picnic basket full of fried chicken for the journey. She dressed Jimmy in his pajamas, let down the seat into a bed, and off we went to Columbus. After settling them there in Columbus, I returned to Fort Lee to receive my assignment – to stay in Fort Lee and give character guidance lectures to the arriving troops. The lectures were somewhat like sermons. With my developing speaking abilities, I gave every soldier who came to Fort Lee character guidance lectures. That was my total assignment.

Vonzeal and I had learned that we both had RH negative blood factors. The doctor had warned us that this second child might be a "blue baby" and might require a complete blood transfusion at birth, with only a fifty/fifty percent chance of survival. Vonzeal would require a caesarean with doubts of her survival. Armed with all this information, I sought a transfer from Fort Lee, Virginia to Columbus, Georgia. Weeks went by, but the transfer could not get worked out and I soon realized that I might not get the transfer in time. Drawing on my military and ministerial training, plus determination learned from my constant fight to get through school, I decided that I needed to take matters into my own hands and go directly to the Pentagon to learn why I couldn't get my transfer. I polished up my brass, had my pinks and greens (army officer's dress uniform) prepared and left just after midnight to make the one hour trip to Washington, D.C. Once there I located the Pentagon, then found a little cafe for breakfast and waited for the offices to open.

I only knew one man there, Major Robert C. Duke. He had been the assistant professor of military science and tactics at Mercer University while I was going through ROTC. When I located him, he addressed me by his favorite nickname for me, "Rabbi, what in the world do you want in the Pentagon?"

"I want to see General Feldman, my commanding general!"

Laughing he said, "You didn't learn a lot in ROTC, did you? You don't just walk into the Pentagon and see your commanding general."

"Why?"

"Well, you just don't do that"

"Oh? Is there an Army regulation against it?"

"No. Not that I know of, but, hey, it's just not done."

Undeterred, I answered, "Fine, I'm going to do something for the first time."

When Major Duke realized I was serious, he took me to the Colonel's office and introduced me as Lt. James O. Dorriety, a former student. Then laughingly he added, "Colonel, he wants to see General Feldman."

The Colonel immediately said, "What would you like to see him about?"

"A personal matter."

"Well, Lieutenant, you just don't walk in off the street to see the Commanding General."

"Sir, I just want to see my Commanding General for

one moment."

"Well," he said, "Let's go down the hall and talk to his Secretary." And we did and the secretary invited me in and asked, "What do you want to see the General about".

Again I answered, "I just want to talk to the General for a moment, just a stand-up conference about a personal matter. And if there's some reason why I should not see the Commanding General, then I'll be glad to leave. But no one has shown me any army regulation that says as an officer I can't walk into the Pentagon and see my Commanding General if he's available."

The secretary excused herself, was gone for a few moments, returned and invited me (with the Colonel) to come in and meet Major General Herman Feldman. She opened the door and stood aside to allow us to enter. Then she closed the door softly. He was standing at his very organized desk and as I walked into his office, I saluted and he returned my salute then reached out and shook hands with me. His grip was firm and confident. " At ease, Lieutenant. What can I do for you?" He made no move to offer me a seat.

"General, I have a copy of my request for transfer." I reached inside my briefcase which contained all my documentation on Vonzeal's health and my transfer request forms, "I'm here to find out why I cannot secure a transfer to Columbus. I'm in a critical situation."

I leaned forward and offered the documents to him. He accepted them and sat down at his desk, reared back in his chair and began closely inspecting all my information while I continued to stand at parade rest. He turned his swivel chair and without any hesitation, picked up the phone and had my orders cut. I was astounded and so very grateful.

I was transferred, beginning immediately, from Fort

Lee, Virginia to Fort Benning, Georgia with an assignment to the quarter master corps. In addition, he allowed me a fifteen day furlough in route. He called the commanding officer at Fort Lee and advised him to sign me out "in absentia" so that when I came through that afternoon, I would only have to stop long enough to pick up my personal belongings from the BOQ and be on my way to Columbus.

I had lunch at the Pentagon before leaving for my new assignment at Fort Benning, Georgia.

At Fort Benning, I was assigned as assistant property officer, which meant that all the installed property at Ft. Benning was under my signature. It took me almost a month to sign for all the installed property, every stove in every mess hall, every garment in every clothing store, every cooler in every area, etc. In addition to that, the army felt I would be the ideal one to serve as mortuary officer which entailed advising families of deaths, selecting escorts, cutting the orders, inspecting the body before and after autopsy, and seeing that it was properly processed. I was twenty eight years old.

On February 16, 1952, our second son Jerry was born, praise the Lord, without any complications, and Vonzeal, baby Jerry, Jimmy and I moved into housing at Ft. Benning. Everything was going fine. We were settled and happy.

Then I received notice for overseas assignment to Korea. In April 1952, I left for overseas duty via a transport to California. The night before my departure, we said good night prayers with Jimmy, and on the following morning Vonzeal carried me to Montgomery to catch a military plane from the base there. To minimize the trauma to Jimmy, we decided we would just say a casual goodbye in Montgomery, so I gave her a quick goodbye kiss and turned to Jimmy, "See you later, big guy."

He jumped into my arms, wrapping his arms and legs around me in a death grip and wouldn't let go. He began to weep, and as Vonzeal pulled him from me, arms and legs flailing, he screamed, "I want my Daddy! I want my Daddy!"

That was the memory I took with me to Korea. Every time I closed my eyes to sleep, I heard his little voice crying, "I want my Daddy!" reverberating in my ears.

Korea had divided into two zones after World War II, the Republic of Korea and North Korean People's Republic (supported by Communist China), with the governments of each claiming authority over the entire peninsula. The two republics had been fighting since North Korean troops had moved across the line dividing the two zones in 1950. Seoul had become the puppet.

Most of the conflict was over and truce negotiations were in full swing by the time my division arrived. Casualties for the United Nations were estimated at almost half a million, of which nearly 150,000 were from the U.S. forces.

As the commander of a truck company which carried ammunition to the front and deceased personnel to the rear for grave registration, I saw young bodies pitched into two and one-half ton trucks like cordwood.

General Eisenhower, who had resigned his NATO post in 1952, had run a successful campaign against Democrat Adlai E. Stevenson with his "I Like Ike" slogan and had been elected President.

The commander of our service unit in the service center asked me to conduct a Protestant service for the troops. I was thrilled to do so even though I had no formal sermons with me. I used my Thompson Chain Reference Bible, which I slept on as my pillow, and, strange as it may seem, I found what I thought would be a very simple text to use in Psalms 46: 9-10. "He maketh wars to cease unto the end of the earth; he breaketh the bow, and cutteth the spear in sunder; he burneth the chariot in the fire. Be still and know that I am God: I will be exalted among the heathen, I will be exalted in the earth."

I used this as my text to ask the question, "How Can I Know God Intimately and Personally?" You can come to know God intimately through *physical quietness*, which we had very little of in Korea; you can come to know God through *mental quietness*, if you can leave everything out of your mind and concentrate; and then we can come to know Him *through prayer*, and we can pray and He will respond and we can feel His presence; and finally, we can come to know Him through *positive action for good*. We serve the Lord when we do something for our fellow man

I didn't realize the need for that sermon at the moment I began to deliver it. Along the Puk Hon River, the small Hon River, in the forks of those rivers there were five thousand troops assembled. When it became apparent that there would be a regular army officer to conduct this service, the soldiers all turned out for some reason, perhaps only curiosity. It was an open-air type meeting. I mounted the podium and laid my forty-five, which was strapped to my belt, and my carbine aside and picked up my Bible and preached. The troops were overwhelmed by this sermon. In retrospect it appears that all these troops were in want of an answer to the question – "How Can I Know God?"

The word of that message began to spread. Some

chaplains over in Seoul heard of this lieutenant who had preached a sermon. One of them was a Southern Baptist, Chaplain Price,[9] stationed in Seoul, Korea at the 443rd base depot, our headquarters company. He made inquiry by field telephone about the lieutenant who preached the sermon. We got in touch, and he asked me to come to Seoul and take his place while he went on R & R. My commanding officer agreed to excuse me from my duty and allowed me to go to Seoul to serve as acting Chaplain for the 443rd base depot. That's where I encountered his jeep driver, Sergeant Bill Fallen, a Georgia boy with a beautiful tenor voice. We began preaching, singing and visiting the orphanages to deliver goods and toiletries sent by Americans.

On my wedding anniversary in 1952, I spent the night in a bombed out building in Seoul, Korea. The structure was an old Masonic Temple, and one end had been totally destroyed. The roof over the back-end was still intact, and I slept in a sleeping bag inside that building. We were unable to have any contact with home, and I went to sleep with Vonzeal and my family on my mind and in my prayers.

The summer passed into fall; Christmas was approaching. Since our company was not in the direct line of fire (even though there were occasional breakthroughs), we had some free time. I found a group of men who wanted to sing, and we formed a choir to sing carols. We began preparing for our Christmas service.

---

[9] I've never been able to locate Chaplain Price since then and continue to search for him. I found Bill Fallen a couple of years ago in a revival meeting in Milledgeville, Georgia. He came on a Tuesday night and we stood in the pulpit of the church and reminisced of our encounter in Korea and we sang an impromptu duet. The congregation gave us a five minute standing ovation.

But before Christmas arrived, our troop learned that we were being shipped back home. Even though the peace treaty had not been signed in Panmunjom, Ike was going to Korea personally to work out the peace agreement. There continued to be prolonged and unsuccessful negotiations regarding the repatriation of prisoners of war. The North Koreans insisted upon the return of all captured prisoners taken by U.N. forces. The U.N. upheld the right of the prisoners to refuse repatriation.

Our transfer happened so quickly that we arrived back in the United States before my letter reached Vonzeal. I'll never forget that day, coming from Korea and arriving in California, going to the airport and making my arrangements for my flight to Atlanta. After I had my ticket in my hand, I went to the pay phone and dialed Vonzeal's number in Columbus.

"Meet me at the Atlanta airport at 6:00p.m. this evening!"

That was the first opportunity I'd had to notify her that I was coming home from Korea. And when I came off the plane, she was there with first grader Jimmy, and what a reunion we had. I was able to stay a few days in Columbus with my family, catching up on my two sons' progress and growth.

I reported back to Ft. Jackson and was discharged from active duty and transferred to the reserves. When I checked out I weighed one hundred eighty-five pounds. The army had been good for my waistline.

On Christmas Eve morning, I drove back to Columbus, Georgia to spend Christmas with my family.

I contacted Dr. Dowell and was invited back to Mercer, so we returned to school with the hope of finally graduating in the June exercise.

My first Sunday back I preached to our beloved flock at Lizella Baptist Church.

The armistice was signed on July 27, 1953, but peace negotiations collapsed and Korea remained divided. I remained in the reserves until my discharge in January of 1954.

Chapter 9

1953-1954

—————>•0•<—————

ithin one week of my enrollment, Dr. Dowell called and asked if I could go out to Warner Robins First Baptist Church on Sunday as a fill-in pastor. I found out later that someone at Lizella had recommended me to Warner Robins. The pulpit committee asked if I could meet with them Sunday afternoon, and I did. Another invitation to meet with them came later in the week, and First Baptist Church of Warner Robins, Georgia called me as their pastor.

I was really excited that finally, after seven years, I would be graduating from Mercer with an A.B. degree. This step was a huge milestone in our lives. My parents had never had a child graduate from college, so I piled Vonzeal and the boys into the car and we drove to Dothan, picked up Mama and Papa and brought them home with us so they could attend the graduation. Scott and Francis Long, the couple from Lizella who had always kept us in eggs and fryer chickens, purchased my class ring for me and gave me the funds to buy a solid white suit for my graduation. They always took such an interest in us and I'll never forget them for it.

Finally, the date came for my graduation, June 8, 1953. I was ecstatic to finally walk down that aisle and receive that piece of paper we'd been working towards for so many years. Vonzeal and I had the greatest celebration of all — we had made it, and we were on top of the world.

After returning my cap and gown, I rushed out to the car to meet my family, but Papa was having a chill. It was frightening. He was freezing. We rushed him home and got a doctor. When he was able to travel, he insisted on going home to Dothan. He was never well again and died in 1956.

My ministry began to produce material benefits. First Baptist Church of Warner Robins had a lovely four bedroom pastorium. What little furniture Vonzeal and I owned had been stored by the army somewhere in Tennessee, with the exception of one bedroom set, a youth bed for Jimmy, a baby bed for Jerry and a small dinette set. So with this limited furniture we moved into that giant pastorium saying, "We'll have open house when our furniture arrives from Tennessee."

We had all those empty rooms, empty living room, empty dining room, empty den. Fortunately, there was a furniture dealer in the church that became a very close friend, Joe Morris and his wife Edna. Joe decided that he would help us get the proper furniture for our growing family, and before long our home was well furnished at a minimum cost to us.

It was amazing to see the church growth. Almost immediately the building was filled to overflowing and we had to open the doors and seat people in the vestibule. After that filled, we opened the front doors and seated people on the sidewalk using outside speakers. We determined we could solve this magnificent problem by having two services on Sunday morning. Soon both of those services were filled to capacity, and again we began to open the doors and put people outside. It was a marvelous feeling.

We had plans for a new building which would seat one thousand people. There was a small building fund, but the church had been unable to get the proper funds in place to get the building started.

But being a young, energetic, ambitious (and sometimes aggressive) preacher, I asked that one of our deacons, Mr. Carl Storey a civil engineer and superintendent of the schools, to lay out the building on the property. I wanted it outlined with rope so we could see the shape of it on the ground. Mr. Storey brought his transit and, with the help of several men from the church, laid off the building, placing stakes and ropes along the edges to show the outline of the new auditorium of First Baptist Church of Warner Robins. We brought in sawdust to serve as a floor and a flat bed truck to serve as a platform for the organ, choir and podium. We had several hundred folding chairs delivered and set.

We began to advertise that we would have our first worship service in our *new building* as an open-air service.

The weather cooperated, and the day was beautiful. During that service I invited the men in our congregation to come on Monday morning and help begin digging the footings for our new building. We passed out cards requesting commitments as to how much money we could give, over and beyond our regular tithes, for a three month period.

And we would trust the Lord for the funds.

On Monday morning twenty-six men showed up with shovels and picks and began digging the foundation for the new building. The first day went well, and we did a lot of digging. On the second day we were busy digging when I was informed there was a man in the parking lot who wanted to see me. Dressed in my boots and overalls, dripping with perspiration, I went out to see what he wanted.

"I'm Howard Barry, a contractor from Texas. I've been awarded a contract to install the gas lines for the city of Warner Robins." He was standing next to a great big beautiful sedan.

"Well, Sir, I'm pleased to meet you. I'm kinda dirty and sweaty," I apologized, wiping the perspiration off my forehead. "What can I do for you?"

"What can I do for you?" He replied. "I've received word that this church is constructing a building. How wide are you digging the footings?"

I told him, and he told me to get in the car with him, and we drove out to his site where his big Barber-Greene ditch digger was digging the trenches for the installation of the utility system. We measured the blade on that ditch digger, and it was exactly the same width as the footings for the foundation of the church.

He ordered the operator to stop digging, load the ditch digger on the low boy and follow us.

"Mr. Barry, you know, we don't have any money to pay you for this."

He said, "This is my contribution to the church." I could have hugged him. That giant digger dug every footing. All we had to do was clean out the corners and cut out the edging. Mr. Barry stayed on site with us until all of the foundations had been dug and all the concrete poured.

In the meantime, an insurance company had given us a commitment to loan us fifty-five thousand dollars on the new building. We were moving along just on faith in the Lord. The church was growing so fast in 1953 that it became apparent that we needed some help in the church office.

Enter Jeanne Bentley, stage right!

Or "Ms. B," as my sons, daughters-in-law, and grandchildren refer to her. The most on-fire, energetic 4'11" stick of dynamite the Lord ever placed on this earth.

The Sunday she and her family first visited First Baptist Warner Robins was the beginning of a life-long friendship with my family and Jeanne Bentley. She, along with her husband Charles and their son and daughter, Mark and Marilyn, were new to the community and appeared interested in joining our church. I went to see them that Sunday afternoon and learned that Mrs. Bentley was a conference stenographer at Warner Robins Air Force Base. Her father had been a Baptist preacher, and she was a very devout Christian. I inquired, and she informed me that she might be interested in becoming the secretary of our church. At the committee's recommendation, she was immediately employed as the full-time secretary of First Baptist Church of Warner Robins at about one-half the salary she was earning at the base.

These events began a beautiful friendship which has endured over forty years. The Bentleys became adopted members of the Dorriety family.

As we advanced with the building, we learned of a brick mason's school in Macon. The building committee, Joe Morris, Carl Storey, Charlie Mercer and I, went to talk to one of the teachers at the school. He agreed to do the brick work at a tremendously reduced rate and selected qualified students from the school to lay the brick.

"Rev. Dorriety, if I was a white man, I'd be a contractor," Bill, the teacher, told me, "but since I'm not, I'm just a brick mason. But I'm the best there is. You'll get the best brick laying job possible."

I looked at him, and memories came flooding back. Memories of opportunities and help I had received along the way. I hurried back to my office and convened a meeting of the deacons. They all agreed to give Bill the job as contractor. He was a fine Christian gentleman. Our church was his first contracting job, and he did excellent work.

During this period I had led the Mayor of the City, W. T. Giles, to the Lord. Mayor Giles had a friend, Marvin Griffin, who was running for Governor of Georgia. They had served in the military, together along with General Ignaco who was the commander of Robins Air Force Base. After meeting and speaking with Marvin Griffin, I became interested in helping him get elected, and began travelling all over the state introducing him.

He succeeded in his bid and was elected Governor. He called me immediately after his inauguration, "I didn't see you at the inauguration, Jim, and I just wanted to let you know if there is anything that I can ever do for you, just pick up the telephone and call me and I'll see what I can do."

"Thanks, Governor, I appreciate it, but I don't need anything. Just do a good job for the state of Georgia."

Work on the building continued, and we needed to finalize our loan with the insurance company. Unfortunately, the loan company had heard rumors of a reduction of force at Warner Robins Air Force Base, and the insurance company elected to withdraw their commitment for the loan which left us owing several thousand dollars to the bank who had been advancing funds.

At the moment that this loan was withdrawn and the efforts of financing failed, the idea dawned on me that Governor Griffin might be able to help our church find financing. So I took the liberty of calling and got through to his Aide who immediately put me through to the Governor.

"Preacher, what can I do to help you?" were the Governor's first words as he answered my call. I shared with him the story of the construction of the building.

"Are there state funds that could be available for this church to get a loan?"

"Let me check, and I'll call you right back." He hung up the phone, and a few minutes later he called back. "I called Zack Craven, the Comptroller General, and he said that we are receiving about thirteen million dollars per month in state retirement funds from school teachers and state employees. He says we're investing all that money in two and one-half percent Yankee bonds, and he sees no reason why we can't loan some of that money to a church. So why don't you come up here and let's talk. When can you come?"

I had a friend who owned a janitorial industrial supply company and flew a private plane. He had once offered to fly me anywhere I wanted to go, anytime I needed. I had already checked with him to see if he could fly me to Atlanta immediately, and he assured me he could and would.

"Governor," I answered, one foot already out the door, "I've got access to a private plane and can come immediately, if you'll get someone to meet me in general aviation at the Hartsville airport."

"No problem. I'll have my Aide meet you."

Hanging up the phone, I did a little dance of happiness around my desk.

We flew directly to the Atlanta airport and went straight to the Governor's office. As soon as I arrived, he called the Comptroller General, "Clear your office, Zack, we're coming right over."

And we did. "How much does your church need?" Mr. Zack Craven asked.

I knew I should say fifty-five thousand dollars, which was the commitment we had had from the insurance company. "To be precise, we need about eighty thousand dollars," I told him, swallowing hard.

"No problem. Your rate of interest will be six percent, is that okay?"

"Sure!" I answered as steadily as I could. "We really appreciate it, Sir."

Mr. Craven called in his secretary who worked up the paperwork, and with papers in hand, we flew directly back to Ft. Valley to meet with George Culpepper, Sr., chairman of the loan committee for the state of Georgia. The Deacons of the Church sat down together that evening and signed all the forms and paperwork, and I delivered the signed documents to Atlanta the next day.

Before our plane landed in Ft. Valley, the funds had already been transferred to our bank. Once again the Lord had been one step ahead of us. Matthew 17:20, "For verily I say unto you, If ye have faith as a grain of mustard seed, ye shall say unto this mountain, Remove hence to yonder place; and it shall remove; and nothing shall be impossible unto you."

If it's in the Bible – it's true!

Jimmy was now seven years old. One afternoon he came in from playing and Vonzeal glanced up at him as he entered.

"Your homework done?" she asked.

"Yes, ma'am." He had a sweet little voice. Even his teachers said so.

"Wash your hands for supper."

"Okay." He turned to go.

"Jimmy!" she said so suddenly that I looked up from the newspaper I was reading. "I told you not to play marbles. We've had this discussion. That's gambling."

"Mother! We don't play for keeps anymore," he shrugged.

"Oh, okay. Then go wash up."

I sat amazed at the exchange I had just heard. How did she know he had been playing marbles? "What was that all about?" I asked, folding my newspaper in half.

"They've been playing marbles. When they knock out a marble they win it. That's gambling, and I simply won't let him do it. But it's okay as long as they don't keep each other's marbles," she explained.

"Not that. I know that. How did you know, out-of-the-blue, he'd been playing?"

She laughed. "Easy. The knees of his pants were dirty."

I sat real still for a second and thought about that. I wonder if she can tell when I sneak off and play golf by the trap-sand in my pant cuffs. Gotta be more careful in the future. Nothing much escaped my beautiful, hard-working, thrifty wife!

We finished our building in the fall of 1954, and moved in. The growth in the church appeared to be only just beginning.

I was asked to speak at the State Evangelism Conference in 1954 on the subject, "*Keeping the Fires of Evangelism Burning.*" The invitation gave me a little bit of notoriety, and the Lord gave us a great year. The church continued to grow, develop and mature.

So many people helped to build this church: the Texas contractor, the plane pilot, the Governor, the Comptroller General, the members of the church, the brick mason and so many others. These months were such blessed times.

Chapter 10

1955-1958

―――――>-0-<―――――

T hen 1955 came, and a very tragic thing happened.

Houston County was a "dry county" meaning there was no legalized liquor. Warner Robins was a growing city with an air force base near by. There were those who felt that Warner Robins needed to be able to compete with Macon and other cities in reaching out for conventions and other economic growth potential. The county was losing a lot of revenue, because people were leaving Robins Air Force Base and going to other communities to purchase their liquor. An announcement came out in the newspaper that an "anonymous committee for legal control" had been established for the purpose of getting the county in position to sell liquor through liquor stores as a legal transaction.

The local churches rose up in objection. Since I was the pastor of the First Baptist Church and president of the ministerial association, I was asked to head the opposition to this movement and lead in helping the churches oppose this action.

Of course, being young, energetic and always ready for a fight, I immediately agreed and entered into the fight for victory. I met with other pastors to see what we could do to head off this movement in our county.

We determined the first thing we needed to do was find out the legality of the signatures on the referendum. Reports were that there were already enough signatures to call for a referendum.

With that ringing in our ears, I went down to the probate judge's office in Perry, the county seat of Houston County, and asked to see a copy of the signatures on the referendum. The probate judge promptly informed me that he could not let me see the document. Stubbornly believing he was in error, I asked, "This is where public papers are filed and I'm a citizen of this county. Why can't I see them?" He continued to deny me access to the referendum papers.

Failing to accept this as the final answer, I called Governor Griffin and, through him, reached the Attorney General of the state of Georgia. I advised him I had been denied the opportunity to see papers in the probate judges's office in Houston County. "Can you give us a ruling as to whether they are public documents, and, if so, would it be possible for me to have a copy of them?" All the newspapers within the state waited for that ruling. We were having daily news conferences regarding the battle brewing in our county, and we were one of the top stories in the state.

The Attorney General ruled in our favor. The probate judge had to release copies of the referendum. In the meantime, we had planned our strategy. We decided to afford everyone who had signed the referendum an opportunity to remove his name before we made the list public. This we did by getting sixty typewriters and sixty typists set up in the educational building of First Baptist Church. We prepared a letter to send to every registered voter in the county, stating that we were going to publish the names of those who had signed the referendum for the legalization of liquor in the county. In essence the letter read – "If your name is on there and you wish to remove it before it is published, sign and notarize the enclosed document, return it to us and your name will be removed before we publish it in the newspapers."

Trucks came from the post office delivering sacks of mail to us. As we processed the removal of names, we destroyed the call for referendum. There was not a bona fide call by enough of the citizens. The referendum was defeated – battle won!

An interesting sidelight to this campaign was the extent to which the "liquor forces" went to try to stop our efforts. One day the man who was the chief property owner and leader of the area known as "front street," came to the office to talk me out of the campaign against legalization. He made some very worthwhile offers, which I considered bribes. After some discussion, I suggested he might wish to leave since I definitely did not intend to be distracted from my goal of winning a victory. Some days later this same man entered the police station and found me seated in an old chair from which the rockers had been removed. I was leaning back against the wall. He looked my way and remarked something to the effect that I was responsible for a lot of disruption and confusion – "just sorta a trouble-maker."

I responded "Oh, I don't really want trouble, come on over here and lets talk a while." Saying this I tilted forward and reached for another chair.

He strutted up in front of me and said, "All I want to do is —," and I noticed his fist just in time to dodge back in the chair enough that he, in swinging, lost his balance, hit the floor and cut his head. The Chief of

Police and another officer moved over to restrain him. I said, "Oh, let him alone, he can't even touch me." So strong was the sense of the presence of God's protection, that I felt totally shielded.

There were other incidents of harassment, such as the front yard of the pastorium's being littered with beer cans, etc. None of this aggressive behavior deterred any of us from working towards defeat of the referendum.

Soon afterwards the names of the committee were no longer anonymous, and we sadly learned that a part of this conflict centered in our church.

Refusing to worship with those who had supported the liquor referendum, three hundred and twenty-one members of First Baptist Church removed themselves from the worship service and met in the city hall the following Sunday. Vonzeal and I remained at First Baptist Church. One Sunday the building was filled to capacity with one thousand people; the following Sunday there were only seventy-five in the auditorium. I went to Savannah and spent several days praying and trying to determine what I should do. When I returned home, I was advised that the splinter group was forming a new church and was asking me to be their pastor.

Since I was the leader of the opposition for the fight against liquor, I was confused as to what I should do. I contacted Dr. Louie Newton and John Hurt, both of whom had been interested in the defeat of the liquor movement, and asked them to come to Warner Robins, have lunch and pray with me. It was their advice that, due to the circumstances, I had no choice but to become the pastor of the new church.

The splinter group was waiting for an answer. The church had not even been named.

I resigned from First Baptist Church and accepted a

E. Zimmerman
and Dora Dorriety,
parents of William
Henry Dorriety,
Jim Dorriety's
paternal
grandparents.

Hamp & Lorena
Stanaland,
parents of
Nettie Dorriety,
Jim Dorriety's
maternal
grandparents.

Jim's parents – Nettie and William Henry Dorriety (1954)

Jim Dorriety
at 7 years old.
(1931)

Family photograph made at the time of Jim's father's death. (left to right) Back row: Rex Pierce, Binnie Frank, James Oral, William Hamilton, Edgar Zimmerman. Third row: Willie Eloyce, Mary Gertrude. Second row: Nettie Dorriety (Mama), Allie Mae. Front row: Rena Thelma, Nellie Ermerlene.

Vonzeal Davis, 1941

Jim Dorriety, 1941

Jim Dorriety, 1941

Vonzeal Davis, 1941

Jim, Vonzeal and the boys. (1953)

Jim, Vonzeal and boys when he received the LLD
from John Marshall University (1961)

PERMANENT RECORD—MERCER UNIVERSITY

Card No. 1 (of 2 cards)

FILE No._____

Name DORITY, JAMES ORAL

Date of Birth April 16, 1924

Address 3807 3rd Ave., Columbus, Ga.

Church Preference Missionary Baptist   Member Yes

Parent or Guardian W. H. Dority, Sr.   From Banks (Ala.) Jr. High, Columbus, Ga.

Date Enrolled SPECIAL July 3, 1945.   Address 4103 3rd Ave., Columbus, Ga.   School

Date Graduated JUNE 8, 1953   Degree BACHELOR OF ARTS   Major CHRISTIANITY   Minor HST; Rel.E.Ed.

ENTRANCE UNITS

Subject	Units	Grade	Subject	Units	Grade	Subject	Units	Grade	Subject	Units	Grade
English	4		Algebra	1		French			Biology		
History—World	1		Geometry—Plane	1		German			Chemistry		
History—U.S.	1		Geometry—Solid			Latin			General Science	1	
Government Civics	1					Spanish			Physics		
		Math							Total	15	

COLLEGE UNITS

No.	COURSE	Rt. Lab.	F	W	S	SS	Cr. Qpt.
	1945 Sch						

CHIPOLA JUNIOR COLLEGE, MARIANNA, FLA.

No.	COURSE	Rt. Lab.	F	W	S	SS	Cr. Qpt.
102	Math—El.of Pl.& Solid Geom.	B		5	10		
101-2	English—Reading,Writing,Speaking,Gram.	B	I	5	10		
102-3	Bible—N.T.& Literature;Sermon Construct.	B		10	20		
103	History—Recent American			5	(5)		

ASSISTANT REGISTRAR

unanimous call as pastor of a new church to be known as Central Baptist Church, Warner Robins, Georgia. Mrs. Bentley, and most of the Sunday School teachers from First Baptist Church, had already made their way to the new church.

We formulated a set of rules for the implementation of forming our new church. We would ask no one to leave First Baptist and join with us in our new church. We would take nothing with us and started returning all library books and literature which was in our possession. We would permit no negative comments about anyone or anything at First Baptist. We simply had the birth of a new church – Central Baptist Church. The first service was held in the auditorium of the city hall. The Chairman of the Deacons, Tommy Woods, stood that first Sunday and prayed, "Lord, here we are. In a few minutes we're going to walk down the hall to our Sunday School rooms. Will You walk with us?"

Mrs. Bentley and I were instructed to form a church office. A free-will offering that first Sunday provided thirty-six hundred dollars to purchase furniture, copy machines and other office equipment. One of our members who had served as a chairman of the building committee for First Baptist Church, Joe Morris, offered us office space above his furniture store. And we hung our shingle – Central Baptist Church Office.

After the first few initial Sundays, we moved our services to Westside, the local high school. We would unload our hymnals from the trunks of cars, have our service, then reload the car trunks until the following Sunday. My family had to vacate the pastorium of First Baptist, and Charlie Williams built us a home on Sunset Drive, complete with a small office behind the carport, and we moved the church offices there as soon as we were able to occupy the new home.

Jeanne Bentley offered this memory of that time: *"I remember that we moved our offices into the little space behind Dr. Dorriety's house, and every morning I'd come to work and get a cup of coffee from his kitchen. One morning there seemed to be a lot of tension in the air. I'd never seen Dr. Dorriety and Vonzeal have any type of conflict or marital argument with one another before, so I began to feel uncomfortable and excused myself. Since I had some errands to run, I drove away and returned about thirty minutes later. When I drove into the driveway, I noticed that little Jerry was playing alone on the carport. 'Jerry,' I asked, 'Where are your mother and father. Why are you out here alone?' 'Oh, it's okay,' he replied unconcerned, 'they're in the bedroom on their knees praying.' "*

Vonzeal and I had a rule. We never went to sleep mad at one another. We stayed up late a lot of nights, but we never carried our argument over into the next day.

Since we were meeting on the west side of the city, it seemed to be the area in which the new church should be located. George Norris, Tommy Woods and I decided to ride around and try to locate a place for our new church – perhaps outside the city limits. We found a spot of land which appeared to be ideal for our church. We got out of our car and walked onto the property and looked at it from all directions. The lot faced Watson Boulevard, the main thoroughfare of Warner Robins, and we decided that this would be the perfect location for our new church. George Norris, being a man of prayer, suggested that we just kneel in the brush and claim the land for the Lord. The three of us knelt and joined hands and prayed that God would make it possible for us to obtain the land for Central

Baptist Church.

We located the owner, Bernard M. Lewis, an elderly gentleman who lived in Macon, Georgia, called and made an appointment to meet with him. When I arrived and shared with him our desire to purchase his property for a church, he informed me that he didn't wish to sell any of this property. In fact, because of his tax position, selling the land was impossible. I went away disappointed and reported my finding to Tommy and George, but we still agreed that this was the place for our church. Therefore, we had claimed it for the Lord, and we would wait and ask the Lord to change Mr. Lewis' mind and guide him that he might see fit to sell us this property.

On Christmas morning 1955, I received a call from an attorney, Bill Wisse, in Warner Robins, who asked that I come to his office. He gave me no explanation as to what he wanted to see me about. When I arrived, I was surprised to see Mr. Lewis there, and I saw the plat of the property spread out on the attorney's desk.

Mr. Lewis motioned me over to his side and asked, "Preacher, show me here on this map. Where's the land you had an interest in?"

I oriented myself, found Watson Boulevard and pointed to the acreage we wanted. He turned to his attorney and said, "Just make out a deed for these three acres of land to this church."

I said, "Wait a minute, Mr. Lewis. I'm just the preacher. I'm not authorized to buy the land. I must find out the cost and call the deacons together for a decision."

He said, "Do you have a dollar in your pocket? I'm going to give the church the land, and you can give me a dollar."

Without another word, I pulled out my billfold and took a one dollar bill out and laid it in Mr. Lewis's hand, and he signed the deed, giving three acres of land to Central Baptist Church for one dollar and other consideration.

Oh, what a Christmas that was. Smiling from ear to ear, I took the deed in hand and went immediately to call a deacons' meeting. That following Sunday, the deacons presented to the body of the church the deed to the property that we had claimed in prayer for Central Baptist Church.

Another example of faith in prayer. Matthew 18:18-20, "Verily I say unto you, Whatsoever ye shall bind on earth shall be bound in heaven: and whatsoever ye shall loose on earth shall be loosed in heaven. Again I say unto you, That if two of you shall agree on earth as touching any thing that they shall ask, it shall be done for them of my Father which is in heaven. For where two or three are gathered together in my name, there am I in the midst of them."

If it's in the Bible, it's true.

We designed a large auditorium, an education building and plenty of parking space. The first phase of the plans called for a U-shaped building. We issued bonds to raise the funds, and the funds were raised immediately. The building was completed within a very few months.

As soon as construction was completed, we planned an open-air revival with Dr. Jess Henley as our evangelist. In the U-shape of the building, we set up chairs, brought in sawdust, outside speakers and hired a Canadian evangelistic singing team, Al and Ivey Walsh. During that time of revival meeting, we had one hundred and forty-one additions to the church.

I hadn't been surprised when Jimmy, at age seven, came to be saved at First Baptist Church in Warner Robins.

I guess we did a little better job with Jerry, for in 1957, when he was just five years old, he came forward to receive Jesus as his Saviour. I rejoiced with him and prayed with him on my knees and showed the congregation at Central Baptist Church in Warner Robins that he had come, but I didn't offer him for baptism. I simply said, "We rejoice with him in his salvation."

The following Sunday as we were preparing for baptism, and Vonzeal was getting my clothes ready, Jerry said, "Mother, have you got my clothes ready for baptism?"

"Jerry, you aren't going to be baptised. You didn't join the Church."

Surprised he said, "Did the Lord tell you that?"

Gently, she said, "You go talk to Daddy, okay?"

He came to me, and I explained to him that because of his age, I had not presented him as a member of the church.

A few Sundays later, he resolutely came forward again, stood there and looked up at me with determination and said, "I've been saved. I want to give my life to Jesus. Daddy, will you baptise me, please?"

What would you have done? I baptised him at the age of five in 1957.

The week after he was baptised he was so excited as a young, little Christian. He'd always heard that as a Christian you were supposed to tell others about Jesus. The father of Jerry's playmates across the street was not a Christian, and Jerry knew that. So that next week he walked through the kitchen and headed out the door with his little Bible under his arm.

Vonzeal asked, "Jerry, where are you going with your Bible?"

"I'm going across the street to talk to Mr. McNeal. He needs to be a Christian, and I want to tell him he needs to be saved!"

We don't know what Jerry said to Curtis McNeal that day.

After we left Warner Robins ,we had no other connection with the McNeals until April of 1993. We had brought Vonzeal home from the hospital , when about eight o'clock one Sunday morning we received a telephone call.

I answered.

"Is this James O. Dorriety?"

"Yes, this is James O. Dorriety, Sr."

"Were you once a pastor in Warner Robins, Georgia?"

"Yes, I'm the one."

"Do you know a Mr. Curtis McNeal?"

"Yes, I do remember him. What's happened?"

"Mr. McNeal has been diagnosed with cancer and is critically ill at the Coliseum Hospital in Macon. He asked me to try to get in touch with you and your son, Jerry. You see, I'm the pastor here and I've been witnessing to him, trying to get him to accept the Lord. This morning, while I was visiting him at the hospital, Mr. McNeal accepted Jesus into his heart. And he had a wonderful conversion experience. He asked that I call and let you and Jerry know of his conversion. He remembered Jerry's witnessing to him so many years ago."

He gave me the telephone number of the hospital and as soon as I hung up , I called that number and spoke to Curtis' son. He confirmed the fact that his father had been saved earlier that morning.

After I spoke to Mr. McNeal's son, I called my son in Blakely.

"Jerry, do you remember Mr. Curtis McNeal in Warner Robins?"

Jerry laughed his big booming laugh. "Yes, I remember him well. I tried to save his soul when I was five years old. Why?"

"I received a phone call today. He is trying to find you to let you know that he's been saved." I continued to explain the circumstances.

There was silence on the phone for a moment; then I heard his voice say through choked back tears, "Dad, that is such a plug of energy and love to me."

However, we should not be surprised that this had happened because God said in Isaiah 55:10 -11, "For as the rain cometh down, and the snow from heaven, and returneth not thither, but watereth the earth, and maketh it bring forth and bud, that it may give seed to the sower, and bread to the eater: So shall my word be that goeth forth out of my mouth: it shall not return unto me void, but it shall accomplish that which I please, and it shall prosper in the things whereto I sent it."

So the witnessing that Jerry did in 1957 had left the word of God in the heart of this man and produced the kind of results that God wanted it to produce thirty -six years later. On his death bed, he wanted Jerry to know that his words had not gone unheeded.

If it's in the Bible, it's true!

Jerry preached his first sermon when he was twelve.

Chapter 11

1959-1961

—————⟫•⟪—————

onzeal and I left Warner Robins feeling that our work was completed. We had done all we could do. Yes, we had created some enemies because of the birth of Central Baptist from the split of First Baptist Church. Although Vonzeal and I had not been involved personally, I was the pastor, and we had made the decision to go with the new church. Some people wondered if we'd made the wrong decision; others believed we had made the right decision. No one openly accused us of doing anything wrong because we hadn't.

But we graciously bowed out of the community and went to Atlanta to a little mission known as Headland Heights Baptist church. Here was a church that owned twelve acres of land, two big, old white frame dwellings for Sunday School and a stable once used for milking stalls and now used as their auditorium. It only seated about sixty people on the concrete floor, with drainage ditches down the middle, but that was no problem because there were only a handful of members in the church anyway.

The Directors of Missions in Atlanta, Dr. James L. Baggett, insisted that I was the kind of pastor who needed to take that church. It was a mission, and it needed to grow and become a church. I had enough building and financing experience that "missions" felt I was the only man to take the job.

But ego involved itself, and I was insulted that they wanted me to go preach in a milking stable after leaving those two big, beautiful churches in Warner Robins.

Dr. John Hurt, the editor of The Christian Index, came to show me around the area. We saw gorgeous homes being built on the outskirts of Atlanta but no church in the midst of this growing community. But the Lord had provided twelve acres of prime land and a handful of people with the dedication to start a church.

Making their best offer, the church committee guaranteed us one hundred dollars per week, but, to sweeten the pot, they offered us a raise every month, based on the percentage of increase in the offerings, until the salary reached a designated cap. The Director of Missions assured me that he would use all the resources of the Atlanta Baptist Association to stand behind and assist us in the building of this church. John Hurt at The Christian Index promised that if there were anything he could do to help us in the publicity department, he would be ready.

Our family did a lot of praying. From within Headland Heights, a subdivision builder named William C. Cato told us that he would build us a house within five weeks. The church could worry about paying him later, if we'd only answer the call.

Never ones to retreat from a challenge, and with a lot of promises outstanding, we accepted.

Cato brought in crews and generators to light the area at night, and within four weeks and five days, my family moved into that beautiful home which is still the pastorium of Headland Heights Baptist Church outside of Atlanta.

On the first Sunday we were there, some dear heart had brought an extra large floral arrangement for the communion table. It protruded about two feet above the pulpit from the communion table. "I can't preach through that," I thought.

I kept watching that basket during the Sunday School Assembly, and afterwards , I walked down the aisle, looking and thinking about where I could move those flowers. I became conscious of a woman walking up behind me. She said, "Preacher, I know you're thinking the same thing I am . . . those flowers have got to be moved."

I started shaking my head in my old Slocomb way and said "Yes ma'am, they sure have, because if I have to preach through these flowers I'll be as cross-eyed as a bat."

When I turned around and looked at her, I almost fell through the floor, for there she stood, the only cross-eyed woman in that congregation. She gave me a bemused smile.

"Off to a great start, you are, preacher." I muttered mostly to myself.

From that day forward, whenever she phoned me, she would say, "Preacher, this is your cross-eyed bat calling."

That was the same Sunday that our family moved our membership to Headland Heights. I stood at the altar and nodded for Vonzeal and the boys to come forward, so we could offer ourselves as members of that church. The chairman of the deacons stepped up to moderate and to welcome us as new members of Headland Heights Baptist Church. The weather was nice and the front doors were open during the service.

As my family left the pew to come forward, my eye caught a little movement towards the open doors. In horror, I watched as our family pet, Hattie, a little black terrier, slowly walked right into the church and down the aisle. She trotted forward straight to me, cut her brown eyes up at me, glanced over at Vonzeal, then up at Jimmy, then casually took her place in line beside Jerry. We were so embarrassed to have this little dog in line with us. But, finally, when I noticed all the wide grins coming from the membership, I simply said to the congregation, "Well, I'm sorry, but it appears Hattie wants to be a member of our church, too. We hope you will accept our family for membership, and that includes our dog, Hattie." Everyone laughed and had a wonderful experience watching Hattie sit there. The chairman of the deacons said, "All those in favor of receiving Brother Dorriety, Mrs. Dorriety, Jimmy, Jerry," he waved his hand on down the line, "and Hattie, would you please raise your hands?" So Hattie joined Headland Heights Baptist Church that day. Jerry picked her up, and everyone came up to greet us and, of course, fell in love with Hattie. Every member of Headland Heights Baptist Church knew Hattie and occasionally asked about her.

We had very few members in our church. How in the world were we going to expand? My mind began to work, and as usual, came up with an outlandish idea. I asked Cato if he would be willing to buy a trailer truck load of bricks, which is about ten thousand bricks, and unload them on the property as his contribution, towards the new building. He agreed.

I approached another church member and sold him on the idea of buying a truck load of concrete blocks and delivering them to the site. He agreed.

Both men were told that the primary reason for the

gift was to generate publicity, and, of course, to ultimately use in the new building.

Cato got his subdivision architect, W. C. Corley, to draw up working plans for the new building, which included an auditorium capable of seating four to five hundred people, and which could later be converted into Sunday School space.

Then the plan went into motion. We started calling in all the promises. John Hurt was asked to designate four weeks of The Christian Index to Headland Heights.

"Sure, I'd be glad to. How many copies are you going to need?"

"I want three thousand copies!" I replied.

"Three thousand! For what?!" he gaped.

"I want to send three thousand copies to people in our community."

"But you don't have three thousand members"

"John, I want to send The Christian Index with Headland Heights on the front page and the back page, to every resident in our community."

"But, Jim, all the residents of your community are not Baptists."

"I know that, John. We've got Catholics, Jews, Mormons, non-christians, all kinds of folks. But we want everybody there to know that we're going to build a new church at the corner of Headland Drive and Ben Hill Road. Besides, you said you'd do anything to help when I took this church." I gave him my most-practiced petulant look. "Well?"

"Okay, I'll do it, but it's going to cost us a lot of money," he agreed reluctantly, shaking his head from side to side.

Smugly satisfied, I went back to Headland Heights and had a bulldozer and backhoe delivered. We made photographs of all the bricks, blocks and construction equipment, and featured a picture on the front page of the Headland Heights edition of <u>The Christian Index</u>. The headline read, "One half million dollar construction of Headland Heights Church to begin . . ."

Three thousand residents in the community received the initial edition and another copy a week later with additional information about Headland Heights. The first Sunday we doubled the membership of the church – we had approximately thirty new additions. The Baptists began to attend. They decided that if there was going to be a hard-working church in their own community, that was the church they wanted to belong to. Every Sunday we began to add family after family to the membership. The church was growing in leaps and bounds.

One Sunday, a new family visited us at Headland Heights and I took their visitor's card and and went out into the community to visit. When I got to their house, I thought I'd better refresh my memory so I pulled the card out of my pocket and reread it. "Okay, I've got it."

I knocked on the door, went inside and visited with the man and wife for awhile until it was time to leave. "Brother Butts, it's nice to have had this visit with you." I extended my hand.

"The name is Bottoms!" He said huffily. "Bottoms!"

I beat a hasty exit, blushing to my ear lobes. My hoof and mouth disease had struck again.

The church issued bonds to raise the money for the building. We had the plans all ready and started construction with Cato serving as building superintendent. During the four months of construction, we never had a drop of rain during a single working day. We began to notice that rain came on Saturday or Sunday. The building crew never missed a day's work from the moment the building began until the dedication service. In less than one hundred and twenty days after the church started construction, Dr. Louie Newton, Dr. Dick Hall, President of the Georgia Baptist Convention, and John Hurt came and dedicated the building .

Membership had grown unbelievably to one hundred fifty in Sunday School. We added to the staff and, of course, Mrs. Bentley became Minister of Education; Mary Morris served as our secretary; and, George Mitchell, an outstanding musician, came as our minister of music.

Simultaneously, several business men, members of Headland Heights Church, developed Lakeside Country Club, and I was asked to help promote the new club and become a charter member – number forty-eight. One of the members supplied me with a free locker; another kept my golf clothes cleaned and pressed; another picked up all my caddy fees . . . Our family was experiencing such a joy in our new community and we were able to enjoy many recreational opportunities.

Headland Heights became one of the fastest growing churches in Atlanta.

A very prominent wedding was scheduled for July in our brand new air conditioned auditorium. As soon as we arrived that morning to prepare for the wedding, we realized that the air-conditioning was not working. The service men were called and they came out to fix the A/C unit. I stayed with them until the repair work finished around three o'clock in the afternoon. "Dump all that cool air into the auditorium because we've got to get ready for this wedding," I told the men as I rushed off to finish the last minute details.

I arrived at the church about 6:00p.m. and the wedding was scheduled for 6:30. The ushers were already seating people and I noticed the guests were fanning furiously. The A/C servicemen had gotten the wires crossed, and the heat was on.

The ushers asked what they should do. I shrugged helplessly, "Shut the system down and just tell 'em it's hot."

I rushed around and got into my pulpit robe. Ten minutes before the wedding ceremony was to begin, I remembered, "Oh, my, I promised that precious bride that I'd get that tape recorder and record this ceremony for them."

So I raced downstairs, back to the other end of the office, grabbed the tape recorder, and raced back up the stairs and through the choir loft. With my pulpit robe on, I was boiling hot, and perspiration began flowing. I saw one of the ushers coming down the aisle with the candles. The wedding was about to start, and I still didn't have the recorder set up.

That's when I made my mistake. I decided that I'd crawl out on my hands and knees and sneak under the table cloth. No one in the auditorium could see me or know that I was there, and I'd set the recorder under the table and get out quickly. I eased beneath the table near all those candelabras and set the recorder just as the usher was touching the flame to the first candle.

Well, when I tried to turn myself around under the table, the south end of me bumped a candelabra. I couldn't see it because of the table cloth, but I heard it fall against the next candelabra. One caught another and another, and like dominoes, the whole works started falling. All those candelabras crashed to the floor at the side of the altar.

I didn't know what to do next, and when the usher leaned over and peeked behind the table, he saw me. I was so embarrassed that I just put my head down on the floor. The usher's eyes got real big. He was scared to death. There I was under there with that pulpit robe all bunched around me. All the candelabras were on the floor and all he had done was touch one candle and everything was in chaos.

Fortunately, the florist was still there in the vestibule and came running down the aisle. In an accusatory voice, she demanded of the usher. "What in the devil happened?"

And all that usher could do was point down at me still crouching under the table.

He whispered, "Preacher, what we gonna do?"

"Come on down here and hide with me." There was no doubt in my mind. "Come on down here and hide with me," I motioned to the usher.

The florist said, "Get up, preacher, and we'll fix it."

"Uh uh" I said. And I left just exactly the way I came in. I crawled out. No one in the auditorium saw me, and I never admitted to anything.

One cold Sunday evening our dog, Hattie, decided to give birth to a litter of six pups. We had been watching her carefully for several weeks, planning for the blessed event. Hattie used a big wooden box in the kitchen as her bed, and every evening when Vonzeal told her to go to bed, into her box she'd go. She'd snuggle down and was happy for the whole night. During her period of expectancy, we had been very careful to make every little thing in her life comfortable. The boys were looking forward to the litter of puppies, and Vonzeal had prepared her bed with extra blankets for the birth of our new family additions.

But, for some reason, Hattie had other plans. We had spent the cold, sleeting Sunday afternoon in leisure. After lunch, I watched a little football with

Jerry and Jim, napped and studied the Sunday evening materials, then napped some more. Sometime in the late afternoon Hattie had asked to go outside, and Vonzeal had opened the kitchen door, let her out and then got busy with other projects. She was always working on crafts or reading recipe books, and this particular Sunday afternoon time just slipped by in peaceful lunch digestion.

Vonzeal looked up from her project and spotted the clock. "Jim, wake up – we're going to be late for the evening service. Jimmy, Jerry – get ready to go!" She tossed aside her crafts and raced to the bedroom. Startled out of our naps, we boys jumped up in confusion, then began rushing to get dressed.

But before I made it to the bedroom, I heard a whine at the back door that I recognized as Hattie. "Is Hattie outside?" I called to Vonzeal, already knowing the answer.

"Oh, yes. I forgot all about her. She usually comes right back —" Vonzeal followed me into the kitchen and saw a slim, but exhausted Hattie.

"Oh, she's had her pups outside in the freezing cold. Jerry! Jim! get your coats on. We've got to find Hattie's babies!" I was already heading out the door without my coat, still in my sock feet from my nap. "Honey, make sure Hattie's all right!"

A blast of icy sleet hit me, but the circumstances being what they were, I barely felt the cold wind. The safety of Hattie's pups was the only thing on my mind. I looked around the carport first, without luck, then headed out into the yard.

Hattie hadn't gotten far because nestled under a big shrub lay six little half-frozen pups. Jerry, Jimmy and I each picked up two and carefully carried the near dead pups into the kitchen. Hattie was frantic! Vonzeal was frantic! Jerry and Jimmy were frantic! I was in control.

"Hurry, put them into their box, and Hattie can get in and warm them up."

"No!" Vonzeal insisted. "Hattie's a nervous wreck! We've got to get these pups warmed up fast. Oh, look – I'd don't think this one will make it!"

"Here, I have an idea. Let's put the box on top of the radiator, turn it down real low and see if that will save them." I suggested.

"Oh, good idea!" Everyone nodded and agreed.

"And, in the meantime, let's hurry and get dressed for church. It starts in fifteen minutes." We began to hustle around, throwing on clothes and shoes and heading out the door.

Jerry said, "I want to stay home and make sure the puppies are all right. Okay, Mom, please?"

"No way." She answered. "You're going to church with the rest of us."

"But, Mom —"

"No! We must go to church as a family. The puppies will be fine where they are, and by the time we get home, they should be stirring around."

"But —-" he pleaded. In his heart he knew he should stay home with them.

"No!"

"But—-"

"No buts, get your buts in the car right now! All of you!"

Vonzeal never swore. From the day I met her, she had been the proper young lady, and foul language was not her style. However, with her sharp intelligence and keen sense of humor, she enjoyed an occasional play on words – especially in the safety of our home.

Years later, when our teenage granddaughter was visiting, Vonzeal and Terri were in the kitchen cleaning up after lunch when Terri said a word she shouldn't.

Instead of using it as a negative, Vonzeal, in her way, tried to turn the moment into a chance to give her granddaughter some positive direction. She began ministering to Terri about the way a real lady acts and speaks. And Terri, who was always respectful, listened politely to Vonzeal's gentle lecturing. "You are judged not only by the way you treat others, but also by the way you treat yourself. You don't show self respect if you use the word _ _ _ _!"

Vonzeal had never uttered that word before. The word left her mouth, raced around her head, flew through her eardrums, stopped briefly behind her eyes long enough to register in wide-open astonishment – then fled down her arm to lodge in the funny bone of her elbow.

I was sitting in the easy chair in the den watching the Braves, when I heard the peal of giggles coming from the kitchen. Grumbling, I grabbed the remote control and turned the television volume louder. The kitchen giggles got louder! Finally, in desperation (and mostly curiosity), I flung myself out of the easy chair and into the kitchen. There were two women, one grown, one almost grown, lying across the counter laughing so hard they were holding their sides.

As a man, I've never really understood women, but years of living with one had taught me that sometimes I just don't want to know. And this was one of them. Without a backward glance, I retreated to my baseball game, leaving them gasping for breath.

That evening as I kissed Vonzeal to sleep, lay down on my pillow holding her hand, I felt her squeeze my hand gently. "Jim, did you hear Terri and me laughing in the kitchen today?" she whispered.

"Sorta." I non-committed, waiting.

"Jim, I said a really bad word today! Accidentally! It was awful!"

"Couldn't have been too awful . . .I heard you and Terri Belle laughing like hyenas out there."

"I was trying to counsel her, and it just slipped out!"

"Honey," I squeezed her hand real hard. "It couldn't have been too bad if you two had such a good laugh over it. That's something Terri will remember for the rest of her life – every time she hears that word. Remember, there's no laughter in hell."

She lay there quietly for a second, then, "Thank you, Jim!" she whispered and fell asleep. Moments later I glanced over at her in the semi-darkness and saw a little smile on her sweet, sleeping lips.

Did I forget something? Oh, yes, the puppies.

When we arrived home from church that Sunday evening, Hattie greeted us at the door running in circles. "Oh, Jim, she needs to feed her babies!" Vonzeal's motherly instinct was right on cue.

But over at the box on the radiator things weren't looking so hot. Or maybe they were looking a little too hot. Jerry let out a wail you could hear in Birmingham; Jimmy got all teary eyed and I rushed back outside to execute (excuse the pun) a quick burial of six little hot dogs before Hattie could learn the truth.

It was too late. She already knew what I had done to her babies. In the week that followed, she lay on the floor with her head resting on her paws, looking woefully at me with one eyebrow cocked. It was her evil eye, and I couldn't face her and she knew it.

And Vonzeal could never ever convince Hattie to go back into her box.

Unfortunately for our family, Hattie died during the construction of our new auditorium. One of the workers took her little body and buried it beneath where we believe the podium now stands. Hattie was the only dog to ever join the Headland Heights Baptist Church and the only member to be buried on the property.

During the time at Headland Heights, Jimmy and his friend enrolled at Gordan Military School. For the first six weeks, we could not visit them. This separation policy allowed the inital shock of loneliness and home sickness to pass, and properly prepared the students to continue their education. We didn't realize how long six weeks can be when you're away from a loved one for the first time. We were anxious for that six weeks to pass and, as soon as it did, he immediately came home, dressed in his uniform and excited about his military training. I had a dear pastor friend, Dr. Howard Ethington, who was pastor at Barnesville First Baptist Church in the city where Gordon Military School was located. I spoke with Howard and asked him to keep an eye on Jimmy, and he assured me he would be happy to look after him. So Dr. Ethington became the one to whom Jimmy went when he was homesick.

One Saturday I decided to visit Jimmy by myself and take him to eat, and since he had received his temporary driver's permit, I thought he might enjoy driving our car. We rode all day long, had lunch together, bowled a few games then had a steak in the late afternoon. As I prepared to leave to go back to Atlanta, sitting there in the car, I said, "Jimmy, I must get back to Atlanta to get ready to preach tomorrow."

"Okay," he replied, "It's been a great day – I've enjoyed it."

"It has for me too, and we'll look forward to you coming home to visit as soon as you can. "

At that point, Jimmy said, "Dad, let's have prayer before you leave."

Thinking there might be a problem he needed to discuss I said, "Is there anything you need to talk to me about or something you want to share with me?"

He shocked me when he said, "Oh no. I don't have anything I want to talk to you about. It's just been a long time since I've heard you pray . . . and I just wanted to hear you pray!"

After he got out of the car and I started driving back to Atlanta, I began to reflect upon that moment. I consider it one of the highest moments in my relationship with my son, Jimmy. I wept as I drove. I would rather hear my son say, "Dad, I just want to hear you pray," than any other thing in the world."

Chapter 12

1961-1962

———⇒»◦«⇐———

[[W]]e received a call that my father in the faith,
Brother M. G. Wilson, pastor of Second Baptist Church
in Huntsville, Alabama, was critically ill. We had been
together in revivals for all those years, and he wanted
me to come to his bedside. Vonzeal and I were prepared
to leave for vacation, so we decided that we'd drive to
Huntsville, see Brother Wilson, then continue to
Panama City, Florida.

When we arrived in Huntsville, we visited him in
the hospital. He was sixty-two years old. "Son, you
know I have cancer," he told me, "I'm not going to
get well."

"Oh, you must, Brother Wilson. I need you in revival
at Headland Heights. This is the only church I've had
that you haven't preached revival."

"No, I won't be able to make it this time. I'm going
to leave from this bed to go home to be with the Lord.
Now go on with your vacation, but leave word with
Clarence Carroll, the chairman of the deacons, where
you'll be. I want you to preach my funeral. Remember,

I've always told you I don't want any slow walking or low talking at my funeral. Get up on your hind legs and preach. I've told Donald, our minister of music, what I want to be sung. I want you and Donald to make it a great worship service."

Vonzeal and I knelt beside his bed, and he began to pray for us. He prayed that we would have a wonderful vacation. He prayed that I would be available to preach his funeral. And then he prayed that I would become the pastor of his church and continue the kind of work I had begun in many other churches.

"Lord, you know, "he continued to pray, "that I've spoken with you many times about Jim. And he is to be the one who will continue my work."

Vonzeal and I were astounded. "Brother Wilson, I don't know about that!"

"Don't worry about it. God will take care of it."

"But, you're trying to say—" I stammered.

"The Lord will take care of it. You're going to be the one to take my place when I'm gone. This church will need you, and you'll be able to lead this church where it needs to go."

Within a few days, Brother Wilson lost his fight with cancer and, as requested, I conducted his funeral. He was the pastor who had baptised Vonzeal when she was a little girl and had been her only pastor until I acquired the honor. He was the one who had counseled with me when I made my commitment to enter the ministry. He had married us. I referred to Brother Wilson and Brother E. R. Broadwell as my "fathers in the faith."

After his funeral at Maple Hills Cemetery, I suddenly found myself surrounded by the twelve deacons of Second Baptist Church. Clarence Carroll said, "We've all made arrangements to have dinner with you and Vonzeal tonight at six o'clock. All of the deacons and our wives."

We were honored.

Dinner was served, and we chatted away pleasantly enough, but we were absolutely shocked when Clarence stood and said, "You all know that we have our next pastor and his wife here with us tonight." Vonzeal and I looked at each other in surprise, and an unspoken communication passed between us that perhaps these deacons were just following Brother Wilson's instructions.

I asked Clarence if I could have a private conversation with him. "Man, you don't have to do this just because it was Brother Wilson's wish."

"What wish?" he was mystified. He had no idea what I was talking about.

"Brother Wilson's wish that I come as pastor."

"I don't know what you're talking about, Brother Jim. He never mentioned it as far as I know," he insisted. In fact, all the deacons were as puzzled as Clarence and swore that they'd never heard Brother Wilson make any reference to me as the church's next pastor. Mysterious events were beginning to happen.

They invited me to return to Huntsville to preach for them as soon as possible, but I made no promises. Vonzeal and I left Huntsville the next day, totally confused, yet determined that we were not going to leave Headland Heights. Brother Wilson had been a completely different pastor from me. He didn't believe in watching television or movies. Although he was one of the sweetest Christian men and greatest soul winners I've ever known, he was an extreme fundamentalist. We were so different in our styles of ministry.

I told the deacons, "Brother Wilson taught a negative ministry. For instance, you don't go to the movies, you don't do this, you don't do that; therefore, you're a Christian. I take the opposite approach. I preach a positive gospel. You fall in love with the Lord Jesus Christ, you receive Him as your Saviour and then, with the leadership of the Holy Spirit in your life, you alone determine whether or not you can or cannot do things. And the Lord doesn't lead me to oppose television nor movies. No, Brother Wilson and I are totally opposite."

Their response was, "But you don't understand. We loved him so much that we never opposed anything that he did. But we realize now that we need what you have to offer. We want you." They insisted.

The year was 1962. We went back to Atlanta, committed that we were not about to go to Huntsville, Alabama.

I received a phone call from Clarence Carroll, once again inviting me to come preach a sermon for them, but I continued to stall. Picking up the phone, I called Dr. Louie Newton, my counselor of many years, and told him exactly what had transpired and asked for his advice.

"But, you do need to go over there and preach for them," he answered. "Who knows, after you preach a trial sermon, they may become convinced, along with you, that they don't *want* you."

I gave his proposal heavy thought, weighing the pros and cons. I didn't want to go preach for them, then have them not *want* me. To be wanted, then rejected, might hurt my ego. But after considering my options, I sighed, "Well, that sounds like good advice. I'll do it."

Finally, Clarence Carroll and I set a date for me to preach the morning service at Second Baptist Church, Huntsville. Vonzeal and I drove over on Saturday, after leaving Jim and Jerry with my older brother Frank and his wife Eva. When we arrived, we found the church had reserved a big suite at the motel for us, and the deacons held another dinner that evening. "Brother and Mrs. Dorriety, we want you both to open your hearts and minds to our proposal."

They were courting us.

Sunday morning Vonzeal went into a Sunday School class, and I spent the time visiting all the classrooms and meeting people. I didn't have an opportunity to see Vonzeal until service time. I entered the auditorium and was amazed; it was filled with people. The pews were packed. There were chairs up and down the aisles all the way to the platform; extra chairs on the platform; people were standing two deep around the outside walls, around the front of the church and down the other wall as long as people could get in the building. An overflow room was packed with people. Never in my life had I seen such a wonderful demonstration on behalf of a church.

As always, the first thing I wanted to do when I got on the platform was to locate Vonzeal. Every time I'd stood in the pulpit to preach, from the time of my first sermon, when I had finally found the top of her head, until today, I'd always located her first and got a nod or wink from her. But there were so many people there, I couldn't find her. She knew I was trying to find her, and she was straining up in her seat. Finally, I saw her, and there were tears flowing from her eyes, and then my eyes filled with tears. We began silently weeping. We knew something unusual was happening. We had already decided that we were only coming to enjoy their hospitality, preach the sermon and go on back home to Atlanta.

And yet, something was saying to us, "You ain't fixing to get out of here!"

I delivered my sermon, and it was genuinely received. We left immediately after lunch, driving back to Atlanta. Traveling that afternoon across Sand Mountain, we didn't do much talking. We'd thought we'd already made the decision, and now we had satisfied our obligation and this was behind us.

Back in Atlanta I preached at Headland Heights that same evening. The next morning John Hurt at The Christian Index phoned me. He asked, "How'd it go yesterday in Huntsville?"

"Well, I went over there and preached."

"Well, are you going to Alabama?"

"Noooo. I'm not going to Alabama."

"Good. I just wanted to know before I went to press with The Index because I wanted to put it in if you were leaving. How 'bout meeting me for lunch, and I'll buy you a steak after the pastor's conference?"

Later that day at the pastor's conference, I saw Dr. Newton. "How'd you do, yesterday?" he inquired.

"We got it behind us. We don't have to worry about that anymore."

"You going?"

"Nooo. I'm not about to go. No way am I going. No intention of going," I insisted. But forces were already at work.

That evening, Monday night, Headland Heights had a Deacon's meeting with all twelve of our deacons and there seemed to be some unrest. One of the deacons brought up a proposition that was unbelievable.

"You know, brethren, I've been noticing that our pastor has been gone to several revival meetings, and I know he must have a time deciding whether to go or not. I think we need to help him by letting him know that he doesn't have to take every revival request. Let's just put a limit of two revivals a year, and then he can tell a church when they call he's sorry, but he only does two revivals a year, and he's already booked. Then we could help him keep from having to go to so many revivals."

I interrupted him, "No, we don't need that sort of

thing. I simply go on the basis of what I feel the Lord wants me to do. I already limit myself to four revivals per year, and I insist on two of those being in the immediate area so I can be at home during the week in case I'm needed."

He again insisted that the number should be limited and the deacons began to talk about it, some agreeing with him and some agreeing with me. Finally, after this discussion had consumed our entire evening, I said, "Look, I don't want to pastor a church that would put a limit on me because I don't work for the church, I work for the Lord. I went to work for Him full-time in 1945, and I haven't changed employers since that day."

"If," I continued, "you were to vote to put a limit on the number of revivals I attend, then consider that a vote to accept my resignation, because I could not even preach the next service for you."

That statement shocked them and they chose not to vote. But when the deacon's meeting was over, I sensed a lot of unrest. Battle lines had been drawn. Needless to say, I was very upset, and Vonzeal and I discussed the meeting and prayed before bedtime.

The very next morning, Tuesday, I received a call from Ray Moore from WSB Television. One of the most respected newsmen in Georgia, he'd been anchor for Channel 2 News for years and had even turned down a job offer from a national network because he wanted to stay in Georgia.

Ray said, "Jim, did you watch the eleven o'clock news last night?"

"No, I didn't. What's happening?"

"Listen, you won't believe what happened! Come down to the station right now. I saved it on tape so you could see it yourself. Friend, if anybody ever had foundation for a lawsuit for slander – you have. Get down here!"

I went immediately to the station and found Ray in the control room, and he replayed the news program for me in its entirety.

Zack Craven, the Comptroller General, was being opposed in the upcoming election by two candidates, and there had been a tape recorded public political forum the night before between the three opponents. Ray Moore had been the moderator. These two opponents, one a lawyer, had accused Zack Craven, the Comptroller General of Georgia, and a Baptist preacher by the name of James O. Dorriety of stealing funds from the state for churches.

Somehow they had found out how we secured the construction loan for First Baptist Church of Warner Robins through the Governor's office. Other churches had inquired about loans, and as the requests came in, Mr. Craven would call me and ask if I knew the church and ask that I check them out for him. Methodist Churches, Presbyterian Churches, all denominations. Many millions of dollars had been loaned to churches in Georgia from the Georgia Retirement System for school teachers and state employees. Of course, the state was receiving six percent interest, rather than the previous two and one-half percent interest on these loans.

These two opponents were making accusations that we, Zack Craven and I, were getting kickbacks from the churches in the state.

Ray said, "I'm gonna keep the transcript just like it is just in case you need it."

"Ray, as far as I'm concerned, the only thing I want," I replied, "is a chance to answer the accusations."

"Okay," he promptly agreed. "I'll prepare a promo that says you will answer the charges tonight on the six o'clock news."

In the meantime, I spoke to Mr. Craven and got all the details and facts together, and I went on WSB Television and gave a retort to the accusation to the people of Georgia. I described in detail how I had first obtained the loan for First Baptist Church in Warner Robins. I explained how I had helped the Comptroller General, in a very limited way, by checking out the solidarity of a few churches, strictly for the purpose of giving a verbal inspiration as to the viability of that church.

When I got home, our telephone was ringing off the hook. We couldn't hang it up before it rang again. We were so concerned; we didn't know what to do. The state began to support me and the opponents began to back up. The scenario began to turn around in my favor.

Suddenly, it seemed to us that everything was going sour in our lives. This loan controversy and false accusations had occurred the very same night the deacon body had begun arguing.

Vonzeal, in her arm chair, had been reading her Bible and praying when she looked up at me and said, "Jim, do you think we made a mistake by not going to Huntsville?"

I burst into tears and fled to our bedroom where I fell across the bed weeping. She came and lay down beside me, "All day long, today, I've been praying. I believe we've made a mistake. Do you think the Lord is trying to change our minds? Tell me what you really feel," she whispered.

"Honey, when I got in the pulpit of Second Baptist Church on that Sunday morning and found you, and my eyes filled with tears as I saw all those eager people looking at us -wanting me as their pastor – I knew that I should go to that church as pastor. Yes, we've made a mistake by not going. We should have gone."

"I believe so, too," she assured me. "Why don't you call Clarence Carrol and talk to him?" Clarence had been chairman of the deacons for forty-eight years and was like an associate pastor.

"Vonzeal, I'm not wishy-washy. When I make a decision I live by it."

Finally, about eleven o'clock, I said, "No relief is coming; I guess I'll be awake all night long. You know, it's only ten o'clock in Huntsville. Why don't I call Clarence and just talk to him and see how things are going?"

Clarence answered the phone. I said, "Clarence, this is Jim over in Atlanta."

Before I could say another word, he said, "You've changed your mind, haven't you?"

"Well, I don't know. I just wanted to call you and see how things are."

"Before you go on, let me tell you what happened. We had a joint meeting with the pulpit committee and deacons, and I polled every single one there. We all agreed that you're the one to be our pastor. So we decided that we would just commit you to the Lord. We got down on our knees and joined our hearts and our hands and agreed that we'll just wait until the Lord changes your mind. And when he does, we're ready for you."

He took a deep breath and added, "How are things going with you?"

"Clarence, I guess I need to come back and talk with you again."

We made an appointment to go back to Huntsville to meet with the committee. We learned that there was not even a pastorium for us as the church had deeded it to Mrs. Wilson when Brother Wilson died.

But the church was willing to let us start all over, come and pick out a lot, pick out our own house plans.

They would build a brand new pastorium for us. So we agreed to come to Second Baptist Church, Huntsville.

Before the weekend was over, we had selected the lot and plans for the new pastorium. We made arrangements to stay in a motel efficiency apartment during the three months our home was being built.

We resigned at Headland Heights with a thirty-day notice in September, 1962 . Jimmy was sixteen years old, had been in military school and had his driver's license. We had three cars to transfer, and he made his first long trip, driving from Atlanta to Columbus to Huntsville. Jerry, who was working on perfect Sunday School attendance, insisted we stop for church, so we attended Sunday School and had lunch in Wedowee, Alabama on our way to Huntsville.

Chapter 13

1962-1973

I was peeling potatoes for my world famous potato soup. Vonzeal, in her effort to clean up after me in our tiny efficiency kitchen at Myricks Motel, was giggling because we kept bumping into each other. "Don't you think it's weird that Charles Bentley got transferred from Atlanta to Red Stone Arsenal a month before we did?"

"Weird, Jim? There's nothing weird about it."

"Coincidental then. I didn't mean weird."

"There's nothing coincidental about it, either," she carefully put the dish above her in the cupboard in her very meticulous way. "The Lord made it all happen. He has a plan for Second Baptist and obviously Jeanne Bentley is as big a part of it as you are."

Jeanne had been with us at First Warner Robins, then Central Baptist and Headland Heights. A total of ten years. Now we were in Huntsville, and she was already here waiting for us.

"A modern day miracle?"

"Call it what you want, but the Lord's had a big

hand in all of this."

"She's going to be a great minister of education here. This church needs to wake up. Guess what? I saw the books today, and there's $60,000 sitting in their checking account."

She looked quizzically at me. "Savings account," Vonzeal corrected.

"No! Checking account. Just sitting there, not drawing any interest at all." I dumped a handful of potatoes in the boiling water on the stove. In 1962 that was a lot of money.

I asked, "Where did the church get the name Second Baptist Church. This used to be Fifth Street Baptist Church. I don't like to be second in anything. I want to win. What about this name?"

"Well," the deacon explained, "the city grew and changed the name of the street from Fifth Street to Jackson Way Boulevard, so Brother Wilson renamed the church Second Baptist since it was one of the oldest churches in the city. No, the congregation never did vote on it, but no one would oppose Brother Wilson. If that's what he wanted to name the church, that was fine."

"Do you suppose the congregation would be amenable to changing the name of the church?"

Everybody started jumping up and down. Nothing would please them more. We found out that nobody liked the name Second Baptist Church. So we formed a committee, as Baptists always do, and decided to wait a full month before we voted to change the name, and, in the meantime, we advertised the upcoming vote so everyone would have an opportunity to be involved in the renaming process. After four weeks, the vote was unanimous to consider changing the name of the church.

Then we set aside three months for anyone to suggest any name to the special committee. If there were three choices that surfaced as the top recommendations, we would vote on those three names.

Someone recommended Wilson Memorial in honor of Brother Wilson, Davis Memorial for the pastor before Brother Wilson, Dorriety Memorial for yours truly. Even the textile industry that once operated in Huntsville was suggested.

And, of course, Jackson Way was a popular name because Jackson Way Boulevard was the name of the four-lane highway that went right past the church.

Three months later we unanimously voted to change the name to Jackson Way Baptist Church, 1001 Andrew Jackson Way, Huntsville, Alabama.

One of the most miraculous things was the fact that their beloved pastor, M. G. Wilson, had been loved so much, they never opposed anything he wanted to do. For ten years the church had sat dormant. Meanwhile, Huntsville, the little city in North Alabama, was growing fast. In 1950 the population was a little over sixteen thousand; by the time I arrived in 1962, it had grown to one hundred thousand, thanks to Redstone Arsenal. From there the number rose to one hundred seventy five thousand, so the city was expanding quickly. But here was one of the oldest churches in the community – not growing at all.

We did a study of the past ten years and saw that basically the yearly income had remained the same – at between forty-eight to fifty-two thousand dollars. Yet, while the Sunday school enrollment had decreased in that ten year period, their baptismal ratio was extremely elevated. For instance, in ten years, Brother Wilson had baptised over thirteen hundred; at the same time the Sunday school enrollment had declined. This was way out of kilter.

In studying the previous years, I began to realize this church had not been released to develop and grow. I didn't believe any of this was the fault of Brother Wilson. He was a victim of the times in which he lived – as well as his own dedication and conservatism.

This was a sleeping giant—a church that was dormant and needed to be awakened. After looking at their finances, we learned that there was sixty thousand dollars in the bank, and there was no debt. Yet, the buildings were inadequate, and the church was not ministering to the community. They were saving money but didn't know why. The sixty thousand dollars, as I had told Vonzeal, was not even in a savings account drawing interest . . . it was in the checking account.

Later we learned that very few members of the church even knew how much money was in their coffers. It was a situation where the pastor, the deacons and the secretary were in control and no one else really cared to find out. There was no problem; everyone was extremely honest and sincere. There just seemed to exist a general lack of interest on the part of the congregation.

I determined that since I'm different from Brother Wilson, I'd better let that difference be known and see what would develop.

The very first thing we did was to develop a stewardship emphasis in a Forward Program of Church Finance. We were amazed to see over three hundred percent increase in tithing that first year. That was a tremendous increase. This, of course, gave absolute assurance to the fact that we could build the needed buildings, because now we knew we had the financial ability. Immediately, we began to plan to enlarge. Increased stewardship means an increase in missions; an increase in missions always means an increase in numbers; an increase in numbers means an increase in buildings.

In 1964 we had plans drawn for our first educational building, three stories high. We had some sleepless nights worrying about the financing. The Chairman of the Deacons and I went to the bank to borrow funds for the new building. We calculated that about $200,000 would be needed over and above what we had accumulated. The banker agreed to loan us $150,000, but we figured when we got down to the end, he would agree to loan us the remaining $50,000. Just building on faith – it had never failed before.

When the construction reached the point the extra funds were needed, we approached the banker, confident there would be no problem. Instead, he refused us saying we had reached our legal limit. He said, "Just stop construction and finish it yourselves as you receive the funds from the pledges." The banker waved his hand as if to dismiss us and looked away from our disappointed faces.

I opened my mouth to protest but something told me I'd get nowhere with this banker. His body language told me that his ears were closed to any persuasion. Never one to take no for an answer or give up easily, I took the liberty of going down the street to First Alabama Bank and asking if they could get involved with our loan. No, I was told; ethically they couldn't get involved in a sister bank's policy.

Down, but not out, I picked up the phone and called my banker friend in Atlanta, Ray Houston, and explained my problem to him.

"The banker told me one hundred fifty thousand was their legal limit!"

"Wait a minute, and I'll look it up and tell you if it's their legal limit or not." He put me on hold for a moment, then came back, "No, he has no legal limit; he can loan you any amount he wants. That's just his way of saying that he doesn't want to loan you any more funds."

"But, we've got to get these additional funds. Can your bank help us?"

"I'll see what I can do and call you back in about an hour."

An hour later my phone rang. "I've talked to the President of First Alabama Bank and he's waiting for you to come immediately," Ray said into the receiver. "He will talk to you again. I told him who you are and what you accomplished at Headland Heights and Warner Robins. I assured him he can trust you because you know what you're doing. So go down there right now."

I couldn't get down there fast enough. The bank president was waiting, and we began to talk. "I have figured out a way that we may be able to help."

"Good, fine. We'll just transfer over to your bank," I answered, impatient to end this problem.

"No. I want you to go back to the other bank and tell him you've talked to me, and that we will participate with him in the loan. If he wants to make the loan for one hundred fifty thousand, we'll provide an additional fifty thousand dollars. He can hold the paperwork and make the two hundred thousand loan, and one fifty will be their loan and the other fifty will be ours."

I'd never heard of that before. "Do you think he'll do that?"

"No, I don't think he will!"

"Then what good will it do for me to go and ask him?"

"Simply because if he won't agree to it, our bank will make the two hundred thousand loan to your church. But ethically, we can only make the loan after he refuses to participate with us in the loan."

"In other words, if he says 'yes,' you'll participate?"

"Oh, yes! We can work out our agreement."

"And if he says 'no,' you'll loan us the full amount?"

"If he says no, you come back, and we'll fill out the paperwork today, and you can pay off what you've borrowed from his bank."

Stunned, I went back to the original bank and met with our banker. I explained all that the President of First Alabama Bank had told me. This banker became very angry and demanded to know why the Chairman of the Deacons, Clarence Carroll, wasn't there to meet with him.

"All we're going to loan is one hundred and fifty thousand dollars. That's it!" And he invited me out of his office.

So back down the street to First Alabama Bank I went and filled out the paperwork. That evening the deacons met and the next morning I went to First Alabama Bank to get the loan.

Our financial secretary, Maureen Alverson, went with me to the other bank, and she wrote a check to pay off our principle. We wanted to pay off the interest, too, but he refused to figure it for us.

While we were there, we closed and moved the church's bank account to First Alabama Bank. I moved my account at the same time.

Before the dust settled, sixty-plus accounts from our church family transferred to First Alabama Bank.

For the next eleven years that I was there, our stewardship saw an increase of three hundred to four hundred percent. When we started in 1962 our stewardship was $53,438. The following year our stewardship was $219,026. When I left in 1972, our stewardship was averaging approximately $160,000 per year. The growth pattern of stewardship was keeping up with the growth pattern of the church.

An auditorium in the church plant was referred to as "the new auditorium," even though it was over thirty years old. It had replaced the original one, a little yellow stucco chapel, that was still free-standing and highly unattractive.

The thirty year old "new auditorium" didn't have one piece of steel in it: it was a wood-frame brick veneer building. Very attractive and very comfortable, it didn't have much educational space. Brother Wilson built a church on a preaching ministry, as opposed to my philosophy of building a church on an educational ministry. The difference was being seen in Huntsville. Mrs. Bentley, our minister of education, started training classes in leadership. She designed a curriculum specifically to develop teachers. The teachers began to study and learn how to teach. Units were developed, and the Sunday School kept growing and advancing.

A good example was a new approach to training called "Sunday Afternoon Sunday School." In January 1963 the training session met for the first time. Out of one hundred twenty one officers and teachers serving, one hundred and ten gathered each Sunday afternoon for four Sundays for two hours of study.

The more people we reached...the more money we received...the more money we spent...the more people we reached...the more money we needed. And the whole thing mushroomed into a rapidly growing church.

In 1963 my son, Jimmy, and I went into big business together and formed a corporation called Dorriety Enterprises for the purpose of selling an apparatus called an automatic sliding glass door closer. Jimmy was in high school and looking for a way to earn money to purchase his 1964 1/2 Mustang and to save for his college tuition. We thought we would earn our first million with this apparatus. A very simple device, it attached to a full length sliding glass door and, piston activated, automatically closed the door. A friend in Atlanta had introduced this item to me, and I thought it might help give Jimmy some business experience as well as finance his automobile. The closures cost us twelve dollars apiece and we sold them for thirty-nine ninety-five installed. Jimmy sold them right out of the back seat of our Volkswagen and installed them on his days off. We enjoyed a nice little profit until he left home for college, when I was left with several hundred boxes full of automatic door closers with no salesman. So there they sat. Every time Vonzeal wanted the garage cleaned out, Jerry and I would grudgingly complain under our breaths as we moved the hundreds of boxes of door closers from one side of the garage to the other.

One day I was out on the municipal golf course in Huntsville playing a little golf when I noticed some light planes landing and taking off in the adjacent airfield. Remembering how I had enjoyed flying on my friend's plane in Warner Robins, I was suddenly inspired to learn to fly. I thought, "Well, I've never tried it, but if somebody else can fly a plane, I can too. So I'll just prove to myself that I can."

I immediately packed my golf clubs, threw them in the trunk of the car and drove thirty miles to Fayetteville, Tennessee. I had heard a radio advertisement for a flying school there. After I arrived, I found the instructor, Reese Howell, and asked about the possibility of enrolling that very day for a flying lesson. I filled out some paperwork, and he took me outside to a little Cessna 150 sitting there in the hangar area. Without hesitation he gave me instructions for a preflight inspection, then told me to sit down in the left front seat.

Shocked, I replied, "Reese, isn't this left seat where the pilot sits?"

"Yes."

"But I told you I want to *learn* to fly. I don't know how to fly so I think you're putting me in the wrong seat!"

"Oh, no. It has dual controls and can be flown just as easily from one seat as the other. I want you in the pilot's seat."

Satisfied that he would still be in control, we went through the check list for the preflight run-up, all the things which need to be checked before the plane takes to the air, i.e. fuel and instruments. Next he gave me instructions for obtaining directions from the tower for taxiing to the end of the runway. My adrenaline was pumping as we waited for permission to take off. He assured me that he would be in complete control of the airplane but asked me to place my hands on the yoke and my feet on the rudders, so I could "feel" the controls as we lifted into the air and began to sail away. The little Cessna gracefully lifted off the runway, and I was getting my first lesson in flying.

As soon as we turned out of the pattern and reached desired altitude, he said to me, "Okay, you have the controls, Jim. I'm going to turn everything loose and let you fly the plane." As I maneuvered the controls, he continued to constantly instruct me how to level the plane and turn, how to control the throttle and change the RPMs of the engine when climbing or descending. Then we practiced a few stalls. I realized I had just spent one of the most enjoyable hours of my life as Reese brought the plane back and landed it safely on the runway.

I was hooked! I went back the next day for another lesson and continued almost daily for two weeks.

During the process of my flight instruction, one of the procedures was for the instructor to say to a student pilot, "Assume you are losing your engine, where would you land? Pick out a spot you can see at a forty-five degree angle, any place around the plane, and assume you need to make an emergency landing."

I looked down to the left and spotted a field. "I can land over there on the left."

He said, "Fine, go to it," and he pulled the throttle back which made the engine idle.

I turned and immediately went towards that field for a simulated emergency landing. In my descent towards that emergency landing sight, I became a little concerned that it might be too short, and I might have some trouble with the wires. Beyond that I spotted a church building and beyond the church steeple I saw a ball field. Immediately I thought, "Well, that would be a better spot," and pulled back on the yoke, flew over my first selection and on towards the church.

Reese began yelling and cursing at me, "What are you doing? What the *&$# are you doing?"

"I'm going to the other side. I believe I can make it better at the field at the church."

"You don't ever change your *&%# decision. You go with your first sighting. You wouldn't have enough air speed to reach the other *&$# sight." He screamed.

"Yeah, but I'll feel safer crashing at the church than I do in the field."

He started laughing and grabbed the controls and brought the RPMs back, pulled the plane out, and we went around for another lecture on selecting emergency landing spots.

After we were safely back in the pattern, I glanced over at him and said, "You know, Reese, you shouldn't curse so much! Have you been saved? Do you have a church?"

This initial conversation ultimately led to his salvation. He joined Jackson Way Baptist Church and remained a member as long as we were there.

After six hours and eighteen minutes of flying time, Reese and I were up for a lesson and he said, "Do you see the runway down there on your left?"

We were flying at seventeen hundred feet, and I assured him I could see the runway.

"I'm wondering if you can continue down wind and at the appropriate time turn left on base."

This entailed turning from the current three hundred sixty degree heading to a two hundred seventy degree heading. We had been practicing it for days. "Yes, sure I can," I answered.

"Okay, I want to see you do that and land on the end of the runway." He reached over and turned the engine off.

That's when I learned what the propeller is really for – to keep the pilot cool, because the moment the propeller stopped, I began to sweat.

As I had been instructed, I went forward on the yoke five degrees and continued to descend executing, a turn to a two hundred seventy degree heading. I turned one hundred eighty degrees, and saw the runway ahead and continued to descend and brought the plane safely down on the end of the runway. It was an exhilarating experience.

As the Cessna rolled to a stop, Reese opened his door and said, "Okay, go back up and do at least three touch and goes. Each time as you turn final, you'll be able to see me standing on the edge of the runway. But if I put both hands up in the air to form a 'Y' with my body, it's an indication that something is wrong. Push your throttle in, pick up your flaps and fire-wall it. Just go around and try the landing again." He got out and left me alone for the first time. I taxied to the end of the runway, waited for permission from the tower, then lifted off on my first solo flight.

I performed three perfect touch and goes just as he had instructed me to do. On the fourth touch and go, I didn't see him standing at the edge of the runway, so I decided everything must be fine and decided to fly off and see the world. I flew out of the pattern and made a heading towards Huntsville thirty miles away.

As I flew over Huntsville enjoying the beautiful mountains, I became aware of another airplane flying in my vicinity. The pilot radioed me and he was Reese Howell, madder than a wet hen. He ordered me to follow him back to Fayetteville. After we landed, I received a most explicit chewing out, complete with adjectives not deleted. While I suffered through his tirade, the other flight instructors and ground crew circled around me and began cutting off my shirt-tail. I was apologizing and laughing, yet frightened and confused. They told me of the "tradition" to cut shirt-tails after one's first solo flight. The piece was then sliced in half, and the date of my first solo was recorded on both halves – one to be my souvenir and the other to hang in the hangar.

I enjoyed flying but soon learned that a preacher's salary didn't allow me to fly often. A friend in Columbus, Georgia, Bob Garrett, who operated a railway salvage business, owned a beautiful little 140 Cherokee, and I would go up with him every available opportunity . As his business grew and he found it necessary to fly nights and longer distances, he purchased a twin engine and placed the Cherokee up for sale. He generously decided to bring the plane to Huntsville to try to sell, thereby allowing me an airplane to fly during the time he sought a buyer. He flew to Huntsville and picked me up in his new twin engine,, and we returned to Columbus. I flew the 140 Cherokee, designated November 9720 Whiskey back to Huntsville and tied it down at General Aviation. For several weeks I enjoyed every opportunity to fly the little plane around.

One day as I taxied to a stop at the hangar I continued to sit in the little plane, and I began to pray. "Thank you, Lord, for the opportunities which have been mine and thank you for providing me with such a wonderful recreation. I would love to own this particular plane, and if it can be made possible I will never misuse it, but use it only for Your honor and glory. Amen."

I climbed out and went about the business of securing the plane at tie-down and as I walked away, I turned and looked back at it and thought, "Isn't it wonderful and beautiful that God is going to make it possible for me to have this airplane for my own?"

Of course, I had spent no time in determining the cost of such an asset or where I would find the money on my limited salary. I just went home, rejoicing that somehow it would be possible.

A week or so later Bob Garrett flew over to check on the plane and I invited him to share a meal with my family. As we were leaving to drive him back to the airport for his flight to Columbus, he spotted the hundreds of boxes stacked in the garage. He asked, "What in the world do you have stored down here?"

So I introduced him to all those sliding glass door closers.

"What are you doing with them?"

"Moving them from one side of the garage to the other every time Vonzeal wants the garage cleaned out," I laughed. "Jimmy was our salesman but he's off in college, so here they sit."

"Do they work?"

"Sure they work. Come back upstairs, and I'll show you the one we've got installed on our door."

We took the steps back up, and he examined the gadget installed on our sliding glass door. "Jim, I could sell these in my railway salvage business. How much do you want for them?"

I shrugged, "I don't know."

"Well, how about a swap? All these door closers for the November 9720 Whiskey," he suggested.

My heart started pounding. Was he serious? Without hesitation, so he wouldn't have time to change his mind, I struck the deal. My door closers for his 140 Cherokee. The Lord had answered my prayer. I wasn't surprised that the prayer had been answered, but I was surprised at how easy it had been. For the next three years I enjoyed the prestige of owning my own airplane.

Mark 11:23-24 "Jesus said for verily I say unto you That whosoever shall say unto this mountain, Be thou removed, and be thou cast into the sea; and shall not doubt in his heart, but shall believe that those things which he saith shall come to pass; he shall have whatsoever he saith. Therefore I say unto you, What things soever ye desire when ye pray believe them and ye shall have them."

If it's in the Bible, it's true.

Along with Reese Howell's flying service, he was an ATR rated pilot and flew a corporate plane for a construction company in Tennessee. In addition, he owned several agricultural planes which were used for spraying fields with insecticides.

On one occasion one of his ag plane pilots radioed in that he was having trouble with the plane. When the pilot landed, Reese exchanged places with the pilot and took the plane up to try to determine the cause of the trouble. What Reese didn't know was that the pilot had just refilled the plane, and the tanks were full of the insecticide. He took off to give it a test flight around the pattern and immediately determined that the problem was not major. Being in a hurry, he banked to return to the runway. Without realizing how full the spraying tanks were, he turned too steeply and lost control of the plane.

An experienced pilot, he knew he was crashing and sought his emergency landing sight, but the only spot available was towards a wooded area. He guided it to the best of his ability through two trees. He missed the one on the left, but the tree on the right caught his wing and spun the plane around and into the ground.

I received a phone call that he was in serious condition in the hospital; his right leg was almost totally severed, and the entire muscle on the calf of his leg was torn away. I rushed to his side to be with him before surgery. We talked and prayed that perhaps some way his leg could be saved. The surgeon came in while I was there, and we all held hands and, with tears in his eyes, he turned to Dr. Whitehead and said, "Dr. Whitehead, I want you to know I've given my life to the Lord, and my pastor, Brother Jim, and I have been praying. Now I give my leg to you. You do whatever you have to do, and I'm trusting God will lead you."

As the surgeon left Reese's room, I left with him and continued down the hall. I said, "Dr. Whitehead, do you think you'll be able to save Reese's leg?"

As he turned his eyes towards me, I saw a tear on his cheek and he motioned for me to step inside the doctors' lounge with him. He sank to the chair and placed his head in both of his hands and sat with his elbows propped on his knees until he regained his composure. He lifted his eyes and said, "Pastor, I was almost sure we were going to have to amputate his leg, and we may still have to. But oddly enough, while you prayed as we stood there beside his bed, I had the strange feeling that we're going to be able to save his leg. But you keep praying and we'll see."

Reese's leg was saved although the muscle was gone from the calf, and he would always walk with a bad limp.

But that didn't stop him. With a cast on his leg, he asked me to spend a day flying him to different air bases around the area. We spent the day flying from terminal to terminal from Nashville, Tennessee to Gadsden, Alabama. Reese witnessed and testified to the field base operators and other pilots of his faith in the Lord and of the miracle of his saved leg.

During the following months, I flew with him quite often in a plane he had refitted as an ambulance plane.

There was no question that we needed to take down the original stucco chapel; it was of no value to the church and it was an eyesore. So when we began to build the new educational building, we decided to demolish the original stucco building. C. B. Myrick, a member of the church, went to his union meeting on Friday night and found a buddy of his who owned a construction company. "We need to tear down that little yellow stucco building at the church. What would you charge us to do that?" he asked.

"Oh, I don't know. I'll tear the building down for just the material that's in it, I guess," the man answered.

"Okay, it's a deal – except for the church bell. I want to keep that bell myself – I don't think the church even wants it."

"Fine, you got a deal. I'll drive by the church office Monday morning and get them to give me a letter of agreement."

Sure enough, on Monday morning the contractor came by, and we signed an agreement with him to tear down the building for just the material. We felt that we had gotten a tremendous bargain.

Little did we realize, however, that the original bell to the church was in that chapel. And no one had really considered the historical value of that large church bell, except one man in the church, Mr. C. Burke Myrick. As the construction company was demolishing the little chapel, C. B. drove by and saw the bell lying in the yard. He pulled up and said, "I'll just load up this bell."

The man demolishing the building said, "You ain't taking that bell nowhere!"

"Yes, I am. You don't get to keep this bell. I told you at the union meeting I wanted that bell. It's a historical part of our church," C. B. argued.

"Well, I got a piece of paper signed by the deacon of the church saying that all the material in this building belongs to me!" He took a step menacingly towards C. B.

"We had an oral agreement that I got the bell! And I'm taking this bell," C. B. insisted turning and heading for the bell.

"No, you're not getting that bell!" Somebody shoved somebody, and the construction man took a swing at C. B. He saw the blow just before it smashed into his front teeth. Dazed, he shook his head and spit a bloody tooth out onto the ground.

"You knocked out my tooth," C.B. shouted at the man. Suddenly, the oral agreement had turned into an oral *disagreement*. C. B. took a swing back at the man and a free-for-all erupted on the church grounds. Someone ran inside and called the police.

Meanwhile, I was up in my Cherokee 140, flying around over the property inspecting it. It was a beautiful, clear sunny day, and I was enjoying the scenery and solitude.

When my plane flew directly over the church, I looked down and saw a car pull onto the property with lights flashing. I became concerned. Moments later I received a call on the plane radio. "November 9720 Whiskey, Come in."

"This is November 9720 *Witness*," I answered.

"Your secretary just called and wants you back at the church. There's some kind of disturbance going on."

"Call her back and tell her I'm on my way." I turned back towards the airport and got on the approach for final landing. "This is November 9720 *Witness* in bound for landing."

No answer from the tower.

"This is November 9720 *Witness* in bound for landing. Come in," I said louder.

No answer from the tower.

"Tower, this is November 9720 *Witness* in bound for landing. Come in," I yelled into the headset.

"Are you trying to say *Whiskey*?" came the voice from the tower.

"Being a Baptist minister, I'm trying *not* to," I replied.

The voice laughed and gave me clearance to land. Quickly I rolled to a stop at the hanger, tied down the plane, hopped into my car and rushed to the church. Of course, by the time I got there all the excitement was over.

The police officer asked the construction man, "Did you have a deal with this man that he keep the bell?"

"Yeah, but I had to back out cause I'm not making any money off this project," was his answer. "There was a lot of hard work tearing down that old building and I'm going to keep that bell."

Through his bloody mouth, C. B. Myrick exclaimed angrily, "A deal's a deal! The only way I won't file charges against you is if you'll leave the bell here." He was so mad he was lisping through his missing front tooth. "You take *thith* bell and I'll file assault against you in a heart-beat."

Clarence Carroll stepped up, "The church wants this bell . . . why – we wouldn't take anything for this bell." He gestured towards the innocuous bell, lying on the ground as if it were gold. The value of the metal had greatly escalated in the last few minutes.

"But I have a piece of paper——," the man began to argue again.

"*Listhin*," C. B. lisped through the gap in his front teeth, "If you want to sign this bell over to the church, I won't press charges, and you won't even have to replace *thith* tooth."

The construction man didn't have much choice but to agree, and the problem was resolved. Thanks to one member's tenacity, the church bell was preserved and still sits today in the vestibule of the new building.

With a plat of all our property under my arm, I went to the architectural department of the Sunday School Board of the Southern Baptist Convention.

"Don't worry about what we own," I said. "Just worry about what we need to build. Here's the plat of the area, and we need an auditorium that will seat about two thousand people. We also need an educational facility that will handle perhaps fourteen to fifteen hundred people. Tell me what we need to build first,   please."

The architectural department prepared a sketch for us which included acquiring seven houses on one block and four houses on the next block, giving us the land we needed. The deacons formed a corporation and hired an independent agent to purchase those houses. We worked out all the legalities with the church body and trustees of the church that this corporation would purchase the houses, and eventually the church would purchase the property from the corporation. This, of course, put all the risk on the men in the corporation.

The agent for the corporation went from house to house and began purchasing homes. He was able to purchase four very quickly, leaving only three houses on that block. Two others finally sold, but, of course, there was one owner who held out, and the corporation had to pay a little more than the land was worth to secure that property.

Three houses from the second block were purchased, and then we discovered that the new expressway was going to run right over and through the old YMCA building which the church owned. So we quickly bought up the land surrounding it, knowing the government would have to purchase it when they started the expressway.

In the meantime, the architectural department made a recommendation that we build our educational building first, since that need was greater at the time and our auditorium was still very functional. We set to work on the construction of the educational building, completed it and moved the church offices into it.

The old stucco building had been demolished, so now we had the auditorium and the new educational building, plus we still had the old YMCA building on the property.

Then in 1965, we had a terrible tragedy. A heating problem developed in our auditorium, and the repair men came out and worked on the system one Wednesday morning. They got it working again and left about ten o'clock.

At one o'clock that afternoon, we received a call

from the restaurant across the street saying "We see smoke coming from the eave of the auditorium." We raced to investigate and found a large fire in the building. By the time the fire trucks arrived, our pine frame auditorium was consumed with flames. Within two hours the building was totally destroyed . We had been unable to save anything...not the organ, piano, hymn books, nothing...everything in the building was gone.

We moved into the old YMCA building that evening for our Prayer Meeting. As we met there, with the embers still smoldering, the church family pulled together and began to plan for the future. We decided to use the gym floor of the old YMCA as our temporary auditorium. One family offered to purchase the folding chairs for the worship services. The pastor and deacons were authorized to begin plans for a new auditorium.

We hired an architect and gave him the sketch from the architectural department of the Southern Baptist Convention to begin preparations. We had the corporation's houses demolished and prepared the land for our new auditorium.

To build the new auditorium required $750,000 to a million. One of the oldest deacons in the church, eighty-four years old, made the motion to borrow the $750,000 through the bond program.

"Mr. Baucom," I said to this elderly deacon after the meeting, "You're one of the most progressive men I've ever known for your age. That you, at eighty-four, requested to make the motion that we borrow three quarters of a million dollars."

With a twinkle in his eye, he said, "Pastor, you know why I didn't mind making that motion? Because I know I won't be around to pay it off."

Brother Baucom taught me one important thing during my years at Jackson Way. He said, "You know

25 years is a long time in the life of a man, but 25 years is not long in the life of a church. Generation after generation can pass, but the church will stay until Jesus comes again. Let's build our auditorium big enough this time to accommodate growth in our church."

I was with Brother Baucom the day before he died. He told me that as he was lying there on the bed, he was hearing the sweetest music he'd ever heard. "I get so caught up in it," he told me, "that the first thing I know I'm humming along or moving my hands and directing it. It seems to be coming through the pillow. It's the most beautiful music I've ever heard."

During the night, Brother Baucom passed on, and I was in the home the next morning with his family. The oldest daughter said, "Brother Dorriety, I wish you could have been here last night when Papa died. We were all standing around the bed, and he was lying there with his eyes closed. His breathing was very shallow, but he began to lift his hands and move them. He appeared to be directing a choir, and then his hands just went limp onto his chest and he didn't move anymore."

Then I shared with her the conversation I'd had with him the previous afternoon and asked her permission to use his testimony at his funeral. Brother Baucom had gotten caught up in the Angelic Choir, and his family had received a glimpse of the joy that he's now enjoying forever.

So we decided we'd go into bond financing, and we had a bond program and issue. The bonds sold unbelievably fast, and soon we had a contract for the construction of a two thousand seat auditorium for Jackson Way Church.

In 1967 we moved out of the YMCA and into our new auditorium. We all agreed that we would remain a happy fellowship church, and we moved in with that attitude.

I worked out the format for a Sunday evening reflections television show which would feature different pastors from different denominations each Sunday night. When I met with Mr. Smith, the owner of the television station in Huntsville, he asked me if we'd ever considered doing a Sunday morning service.

"Sure, we have. We'd love to. Do you have a remote facility to handle that?"

"No," he answered, "but let me tell you what we've done. We've propositioned the First Baptist Church that if they would buy the remote equipment, and install it and give us the opportunity to use the equipment for unusual outstanding events in the community (maybe four or five times per year), we would give them the one hour to broadcast their Sunday Morning Service for free."

"You mean, they didn't take you up on that?" I couldn't believe it.

"No, it's been over six months since we proposed it to them, and we haven't heard a word."

"Would you give us that opportunity?" I was getting excited. "If you'll give us a thirty day irrevocable commitment, I'll have an answer for you in thirty days – yes or no."

"Fine. I'll send you a letter of confirmation as soon as I check with First Baptist Church about their intentions."

Late that afternoon, the letter of confirmation came by courier. So we began to plan for our television ministry.

On Sunday morning I asked all the electrical engineers in the congregation to meet that afternoon, and I wasn't surprised, this being Huntsville, Alabama, that twenty-eight engineers showed up for the meeting. They divided into several committees: the equipment, the lighting, the audio and others, with each research-ing what was required. The equipment committee decided to buy the components and put the package together themselves. The body of the church gave the committee the authorization to purchase the compo-nents and put together a microwave television system within the church.

JACKSON WAY BAPTIST CHURCH SIGNS TV CONTRACT WITH CHANNEL 31 read the <u>Huntsville Times</u> headline with a picture of Mr. Smith, the station owner, and me signing the contract, witnessed by the station manager and the chairman of the deacons.[10]

We were on the air when I broke my toe. I was preaching a stewardship sermon entitled "FLINT-STONE, SPONGE AND HONEYCOMB."

Moses, speaking to the children of Israel, talks about flint, one of the hardest stones men-tioned in the Bible, Deuteronomy 8:15 "Who led thee through that great and terrible wilderness, wherein were fiery serpents, and scorpions, and drought, where there was no water; who brought thee forth water out of the rock of flint." There are some Christians who have the personality of flint. They won't give anything unless someone strikes them. There are many Christians who are very much like sponge, a porous substance which has a marvelous ability to absorb, but will not give anything unless squeezed. Isaiah 43:24, "Thou hast bought me no sweet cane with money, neither hast thou filled me with the fat of thy sacrifices: but thou hast made me to serve

---

[13]From that date until present 1994, Jackson Way Baptist Church has never missed broadcasting its Sunday service. It has developed its studios into state-of-the-art with three crews. The crews formed a special Sunday School class which meets at 8:00a.m. Sunday morning to allow plenty of time for the men and women involved, cameramen, producers, directors, audio, and lighting people to prepare the equipment, yet still study together.

with thy sins, thou hast wearied me with thine iniquities." And there are many Christians who have the ability to give, and will if you squeeze them enough. But if you quit squeezing, they quit giving. And then the third type of Christian is like the honeycomb, Psalm 19:7, "The law of the Lord is perfect, converting the soul: the testimony of the Lord is sure, making wise the simple" (Psalm 19:10) "More to be desired are they than gold, yea, than much fine gold; sweeter also than honey and the honeycomb." Hearts are like that of a honeycomb. Picture that with its many different sections, all containing something sweet, pure and magnificent. You can touch a honeycomb anywhere, and sweetness will flow from that section. Some Christians are like that. Anytime there's a need, they are willing to give a part of themselves.

As I was preaching, I noticed a young couple whom I knew. The wife was a Christian, but her husband was not. As I developed the point of the flint, he became angry and began to mumble to his wife about leaving. When I got to the sponge part of the sermon, he really got angry and remarked loudly that he would never hear me preach again. His wife, very embarrassed, was trying to calm him. When I got to the development of the honeycomb, the Holy Spirit began to work with him. A deacon and his wife, sitting behind this couple, realized that something unusual was happening to this young man. As the invitation was given, the young man jumped up and left the pew. As he entered the aisle, he turned towards where I was standing. The deacon became alarmed, fearing for my safety, and left his seat to follow the man down the aisle, just in case I needed his help.

As the man got closer, he started to run, and just

before he reached me, he fell on his knees with his hands lifted in the air and yelled, "Preacher, help me!" I began talking to him, and he accepted the Lord as his Saviour.

No one seemed to notice that my smile was more grimace than grin. When everyone had left the auditorium after the service, Vonzeal said, "Jim, let's go. What are you waiting for?"

"I can't move my foot!" I couldn't walk and had to hop to the car. She drove me immediately to the emergency room, and the doctor found I had a broken bone in the top of my foot. When the young man, Phillip, fell on his knees at my feet, he fell with one of his knees on the top of my foot. Oh, pain!

Phillip's heart was healed, and he became an outstanding Christian and my toe eventually healed, too.

Jerry started asking me, "Dad, when are you going to let me preach?" Finally, I found just the right opportunity to allow Jerry his first opportunity to preach. He was twelve years old.

Youth week was approaching so the church decided to let them serve in different roles. For instance, we selected a youth to teach in many of the Sunday School classes. We used the youth for ushers, for leading the music and, of course, Jerry as the pastor. He preached his very first sermon.

Vonzeal sewed him a new blazer to wear for that day. I, of course, tried to help him prepare spiritually. But he wouldn't let me help him. "Jerry," I asked, "are you sure you're going to be able to do this?'

"Yes, sir, Dad."

"Well, what scripture are you going to use?"

"Just be there. You'll find out."

I pleaded with him. "Jerry, what is your subject?"

"Just be there." He never would tell me anything

about his preparation. So I simply had to trust him. I prayed an awful lot, knowing it could be a terribly embarrassing moment if he got up and had nothing to say.

The day came for Jerry to preach his first sermon. Without his knowledge, we set up a tape recorder so every word could be recorded. This, of course, was the first time for me to introduce my young son as Youth Pastor of the Day.

"Prior to the birth of each of our sons, my wife and I prayed together earnestly, first that they would be healthy and normal and that God would use them for His glory. This we prayed constantly, right up until the hour of their arrivals. Second we prayed to give them to the Lord after they came to be with us. I was thrilled in a Florida revival to have Jimmy lead the singing, his first official week-long service with me. And then this morning I have another high honor and glorious privilege of introducing our younger son, Jerry. Jerry is known by practically everyone in the church. If they look at him twice, he is their friend. And I trust that you will hear him prayerfully, as a twelve year old boy comes to bring what God has placed on his heart. And trust that God will use it for the advancement of His kingdom. God bless you, Jerry!"

When he stood he said, "I've looked forward to this for some time, but my father's been asking me to wait awhile. And now it's finally come, and so I'm going to make the best of it." He proceeded to preach the following wonderful little sermon, beautifully outlined:

JERRY'S FIRST SERMON

"I've chosen as my subject tonight – questions on witnessing. If you would, I'd like you to follow as I read Matthew 12:30-37. "He that is not with me is against me and he that gathereth not with me scattereth abroad. Wherefore I say unto you, All manner of sin and blasphemy shall be forgiven unto men: but the blasphemy against the Holy Ghost shall not be forgiven unto men. And whosoever speaketh a word against the Son of man, it shall be forgiven him: but whosoever speaketh against the Holy Ghost, it shall not be forgiven him, neither in this world, neither in the world to come. Either make the tree good, and his fruit good; or else make the tree corrupt, and his fruit corrupt: for the tree is known by his fruit. O generation of vipers, how can ye, being evil, speak good things: and an evil man out of the evil treasure bringeth forth evil things. But I say unto you, That every idle word that men shall speak, they shall give account thereof in the day of judgment. For by thy words thou shalt be justified, and by thy words thou shalt be condemned."

I took my text from verse 30. He that is not with me is against me; and he that gathereth not with me scattereth abroad.

Either you are against God or you are for God. You are either for God or the devil. One way or the other. There is no in between.

The first question I want to ask is "Where are we witnessing?" God said for us to witness everywhere as is said in Matthew 28:19-20 "Go ye therefore, and teach all nations, baptizing them in the name of the Father, and of the Son, and of the Holy Ghost: Teaching them to observe all things whatsoever I have commanded you: and, lo, I am with you alway, even unto the end of the world."

You should go forth in your community and enter everywhere you can go and preach and set a good example.

And the next question is "How do we witness?" We witness by doing what God commanded as he said in the two verses I just read, "Go forth and teach all nations and study and set an example in our community. You can go forth and witness on the playground, school, your office . . . just about anywhere . . . even in your church. But you have many opportunities.

The next question is "When do we witness?" We are witnesses twenty-four hours a day. We are witnessing now. Someone is watching you, every one of us, every minute of the time.

The next question is "Why do we witness?" We witness because God commanded us to witness. As is said in Acts 1:8 "But ye shall receive power, after that the Holy Ghost is come upon you: and ye shall be witnesses unto me both in Jerusalem, and in all Judea, and in Samaria, and unto the uttermost part of the earth."

So we see in this verse that God made us witnesses and told us to go forth and witness.

The next question and probably the most important one is "Who are witnesses?" Everyone is a witness one way or another. In Isaiah 43:10 "Ye are my witnesses, saith the Lord, and my servant whom I have chosen: that ye may know and believe me, and understand that I am He: before Me there was no God formed, neither shall there be after Me."

So you see we are witnesses as stated plainly in the Bible.

Now I want to ask you four questions. Where have you witnessed? Have you ever counseled personally to a person? It's a real joy and there are numerous opportunities. I've been asked questions about the Bible on the way home from school. And, of course, that opens the door to go in and witness.

How have you witnessed? Have you set a good example for that son or daughter of yours, or that friend that looks at you and sees you? When have you witnessed? You should be a living witness twenty-four hours a day. Are you a living witness? Why do you witness? Do you witness for the glory of God or do you witness for the glory of man?

Are you answering these questions correctly? You know if you have. God knows whether you have. It will be on your heart whether you have or haven't.

Now that I've mentioned the where, how, when, who or why of witnessing, I've mentioned the need of witnesses. In the nineteenth century, over one hundred years ago, the statistics were four Christians to every one person won to the Lord that year. In our time these statistics are one hundred Christians for every one person won to the Lord. These statistics for our church alone last year only were seventeen Christians for every person won. We are way above average. There were eight last year, the number of people who were baptised in our church. Other churches don't have this good record.

Are you one of these witnesses? Will you choose to become one tonight? You may not have another chance as was brought out in this poem:

> *The clock of life is wound but once*
> *And no man has the power*
> *To tell just where the hands will stop*
> *At late or early hour.*
> *To lose one's wealth is sad indeed*
> *To lose one's health is more*
> *To lose one's soul is such a loss*
> *And no man can err restore.*
> *The present only is our own*
> *Live, love and do God's will*
> *Personal faith in tomorrow*
> *And the clock will then be still.*

Daddy, I'd like you to come and give a short invitation to those who might like to make a decision tonight."

At the end of his sermon, we had three teenagers come forward to be saved. The service was an exciting time. The interesting thing about Jerry's sermon was how closely it paralleled my own first sermon.

We took the tape home and listened to it with Jerry. Several months later I listened to it again and found that Jerry had added some comments at the end of the tape. He had critiqued his own sermon. For instance, I heard his little voice say, "Well, this has been the first sermon that I've ever preached. I believe I was a little scared when I did it. And I read my scripture too fast and mispronounced too many words. I believe I did not have it planned well enough. I will try to correct these defects in my next sermon which I hope will not be too long."

Just so you'll know, I've preached a few bad sermons. Some I heard about after the fact; some I realized at the time it was happening.

One memorable bad sermon took place on New Year's Eve Watch Night Service. In the previous week, I had found what I thought was a wonderful manuscript about new beginnings so I decided that rather than prepare a sermon that evening, I would just get up in the pulpit and read this piece from front to back to the congregation. I was convinced they would enjoy it as much as I.

"We're going to do something different tonight. I've never done this before, but I would like to share this with you as a beginning for the new year." And I began to read. And read. And read. When I had read it at home, it hadn't seemed so very long; now it continued to stretch out almost indefinitely. I had read for about thirty minutes when I noticed I was losing my audience. One by one their faces had become glazed over with that "when will the school bell ring" look. At this point, I decided to just continue and bully through the rest of the manuscript and hope for the best.

About forty-five minutes into the piece, I heard a loud plop and glanced up. A little elderly lady, who was sitting center front, had fallen asleep, and her head had dropped back onto the pew. And her wig fell off behind the pew. Startled, she woke, dived beneath the pew, retrieved her wig and plopped it back onto her head. Morosely, she slumped down into the seat.

That didn't bother me. What bothered me was that everyone was so far gone nobody noticed. No one except sixth grader Jerry and Mildred and Richard Pinion who were sitting together on the side and had had an unobstructed view of the whole event.

They were rocking with silent laughter.

I decided to end the sermon right then, and never read someone else's material when I was in the pulpit.

One day after a Sunday morning service, I was greeting the congregation as they were leaving and a friend of Vonzeal's named Connie shook my hand. She smelled so good; I loved her fragrance. That afternoon I said to Vonzeal, "Honey, ask Connie what that perfume is she wears."

"Why don't you ask her yourself?" she countered, surprised.

"Oh, no. I can't do that. She might think I'm being fresh or out of line. You know Dr. A. C. Baker always warned me about being careful in those matters."

"Oh, no, Jim, it would be a compliment to her. Feel free to ask her yourself." Vonzeal always said she never minded when I hugged the ladies because I was just a comfortable old man.

So I asked Connie, and she told me the perfume was Opium. I immediately went to buy Vonzeal some but found it was eighty dollars for just a tiny amount. But from that moment until the rest of her life, I kept my sweetheart in plenty of Opium.

When we were out with couples, we men would retrieve our ladies' coats from the closets, and I would always put Vonzeal's coat to my face and breath in her sweet fragrance. The buddies would ask, "Is that the way you find Vonzeal's coat?"

"I have been enjoying her fragrance through all these years. Yes, I can find her and her coat through her fragrance."

Chapter 14

1974-1978

———⊱•⊰———

With all the building at Jackson Way completed and all the financing in place, debt retirement was being met; Vonzeal and I decided it was time to move on. Both sons were adults, Jerry completing college, Jim already married and gone from home. We decided to get out of the way and let someone else come lead at Jackson Way. After building four churches, Vonzeal and I were ready to build a home where we could put down roots and live after we retired.

I had a friend, Scott Hudgens, who was building the new city of Shenandoah, and he asked me what I would recommend if I had an opportunity to give directions to the religious environment of a city. What would I recommend? He continued over several months to pose the same question every chance he had. Finally I sat down with my tape recorder and dictated the things I would recommend for a new city being built from the ground up. Mrs. Bentley took all my cassette tapes and transcribed them into a manuscript. After she and I had edited it to our satisfaction, I submitted it to Mr.

Hudgens. Little did I know that he was going to incorporate my religious environmental study with all of his other environmental studies in his application to HUDD for the fifty million dollars to build the new city of Shenandoah. He had already invested seven million dollars in the property and studies for preparation.

Then he offered me a job as Chaplain to the building of the new city of Shenandoah. Because I didn't want to get outside of the denomination, I agreed to take the position only if the Home Mission Board would appoint me as an Industrial Chaplain . The Board agreed, and I accepted Mr. Hudgens offer and served in that capacity for almost two years.

Personal Testimony of
Scott Hudgens

Some months ago, I came to a very drastic point in my life. There seemed to be only a complete darkness and I had gone down a long road in the wrong direction. This had been going on for several years. The right kind of life seemed like the eye of a needle and the needle's eye seemed to get smaller and smaller; in fact, it seemed to become impossible. I thought I had to bear all my problems and the problems of others alone. I always believed that God was up there but now He seemed to be completely blotted out because of the dark cloud. My life became so confused that on a certain Saturday morning in September, 1972, there seemed to be no way out. The apex of this confusion, however, corresponded with a planned annual dove shoot to be held at my home. A dear preacher friend of mine, Jim Dorriety, was in the habit of attending and had planned to attend this one. Since he arrived before the others, we had a chance to share together and in the process we both got down on our knees and I cried out to the Lord for forgiveness. Because of God's love, as expressed through His Son, Jesus, I was forgiven of my sins and I placed the entire burdens of my life on His shoulders. This I can only describe as God's miracle of forgiveness. Because of this I was able to see the clouds of life begin to lift and daylight began to show again in my life. John 3:16, which says, "For God loved the world so much that He gave His only Son so that anyone who believes in Him shall not perish but have eternal life.", became a reality in my life. I no longer feel that the eye of the needle is small and even though the devil often beats on me I am able to call on God for help and through the presence of the Holy Spirit who lives in me he is soon driven out.

Jeanne Bentley accepted a position as Minister of Education with Highland Baptist Church in Huntsville after our move back to Georgia. Our families had enjoyed one another's fellowship since 1953, and we missed them. Charles, Jeanne's husband, was a quiet, unique individual. Although he never tried to be popular or extremely out-going, he was always there for anyone who needed him or wanted to be his friend. He never became overly involved with church work but always permitted Jeanne unlimited time for her church activities and took pride in her work.

In 1974 Charles Bentley was diagnosed with terminal cancer, and the prognosis was for a very brief time – only weeks. We were heart-sick as we rallied around Charles and Jeanne during this period of their trauma. But Charles accepted the news with resolve and determination, neither spending time weeping nor in remorse. As friends and relations came by the Bentley's home to visit, he anticipated their feelings of sadness and insecurity and spoke openly and calmly about the pain and suffering from which he would soon be free. He anticipated and seemingly welcomed his home going and made others feel comfortable with the news.

Vonzeal and I drove to Huntsville to see him during this period. As we visited with him and Jeanne, he said, "Vonzeal, I have something very special I want to give you as a memento of our years of friendship."

"Oh, Charles, I'd be delighted!" she answered. "What is it?"

He held out a closed fist and asked her to open her palm, and when she did he placed a small three-inch pocket knife inscribed Case on the plate.

He said, "I remember you talking about the Case knife your Mama kept in her kitchen."

"Oh, yes, Mama would ask for the Case knife, and

we'd hand her the sharpest one we had." Vonzeal stated.

"This Case knife came from my personal knife collection," he informed her. "Case is a name-brand and the Case Company makes outstanding knives. I just wanted you to have it as a memento."

She received it with grace and thanksgiving and lovingly placed it inside the change purse in her pocketbook. There it remained for almost twenty years as a reminder of a dear friend, now gone. She took great pride in owning it and the little item became quite a conversation piece. When she and I dined out with our preacher friends and wives, sometimes I would lean over to her and say, "Honey, may I borrow your knife?"

She, dressed to perfection in her formal clothes, would open her purse and, without saying a word, hand me that beautiful little knife. All around the table our friends would stare in disbelief that this petite immaculate lady would carry such an item in her purse. It became the source of many moments of laughter and many moments of reflection as she took each opportunity to share the story of the gift from Charles Bentley.

During that two year period, I began to do more and more revival meetings, and in the process I realized that I was beginning the transition into evangelism. In 1974, Vonzeal and I found and bought some two and one-half acres of land in LaGrange, Georgia, in the woods, overlooking Yellow Jacket Creek. A dam was being built to form a new lake, and the corps of engineers had the contour lines where the water would come.

We began to make plans to build our home. We got the architect who had helped us in Headland Heights to draw up a design for our house. After we got the plans like we wanted, we contacted our old friends Charlie Cornelison, and engineer Ed Keye, and another friend, an earth-mover, Bill Tinsley. I called these men to tell them I was ready to begin building my house, and all three of these men said, "When do you want me to come?"

Bill put the D9 Caterpillar on the lowboy and the backhoe on the trailer behind the dump truck. I drove the dump truck, and Bill drove the lowboy and we went out to the land and cleared it. Within a week's time, we had the total land cleared, the road cut and we were ready for the foundation. Then Bill refused to take payment for his work. He wouldn't even let me pay for the diesel fuel.

Another friend , the superintendent for Scott Hudgens Company, wanted to help. So he came down with his transit, took the plans and laid out all the house, put up all the battle boards and got everything ready to start digging the footings for the foundation.

Bill Tinsley was still there with his backhoe, and we dug the footings, got the leveling stakes in and were ready to call for the concrete. We paid three men twelve dollars each for a couple of hours work to help in pouring the concrete.

Up to this point we had thirty-six dollars invested in our house.

And we built our home there in LaGrange. Our plumber and electrical friends in Huntsville came and helped, and we were able to move into our home three months after clearing the land. So many friends made such wonderful contributions of their time towards building our home. Vonzeal and I were so blessed.

By now we were in full-time evangelism, conducting thirty-five to forty revivals per year in churches, traveling in our motor home. I always liked to say jokingly, "I was in thirty-five to forty odd churches a year and some of them were pretty odd." And we continued in full-time evangelism for six years.

In the meantime, Mrs. Bentley accepted an appointment by the Home Mission Board as a missionary to the Sellars Home in New Orleans, a home for unwed mothers. She served as Religious Educational Program Director and Residence Manager.

Vonzeal developed a nerve injury in her hip and could no longer travel with me.

In Alaska at King Salmon Air Base there were only about fifteen hundred personnel with half of those being civilians. As I preached that week during the religious emphasis week, I began to think. "This can't be the Lord's will. This is the seventh week I've been away in revival meetings, and Vonzeal is there on the lake alone." So, in the process of that revival meeting, I made the decision that after I returned home, if it was the Lord's will, I wanted to return to a pastorate. I couldn't tolerate being away from her, my helpmate.

Chapter 15

1979-1990

———◦———

Vonzeal never opposed anything I suggested, but this time she seemed to be extremely happy about my decision. We were sitting on our front porch swing; it was a frosty early December day, and the reflection off the lake seemed silver. The leaves were off the trees and the view to the lake was unobstructed. I sipped on my steaming cup of coffee, rocking the swing gently, "I'm not the most polished and sophisticated pastor, but I would love to have another pastorate."

"You're right, Jim, you aren't. But what you lack in spit and polish you make up for in conviction and dedication. You're still the best preacher I've ever heard, and I've heard a lot over the years."

"I consider it a failure that I never went to seminary," I confessed.

"Yet all but two of the twenty-two young men you brought to the ministry attended seminary. Is that a failure?"

I looked at her. She always had a way of making me feel so good about myself.

My daughter-in-law found the following speech inside Vonzeal's Bible. It was the words to the only address she ever gave, and she presented it to a meeting of young pastors' wives. Her words express better than mine, the unique ability she had to bolster my depressed feelings and remind us both that God was in charge.

"I count it a great privilege today to be able to share with you the joys that have been mine while being a preacher's wife. For thirty years I was a very happy wife of a busy Pastor. For the last five years I have served as the wife of a full-time Evangelist. The two are very different.

A friend of mine just recently asked me the question, "Vonzeal, if you were the one to make the decision which would you choose to be – Pastor's wife or Evangelist's wife?" I thought a moment and realized the greatest fact about that was, that it wasn't I who had to make the decision. For a number of reasons it has been very good that it wasn't I who had to make these decisions. About thirty-five years ago, God spoke very clearly to Jim, when calling him into the preaching ministry. Jim labored with the call for a while because there were many obstacles to be overcome before he could be used effectively by God. It was in the middle of the night when we both finally surrendered our lives together, for God to use as He saw fit. Jim's was a full surrender to preach the gospel and mine, a full surrender to uphold and follow my husband wherever God led him. It hasn't all been easy. You see, to begin with, we packed four years of college into seven years. Not easy, but, as I look back, it's most rewarding, because – you see – we had made the promise to follow and God was doing the making. God didn't promise a smooth sailing, but He did promise a safe landing if we followed Him.

The first reason it is very good that I haven't been the one to make the decisions about when and where we would go, is, because we would probably be in the first church Jim was ever called to, if I had been the one to say. You see, I am a person who could very easily settle down and live "happily ever after." I have been guilty of putting down deep roots wherever we have lived. We would have missed many opportunities had we not moved on when God led from one place to another. Jim always warned me, when we went to a new church, that we were there for a period of time, to do what God had for us to do at that time and place and never to think of it as a permanent move. However, since I'm me and made the way I am, I could very easily have settled myself down and stayed the rest of my life at any of the churches.

We were very fortunate in having great people to work with throughout Jim's ministry. All the places still seem much like home to me. I even went so far as to tell the Lord that we were homestead in Huntsville, Alabama and, please not to bother to move us again. About the time I was feeling so smug about the situation God began to speak again. This time in a different way. When Jim first mentioned it to me, I said, "OK" for I really didn't think it could come to pass. Again, I didn't want to face change. I didn't want to leave my friends and on and on, I could go. But God did speak, Jim did answer and I did follow. We left and entered into what we call Act Two of our lives. If I told you we had entered a perfect situation, I would be telling an untruth. You see, we are still working with people, but without our own people. This we miss most of all. After being queen of the pastorium for thirty years, and enjoying every bit of it, I don't even get to stay in my own home many weeks out of the year, much less be the queen. It's pack and go and come home for a short while and pack and go again. I truly miss my home in LaGrange. The desire is still in me to settle down, and send my roots very deep. But, when I think of all we would have missed had we not moved on when God called, I'm most grateful that it was my husband who had to make the ultimate decisions. The Lord has been good to us. As I said in the beginning, it hasn't all been easy but, most rewarding. I thank the Lord daily for the life I have had. If I had the opportunity to relive my life, I don't really know of anything I would change. To know that you are in the center of God's direct will for your life, is worth all the sacrifices that are necessary to be made in this life.

Hebrews 13:5-6 "Let your conversation be without covetousness; and be content with such things as ye have: for he hath said, I will never leave thee, nor forsake thee. So that we may boldly say, The Lord is my helper, and I will not fear what man shall do unto me."

Almost immediately I received a call from Glen Shepherd at First Baptist Church, Blakely, Georgia. He was resigning to go to Central Baptist Church in Lawrenceville, Georgia, and some of the membership wanted him to see if I could serve as interim pastor beginning October 1979 through January 1980, with the express condition that I would not seek a full pastorate from them.

I agreed and after several weeks two churches in Montgomery each sent a pulpit committee on the same Sunday. That evening the chairman of the deacons asked me, "Was that a pulpit committee I saw here today?"

"No sir, that was two pulpit committees, all from the same city."

"Are you considering going back to a full-time

pastorate?"

"Well, yes, I guess so."

"Then will you meet with us tomorrow night?"

"You know we agreed that while serving as interim, I would not be available to be your pastor. You wanted an interim who was not interested in being your pastor."

"Let me take care of that," he insisted, "would you meet with us tomorrow night?"

"Yes, but I want you to understand, I'm not trying to get this church to make a commitment to me."

"I do understand. But if you're going back to a pastorate, we want to have the opportunity to chat with you first."

So I met with the committee Monday night. Now there were three pulpit committees interested in us.

I left the next week to preach a revival in Indiana and, to my surprise, sitting in the congregation was the pulpit committee from one of the Montgomery churches. I felt very strongly about this particular church and was very interested in accepting their offer.

In the conference I attended just following the Indiana revival, I brought together my preacher friends Hugh Chambliss, Charles T. Carter, Hudson Baggett and Jerry Gunnells to ask them to pray with me and help me make a decision. These brethren listened to my dilemma and one of them, Jerry Gunnells, said to me, "Jim, when I get to the age and status that you are now, I hope that I can go to a church very similar in type and size church to Blakely First Baptist. That's the most beautiful forum for preaching; with all of their stained glass windows and highly educated congregation, it must be one of the happiest situations that any pastor could ever be in. It's the ideal church for you at this stage of your ministry. That's what I hope and pray will happen to me when I approach my retirement."

I brought this thought home to Vonzeal and she said, "Jim, you believe you can go to Montgomery and lead the state in baptisms?"

"Right!" I was ready to set Montgomery on fire for the Lord.

"Jim, how many heart attacks do you think you'd have accomplishing that?" Almost instantaneously my desire to go to Montgomery left me. And my heart was drawn to become the full-time minister of the First Baptist Church of Blakely, Georgia.

I called Mrs. Bentley in New Orleans and invited her to come as Minister of Education. Since 1953 she had been been with us through those years and Vonzeal and I called and invited her to make one more move to Blakely. Her answer was that she needed to pray about it.

She called back and said, "Preacher," she always called me Preacher, "I'm going to retire when I turn sixty-five."

"I'll be at Blakely that long, and that's just about the time I plan to retire, too." So she resigned as missionary of the Home Mission Board and was called as the Minister of Education of First Baptist Church Blakely. She stayed with us until we had her retirement dinner in 1982.

During our ministry at Blakely, we developed many lifelong friends, as we have at every church we ever served. Vonzeal was especially blessed in that four ladies from that church became special friends of hers. Ann Alexander, Alicia Collier, Delma Houston and Carolyn Fuller were very close friends and continued to enjoy a close camaraderie even after we left Blakely in December of 1985.

In January of 1986 I went to the Georgia Baptist Convention in the Stewardship and Annuity Department to help design a special program on

Cooperative Program Endowment. The only requirement to membership in the Southern Baptist Convention is to give to the Cooperative Program. When a church contributions to the Cooperative Program, those monies are divided. After the state mission budget is met, the funds are divided, with a portion going to foreign missions and a portion designated for home missions. At this time, Georgia Baptist Convention still gives a higher percent than all the other thirty-eight state conventions.

When I attended Mercer University, I received ministerial aid from this Cooperative Program as a ministerial student.

I asked them, "If I accept this aid, when do I have to pay it back?"

"You never have to pay it back," I was told.

"Well, where do I sign because if I don't have to pay it back, I'll take it." I accepted the aid without really being concerned where that money came from. Later in my ministry when I learned more about the Georgia Baptist Convention and programs it supports. When I examined the Cooperative Program Endowment's budget, I saw a little sliver of funds that went to ministerial students.

The Georgia Baptist Convention decided to authorize an endowment fund which could represent additional contributions. I was given the opportunity to write and present this program to the GBC.

I met with Dr. Jim Griffith in Atlanta. "This program looks very exciting, and I'm interested but I don't believe Vonzeal and I want to live in Atlanta."

"You don't have to live in Atlanta. Live wherever you like," he answered.

"You know, I have my retirement home on the West Point Lake in LaGrange."

"That sounds like a great place to live . . . it's the

middle of the state, close to a major interstate. Of course, you'd have to commute two or three days a week to Atlanta, but you're going to be driving anywhere you live."

So I agreed to come on board as the Associate Director of Stewardship, with the assigned task of writing and presenting to Georgia Baptist Convention the Cooperative Program Endowment. During the time of writing this program, I was able to get many people to make a contribution to that fund. I told them, "If you gave anything to your church between the years 1945 and 1952, then you helped pay for my education at Mercer University without even knowing it. Now you have a chance to pay for someone else's education by leaving something to the Cooperative Program Endowment."

Many people have been very generous to the Cooperative Program Endowment.

The most viable group I spoke to were senior adults, and many of them did not have wills. We provided, free of service, attorneys to help prepare their wills for a small gift to the endowment program. Many felt that this was a great way to witness until Jesus came again. When you're gone, the money you leave keeps on witnessing, allowing your funds to be involved in everything the Georgia Baptist Convention is doing.

These senior adults were also the ones in their churches looking for an entertainment program. I began offering my services to their program if they would let me tell them about the Cooperative Program Endowment. I began visiting the churches speaking and generally just telling my corny stories, making people laugh. I stayed with this program until I retired in 1989.

Thus my ministry of humor was begun. I began "entertaining." Almost simultaneously, Bowden Baptist

Church called me as interim pastor.

One of the great things about being a senior adult, I'd tell them, is "we've been everywhere, we've seen everything, we've done everything, we've forgotten it all and we can start all over again."

Then I'd tell them about the old couple sitting on the front porch. She said to him, "I wish I had some vanilla ice cream with some chocolate syrup on top." He said, "I'll be glad to go get you some." She said, "John, write it down." Indignantly he said, "I can remember vanilla ice cream with chocolate on it," and he went to get it. Twenty minutes later he returned with two scrambled eggs. She said, "I told you to write it down. I knew you'd forget the bacon!"

The very reason the Lord won't let senior adults have babies is because we'd put them down and forget where we put them.

In fact, I'm so forgetful I have trouble keeping up with my portable telephone. One day I was working in the yard, and I lost the phone. My neighbor was out in his back yard, and I yelled to him over the fence, "Would you call me on the telephone?"

"For what? Just tell me now and I won't have to call you!"

"No, I don't want to talk to you."

He said, "What do you mean?" I had him so confused, but I couldn't understand why he was confused. I just wanted him to call me for the phone to ring so I could find it.

A young fellow about eighty-four years of age had recently lost his wife, and he was so lonely he decided he'd go over to the senior adult meeting at church. He saw a lady there whom he'd never met before, and she kept smiling at him. Every time he'd look her way, she'd be smiling at him. Finally he went over and introduced himself. She said, "You know, you look just like my third husband!"

Shocked, he asked, "My word, lady, how many times have you been married?"

"Twice," she smiled.

My son, Jimmy, who lived in Kansas City, called one day and asked, "Dad, what do you do when you entertain?"

"Oh," I answered embarrassed, "a lot of corny jokes sort of like Jerry Clower, but with religious overtones. In fact, I'm entertaining a group at Toccoa Assembly at a meeting for senior adults. From there I'm going to Florida where I'm entertaining another group at a stewardship banquet."

He piped right up, "I've got some time off. Why don't I fly in and go with you."

Again I was embarrassed. I didn't know whether I wanted him to hear what I did or not.

He said, "I'll bring my golf clubs, and I'll chauffeur you. I'd love to hear you entertain."

"Okay. Come on. Great!"

So he came and heard me, and we had a magnificent response at Toccoa Assembly, then left for Palatka, Florida. On the way down we played golf and caught up on our gossip. Returning from Florida, Jim told me he was convinced that I should go into speaking full time. "How much do you charge?" He asked.

"Charge? Why nothing. We preachers just go and hope for the most."

"Well, in industry they charge."

"Yeah, but I'm not in industry."

"You ought to be. I've heard motivational speakers not half as good as you are. And they cost a lot of money."

"Yes, but I haven't broken into that yet. You're just prejudiced because I'm your dad."

"No, you're really funny and you need an agent!"

That's when we got started. We printed a brochure and made our promo tape with an introduction by Dr. Griffith of the Georgia Baptist Convention.

As far as entertaining goes, I feel I've been tested many many times in all kinds of groups, all sizes from several thousand to a very small number, from older groups to young groups. One of the greatest tests I ever had took place at Smoke Rise Baptist Church, a large church in Atlanta. They were having a day long senior adult conference and didn't anticipate how many would attend. Lo and behold they had over one thousand to show up that day for the conference. They realized that the dining room could only seat five hundred, so the problem was how they would take care of feeding five hundred while the other five hundred waited to eat. D. F. Norman, Director of Pastoral/Ministry Department of the GBC, which includes the Senior Adult Mission, decided that the best thing to do would be to let me entertain five hundred while the other half ate. And then when the other half were through eating, we'd swap and I'd entertain the five hundred that had just eaten.

"You guys are giving me an acid test," I protested. "You're going to make five hundred people mad because they've got to wait to eat – and you want me to entertain them for an hour. And then when this mad group gets through being entertained for an hour- you're going to bring in this other five hundred who's full and sleepy and have me entertain them for an hour."

And if that's not an acid test, I don't know what is.

After my retirement from the Georgia Baptist Convention in 1989, Vonzeal and I were privileged to serve eight churches as interim pastor: Center Point Baptist Church in East Point, Georgia; Second Baptist

Church of LaGrange; First Baptist Church of Bremen; Bowden Baptist Church of Bowden; Britt David Baptist Church in Columbus; Eastwood Baptist Church in Columbus; First Baptist Church of Tallapoosa; and finally, First Baptist Church of Villa Rica.

During Christmas 1991 we announced to the family that even though our 50th wedding anniversary was coming up in 1992, we did not want a party; instead we felt we would like to go back to Hawaii again. Our oldest son, Jim, insisted on donating his accumulated mileage on his airline frequent flyers program to get the airline tickets and hotel rooms.

Our younger son Jerry, minister of music in the Methodist church, looked at us and said, "That's great, and I'll pray for you."

We had one son to pay for us and one to pray for us. What more could we want?

We got our tickets from Jim in January and confirmation of our hotel on Waikiki Beach in February and planned our trip for September. A limo met us in Honolulu and carried us to our hotel. A beautiful arrangement of flowers waited in our room. The front desk called the next morning to tell us our rental car was waiting for us downstairs. Our sons had taken care of everything. I'm proud of our boys. We've got one son who pays for us, and one son who prays for us. Who could ask for more?

As soon as we returned from Hawaii, Vonzeal insisted I rush to get the pictures developed, and she made the most beautiful fiftieth wedding anniversary album. "Now," she said, "you'll have this when I'm gone."

"Honey, you're not going anywhere. Men die first."

Then she looked at me and said, "Jim, you know I'm sick."

"I know you've not been well."

"It's not going to be long, Jim."

Vonzeal and I have had so much laughter and fun in our marriage over our fifty years together. The most fun we had was when we were alone – laughing and working together in mutual harmony.

The first tape I recorded in my fun ministry was "Laugh With Me," the second one was "Laugh With Me Again."

Now I want to invite you to Weep With Me.

In fact, I don't weep, I squall and I can shake down a good size bed squalling.

Psalms 30:5, "Weeping may endure for a night, but joy cometh in the morning." What a magnificent passage that is.

I've always enjoyed preaching on Heaven. I remember many years ago I came out of the pulpit, and we traveled home in silence. Finally I broke the silence, "I don't think I'll ever try to preach on Heaven again."

"Why?" Vonzeal asked.

"I cannot find words to express what I know the Bible says; I just can't find the words to communicate what I know the Bible tells us about our eternal home. I feel it, I anticipate it, but I have difficulty expressing it even to my own satisfaction, let alone to the satisfaction of other minds. "

She didn't respond, and we traveled on in silence. When we got home, I removed my suit coat and tie and sat down oppressively in my chair of self-pity in the den, and Vonzeal went back into the bedroom. I was clearly depressed. After a few moments she returned and dropped her Bible in my lap, pointed to a verse of scripture and walked on towards the kitchen.

I looked at that verse, I Corinthians, 2:9 "Eye had not seen, nor ear heard, neither have entered into the heart of man, the things which God hath prepared for them that love Him."

I had never really understood that verse until that moment. Suddenly I realized that no wonder I could not tell, I had not experienced it yet. When you begin to meditate upon that scripture, you will see that we have something great to look forward to, something magnificent to look forward to, and we can begin to anticipate that moment.

I've seen all kinds of death. I've been in the military, and I've seen young men die in battle. I've seen people die along the highway. In my files are copies of several letters to families, telling how I held their loved one in my arms during his last moments.

One example was Roy Hood, a man involved in a fatal accident along a Florida highway just moments before I got there. I held his head up in my arms and told him, "An ambulance has been called. Everything will be all right." I began ministering to his soul and quoted a Bible scripture.

Bleeding, he looked up at me and said, "You must be a preacher."

"I am."

"Thank you for telling me everything is all right. I know it's all right because I've made it right with the Lord." And with that he died in my arms.

I've been with friends in their homes as they passed beyond the veil into the presence of God. There is a difference in the way people die. There is a difference in those who die in the Lord and those who die out of the Lord. Rest assured that there's a difference. Medical doctors have agreed with me, some reluctantly, that there is a difference.

Salvation is the base, beginning with trust in the Lord Jesus Christ, being saved knowing that you are in Him. "Weeping may endure for the night, but joy cometh in the morning."

I like the order in which that scripture is written. Weeping just for a night, a given period of time. Joy comes in the morning, but it doesn't mention an ending. Joy to never end. Eternal joy. Forever, forever and forever.

Weeping is an expression of deep emotion within mankind. All of us have shed tears. Hopefully we all have. I feel sorrow and pity for that one who cannot weep. We should not feel less a man when we weep. Our Saviour wept. In Matthew 23:37, Jesus looked out over Jerusalem and said, "O Jerusalem, Jerusalem . . . how often would I have gathered thy children together as a hen gathereth her chickens under her wings," and he was weeping as he said those words.

Paul tells us He wept for the world. The shortest verse in the Bible that we all know, all the children know. John 11:35 "Jesus wept."

There's nothing wrong with weeping.

Ecclesiastes 3:4 tells us that there is a right time for everything "—a time to weep, and a time to laugh, a time to mourn, and a time to dance—." There's a time for us to express all of the emotions that God has placed within us, and we should never apologize for the tears nor for the laughter.

In March of 1993 I was in Reedsville, Georgia, preparing to preach a revival at Plainview Baptist Church, when I received a phone call from Mrs. Bentley, who was staying with Vonzeal, informing me that she and Joyce Yarborough had rushed Vonzeal to Emory Hospital in Atlanta. I immediately called Dr. Seavey, and he asked where I was and what length of time I would be away. I informed him that I was scheduled to be in Reidsville through Thursday. He told me he thought I should get a replacement to finish the meeting and come home. This was not good news, and I feared for Vonzeal. We were in serious trouble as far as her illness was concerned.

The church was able to get a dear friend of mine, Grady Roan, pastor of First Baptist Church, Vidalia, Georgia to come and cover the revival services for me.

I rushed to my wife's side at the hospital.

Chapter 16

March 1993

⚬

THE CHRISTIAN INDEX

*Vonzeal Dorriety, wife of Jim Dorriety who
is the former associate in the GBC's
Stewardship Department, has pancreatic
cancer. She is staying at Emory Hospital.*

One night I heard her whisper, "Jim, are you asleep?" I was at her bedside at the hospital in a lounge chair the hospital had provided. "Come, get in bed with me. You know Dr. Seavy is going to give us bad news tomorrow morning. He lost his smile over a week ago, and I know what it is. It's pancreatic cancer."

I began to weep as she continued, "Listen, just remember we've been preaching all these years and it's time to put up or shut up. Let's prove how Christians should die."

March 29th, our doctor gave us the news that Vonzeal's death was imminent. She did have pancreatic cancer, already through the liver and lymph nodes. The prognosis was anywhere from six to eight weeks. It actually turned out to be eight weeks and one day.

I was sitting in the lounge chair next to Vonzeal's hospital bed. She was resting, but I wasn't. My mind was having a difficult time grasping the reality that this precious woman would not be with me very much longer. Everything seemed surreal, as if happening in another time and dimension. "Please let this just be a bad dream," I thought. Constantly I found myself shaking my head as if to clear it, hoping things would be back to normal, and we would be cooking dinner on the lake.

The room was very dark and still and silent. I wasn't even aware of the activity in the hallway outside the door. There were moments when I felt so detached from life as if it were all so unreal, ethereal, and then the stark reality of the situation would flood me with pain and heartache. Vonzeal had earlier confessed to some of those same feelings, as if a grand drama was being played out, and she was an audience of one.

A crack of light interrupted my foggy reverie and the door slowly opened. Our five year old granddaughter, Maggie, walked quietly into the room followed by Jerry and Beth. Maggie was clutching something in her hand.

"Vonzeal, look who's here to see you." I whispered, not wanting to wake her if she were asleep. "Miss Maggie's here."

Maggie tiptoed up to the bed, but Vonzeal was already stirring up in bed. She sat up straight and arranged her hair with her fingers. She still had the most beautiful hands and hair I'd ever seen, although now she wore her hair short and through the years the lush browns had been replaced with silvery gray. Yesterday while our older granddaughter, Terri, was visiting, Vonzeal had insisted that Terri give her a manicure, therefore, as usual, her nails were perfect.

"Maggie, we weren't expecting you tonight. It's good to see you," Vonzeal said, holding out her arms.

Maggie leaned onto the bed and threw her little arms around her grandmother, and they embraced. "Grandmother, I brought you something very special. Do you want to see it?"

"Of course I do." Vonzeal smiled, playing along with the game. Maggie always wanted to build up her surprises before she sprung them.

"It's very special and it's just for you." She pulled her arms from around Vonzeal, and in one hand was a small teddy bear. "I brought you this teddy bear, and I've kissed it all over. So now when I'm not here and you get lonely, you can get a kiss from it anytime."

"Thank you so much, Maggie. I'm going to keep him right here on the nightstand." Vonzeal said.

"Do you love him, Grandmother?"

"I love him, but I especially love you for thinking of me."

The following day an old family friend, Gayle Myrick, came by to visit. As she sat next to the bed, she spotted the teddy bear. "Where'd you get the teddy bear?" Vonzeal shared with her the story of Maggie's gift.

The very next day Gayle returned again. "Vonzeal, I've brought you something." In her hands was a bunny rabbit. Vonzeal looked puzzled. Gayle laughed, "This is for you to give back to Maggie with your kisses all over it. Then she can get a kiss from you anytime she needs one." Vonzeal and I were both impressed with Gayle Myrick's clever thoughtfulness. Little did I know at the time that several weeks later that little bunny would cause me the loss of a full night's sleep.

The doctor gave us permission to carry Vonzeal home for her remaining time. Joyce Yarborough, our next door neighbor and a nurse, volunteered to administer Vonzeal's pain medication. Joyce made arrangements to have a hospital bed delivered. My son Jerry and I removed the king-size bed from our bedroom and set the hospital bed there. I drove over to Skinner Furniture Store in Columbus and purchased a small sofa which made into a bed. It was delivered and placed beside Vonzeal's bed where, during the day, it provided additional seating for family and visitors. At night I could let it out and sleep beside her. Vonzeal and I had purchased our very first bed and other furniture from Skinners; now fifty years later I purchased the very last piece of furniture we would buy together. It was a circle completed.

She was released from the hospital on April 5th, and I brought her home to LaGrange. During this period we had an unusual time together. I rarely left her bedside, and we talked and talked.

Vonzeal began planning for a "thanksgiving" dinner to be held as quickly as possible, in order to pull her family together for a final thanksgiving celebration. This would give her the opportunity to tell all her loved ones "goodbye."

We planned for this meal to be held on April 15th, and decided to use the exact same menu from the previous Thanksgiving. Our loving neighbor, Joyce, volunteered to prepare the meal precisely to Vonzeal's specifications, and did so with the assistance of her own sister.

The grandchildren arrived from various states; Vonzeal's beloved nieces came, brother L.V. and his wife, Carrie, everyone was there.

We had a wonderful day of laughing, visiting and hugging. She stressed to all her family the joyous anticipation of her homegoing, and with her smile and grace, helped ease the burden which lay heavily on our hearts. She ministered to us.

The five grandchildren performed entertainment skits for her enjoyment, singing and dancing. She hugged and kissed each and every one of them, and told the four older ones how thankful she was for their profession of faith in the Lord. She encouraged them to be prepared to meet her in the glorious resurrection. It was a day of joy.

On the morning of my 69th birthday, April 16th, Vonzeal got out of bed and came into the den where I was sitting and said, "Jim, I have a special gift for you. Will you open your hands, please?"

As I cupped my hands together, she placed the small white Case knife that Charles Bentley had given her almost twenty years before. "Charles gave this to me before he died, and now I would like to pass it on to you. Happy Birthday!" No one knew the heartache I felt at that moment as I received the little knife into my hands. I made a silent vow to carry it with me always until the moment I could, in turn, pass it on to Charles' only son, Mark. The Bentley children, Mark and Marilyn have always been close to us and referred to me as "Preacher Papa." Perhaps Mark will, in turn, pass the little knife on to his son, M. J., sometime in the future, thereby completing a circle of love that no blade, no matter how sharp, can ever sever.

Over the years Vonzeal helped me polish my sermons and one of her very favorites had become "The Value of a Minute." We discussed the contents of this sermon and how we must make the most of every moment together. So much could be lost; so much gained, if we could benefit from the time we had left together.

Our minutes together, from the moment of Vonzeal's release from the hospital until her homegoing, were spent reliving and discussing the wonderful life we had shared together with the Lord, Jesus Christ.

She planned her funeral as calmly and orderly as she did for the thanksgiving preparations. She spoke with Dr. Charles Q. Carter at Jonesboro First Baptist and Dr. Hugh Chambliss from Huntsville regarding her service. She made all the music plans with our son Jerry, who was minister of music at Blakely Methodist Church, and with Sharon Sewell, Minister of Music at First Baptist Church Bremen. The choir would be formed from several different churches – First Baptist Bremen, Villa Rica, Bowden, Tallapoosa and our home church in LaGrange. She selected the songs that she wanted sung. "Redeemed How I Love To Proclaim It", and she asked Jerry and his wife Beth, who has such a beautiful voice, to sing "Amazing Grace" as a victory song. She requested Sharon Sewell select a the song for the choir to sing. She chose "Great Is Thy Faithfulness".

In the process of all that, Vonzeal shared with me so many personal things, how she wanted to be dressed, the jewelry, make-up. Vonzeal asked Beth to sit at her bedside and watch her make up her face because she wanted to be sure she wasn't "over made," and Beth was given the responsibility of checking her makeup with the undertaker before Vonzeal's body was placed in the casket for viewing.

She apologized for leaving me, but said she had stayed far longer than she'd ever anticipated that she would live. She was grateful that she was leaving first because she thought that I would be far more able to manage alone than she could have. She assured me that perhaps there would come a time when I might want to marry again. As I began to weep, she took my hand and said, "Well, we don't have to talk about it, but if it happens it will be all right. And when it happens, you just let it happen."

We talked about the things she did not want me to do afterwards. For instance, she didn't want me to waste any time coming to the gravesite. "You know, we've talked about this all through the years; I'm not going to be there. I'm going to be in the presence of the Lord. So don't waste your time beside my grave."

One of the last things she told me was, "Jim, whatever you do . . . don't quit preaching and don't quit entertaining."

"I don't think I'll ever entertain again," I cried. My heart was breaking.

"But you will," she assured me, "and you'll need to. You're the best preacher I've ever heard." She thanked me for what she had learned under my preaching and she said, " even if it's the day after I'm buried, and you get an opportunity to preach or entertain, don't you miss it." She enunciated the last four words carefully and slowly as was her style when she was making a point.

When you're young you want to live until you're happily married. That happens, and then you want to live to have children. That happens, and then you want to live to see your children happily married. That happens, and then you want to live to see your grandchildren. Then that happens, and your grandchildren make you twice as happy as your own. You're happy when they come and happy when they leave. Grandchildren are fun. In fact, if we'd known how much fun they were, we'd have had them first.

And then there comes a time when you may not be

as anxious to see the things here on earth as you are to see the things beyond here. To me that's "dying grace."

Vonzeal did not weep. Not one tear did she shed until her last breath. Towards the end of Vonzeal's time here on earth she said, "You know, Jim, I understand that sermon on 'dying grace' better now." I was kneeling at her bedside. "You've explained it to me, and now I'm experiencing it. I'm rejoicing in what's going to happen when the end comes because you've told me and the Bible tells me that to be absent from the body is to be present with the Lord."

So many times I've used 1 Thessalonians, Chapter 4, beginning Verse 13 when Paul said, "But I would not have you to be ignorant, brethren, concerning them which are asleep, that ye sorrow not, even as others which have no hope. For if we believe that Jesus died and rose again, even so them also which sleep in Jesus will God bring with him. For the Lord himself shall descend from heaven with a shout, with the voice of the archangel and with the trump of God: and the dead in Christ shall rise first: Then we which are alive and remain shall be caught up together with them in the clouds, to meet the Lord in the air: and so shall we ever be with the Lord."

And the final verse, "Wherefore comfort one another with these words."

There is no way to misinterpret these words. Jesus is coming again.

Hebrews, Chapter 13:20-21, Paul was writing to young Jewish Christians, encouraging them in the faith, and he talks about the Lord Jesus Christ being the great shepherd. "Now the God of peace, that brought again from the dead our Lord Jesus, that great shepherd of the sheep, through the blood of the everlasting covenant, Make you perfect in every good work to do his will, working in you that which is well pleasing in his sight, through Jesus Christ; to whom be glory for ever and ever."

Which leads us immediately to the 23 Psalm, "The Lord is my Shepherd . . ."

On one of our trips to the Holy Land, I asked the guide to find a shepherd and ask if I could go out into the field with him for several hours. I went out and observed him and felt the quietness of that hillside and watched the sheep as they enjoyed the lush grass. I observed the shepherd as he walked in front of them. I glanced back and, it was eerie, but all those sheep were following him, nudging along, licking one another. And I realized that the shepherd was walking out in front so if there was danger, he would encounter it first, and the sheep would have safe ground to walk on.

John 10: 27-28 Jesus said, "My sheep hear my voice and I know them and they follow Me: and I give unto them eternal life: and they shall never perish...."

There's a difference when you know the Shepherd. "The Lord is my Shepherd, I shall not want." I knew of a little boy who misquoted it, "The Lord is my Shepherd, what more shall I want?"

During the brief two months of Vonzeal's illness our beloved Jeanne Bentley came to take care of us. In her very efficient way, she kept a record of every telephone call and every visitor we received. She organized our meals and helped us with our thank-you notes and paperwork. She tended Vonzeal as though she were a beloved sister, and indeed they were closer than most full-blooded sisters.

We were fortunate that our wonderful neighbor of twenty years, Joyce Yarborough, was a nurse, and she tended Vonzeal diligently throughout those weeks.

It was not an easy time for me as I kept watch over my sweetheart, but the Lord had placed Vonzeal and us in the very capable hands of Mrs. Bentley and Joyce Yarborough.

Vonzeal's brother, L. V., her only remaining sibling, and his wife, Carrie, drove their mobile home to LaGrange and parked it on our property. They took over the housekeeping duties, and it was a blessing to have them there during our greatest hour of need.

Mable and Harold Harris, likewise, blessed us with their time and dedication, always there to assist or lend a hand in any way.

First Baptist Church of Villa Rica, Georgia was the church we had been serving since the fall of 1992. Vonzeal encouraged me to continue with the ministry even though it took me away from her bedside during those hours. The wonderful people of Villa Rica ministered to us during Vonzeal's illness. Our kitchen was always filled with food sent by the ladies from the church; our yard work was done by the men from the church; they stayed with us in prayer, meeting every need during this difficult time.

Mrs. Bentley wrote a poem for Vonzeal during her stay with us:

ALL THE WORLD'S A STAGE

Good morning, Lord!
    My name is Vonzeal.
You've walked with me for many years
    And I thank you!
Just now, Lord, I yearn for Thee.
    My arms reach out to you.
So many friends have come to say,
    "Goodbye Vonzeal. We love you."
What a drama Lord, unfurling daily,
    Even now before my eyes.
I lift up to you the love they give to me.

It is an offering unto you.
Except for you I would not be
Receiving it into usefulness.

I see their tears – it seems so strange
That anyone would weep for me.
They want me here but I would go
My Lord, to be with Thee.
Come, receive me into your arms,
Guide me safely home.
Bring down the curtain, Lord.
I give to you their applause.
For all I am I owe to Thee.
Their love I have not earned.
So graciously you revealed yourself,
In this small light of mine.
May it shine on through years to come,
As a spotlight of your great love.
NOW, turn off the stage lights, Holy God.
Your child is ready to come home.

Jeanne G. Bentley
April 13, 1993 – 5:00 a.m.

On the Saturday afternoon of May 22nd , my son Jerry and I were kneeling by Vonzeal's bed, and I showered her with kisses. In a moment her eyes opened in surprise, and Jerry and I felt the presence of the Lord.

Her eyes closed, and one tear rolled down her cheek. I reached and caught it on my finger and brought it to my lips.

"Jerry, mother's gone."

I don't know how he did it, but he started singing, "And when the battle's over we shall wear a crown, we shall wear a crown . . ." and he sang the song all the way through.

As I sat there listening to him sing, I realized that Vonzeal's tear was the first tear she had shed since we had been told of her disease, and it was the last tear she would ever shed. There would be no more pain, no more weeping, for all of the former things had passed away for Vonzeal. It was a tear of joy for she had seen Jesus, and I had shared that moment with her. Revelations 21:1 "And I saw a new heaven and a new earth: for the first heaven and the first earth were passed away; and there was no more sea."

Jerry finished singing, and we prayed together before calling Jimmy in Orlando to break the news to him. Jimmy and Monte had traveled every weekend from Orlando to LaGrange. But this was one weekend when I had asked them to stay home and rest. Jimmy had said "goodbye" the previous weekend.

If you want to beat anxiety in death, you do so in spiritual preparation. And all of us will experience a home-going. And it will be magnificent.

"The Lord is my shepherd, I shall not want." He walks with us through the valley (not into it, but through it) of the shadow of death. "Surely goodness and mercy shall follow me all the days of my life: and I will dwell in the house of the Lord for ever."

THE HUNTSVILLE TIMES
by Bill Easterling

If it was hard being married to a high-profile preacher whose life never really has been his own, she didn't show it.

For the record, her husband has always said without her he couldn't have shouldered the cross God told him to bear.

From the moment they became partners almost 51 years ago, she handled the pressure of being his wife with a grace and a dignity which grew to be legendary.

If he was the hurricane, then she was the eye of the storm, and her tranquil soul and sweet spirit provided safe harbor where he could rest and refresh, knowing full well she would fit together the bits and pieces of family life without him directly being involved except when needed.

He could concentrate on preaching with crystal clear clarity the uncompromised word of God. He could conduct the Lord's business every day without interference. she was his mighty fortress, and the ministry of Jesus Christ prospered and grew because her presence allowed him to heed the call he received as a young man.

It didn't hurt that she was as beautiful outside as she was inside, because the complete package encouraged and influenced many women, married and single, in churches where they served to improve themselves, spiritually as well as physically.

Vonzeal Davis Dorriety was no saint, but she

was the closest to being one I've ever met.

Vonzeal died Saturday, two months after being told she had six to eights weeks to live. Monday, Dr. Hugh Chambliss of Huntsville eulogized her and Dr. Charles Q. Carter of Atlanta preached her funeral. The old First Baptist Church in downtown LaGrange rang with Christian celebration for an hour, and most of the tears that rolled down cheeks and fell to the floor were tears of joy.

Eight weeks ago, when doctors gave the Dorriety family the sad news, she called her husband and her sons to her bedside and said, "We have told people all our lives how to live in the presence of God, and now we're going to show them how to do it."

She never complained and didn't cry during her painful ordeal. Even at the end of her life, she handled the situation with her customary quiet, radiant grace. And she was, again, in the position of being a positive role model.

Terry Dorriety, 24, and a college student, said this: "My grandmother taught me how to comb my hair and how to coordinate my clothes. She taught me how to live life like a lady. Now she has taught me how to die with dignity."

Vonzeal Davis was 16 and they "waited" until Jim Dorriety was 18 before marrying in 1942. Monday, he said they'd found themselves another favorite love song in the last few weeks, a current country hit called, "Like Two Sparrows in a Hurricane." His favorite part goes like this:

"She had his ring on her finger and he had the key to her heart."

Chapter 17

Present

—➤◦⫷—

And sure enough, just as she'd predicted, the day after we buried our dear Vonzeal, I received a call from Dr. George Phillips in Owensboro, Kentucky. He identified himself as a Methodist evangelist, and executive director of the Robert Sheffie Memorial Camp Meeting, an annual event in Pearisburg, Virginia.

"Dr. Phillips, I'm sorry." I croaked, "I'm not in a position to talk to you. I just buried my wife yesterday plus I have laryngitis. But my son, Jimmy, is standing right here. I'll put him on the phone."

Jimmy spoke to him and learned that fifty churches are involved in the Robert Sheffie Memorial Camp meeting. The preacher who had been hired could not attend. Would I come and be the preacher? I learned that Robert Sheffie was an itinerate Methodist preacher. Born in 1820, he had led the Wabash Camp Meeting for years and years until his death. He was so famous for so many outstanding things that Bob Jones University made a movie of his life entitled, "One Saint in the Wilderness."

I had been recommended to take the place of the other preacher. Remembering what Vonzeal had said, I knew that I could not say no.

Within the same hour, a call came from Bowden Baptist Church, inviting me to come back as their interim pastor. This was the church where Vonzeal and I had pastored in 1991.[11] I felt it would just break my heart to go back where we had spent our last ministry.

Then I received a call from Central Baptist Church in Warner Robins, asking if I would preach on the last Sunday in June. Remember, this was the church where I had been the founding pastor in 1955. Over the years I had continued to return to Central for Homecoming every fifth year and had returned during every pastor's tenure, either for revival or a special program.

"Yes," I answered, "I can." Then the caller asked if I could preach the following Sunday, July 4th. "Yes, I can, but where is your pastor?"

"We're without a pastor, but we want to talk to you about the possibility of being our transitional pastor, staying with us for a year and helping us." They wanted me to help them find new direction and get recommitted for the future.

So suddenly, I was faced with many decisions and opportunities. Closing up the house, I said goodbye to Mrs. Bentley, who was returning to her home in Huntsville. My own pain was so great that I, without meaning to, overlooked the pain that she was feeling. She drove herself away from the house that day, mentally and physically drained. Looking back, I should

---

[11]My daughter-in-law, Montez, who co-authored this book, noted that several times I had mentioned when "Vonzeal and I" had been the pastor of a church. I explained that in my mind Vonzeal had been as much the pastor of our churches as I. She helped me with sermons, and her ministry always seemed equal in my mind. Had it not been for her simple faith, my life might have taken a different direction. Her words, "if it's in the Bible, it's true!", directed our life.

never have allowed her to leave alone; but the Lord looked after her and saw her safely home.

At the Camp Meeting I found some of the most wonderful Christian people, in those mountain folks in that area of Virginia, that I'd ever met. I didn't know a single soul in the personnel of the camp meeting – the leader, Dr. George Phillips nor the music director, Dr. Charles Dennis, and yet there was a warmth and connection almost instantaneously established with them.

On the first morning, I shared with the Bible Study group my dilemma regarding the decisions concerning my two beloved churches. This group began to pray with me about the matter, and every single morning someone there would pray and ask the Lord to give me direction. Realizing that God was going to give the answer, I simply put out a fleece based on Judges 6:36-40,

> "And Gideon said unto God, If thou wilt save Israel by mine hand, as thou hast said, Behold, I will put a fleece of wool in the floor; and if the dew be on the fleece only, and it be dry upon all the earth beside, then shall I know that thou wilt save Israel by mine hand, as thou hast said. And it was so: for he rose up early on the morrow, and thrust the fleece together, and wringed the dew out of the fleece, a bowl full of water. And Gideon said unto God, Let not thine anger be hot against me, and I will speak but this once: let me prove, I pray thee, but this once with the fleece; let it now be dry only upon the fleece, and upon all the ground let there be dew. And God did so that night: for it was dry upon the fleece only, and there was dew on all the ground."

Knowing that Central was a large church with over three thousand members, my fleece would be determined as follows: if there were any opposition whatsoever to my returning, then I would not go.

Wednesday night, when I returned to the motel from the camp meeting, I received a call from the vice chairman of the deacons in Warner Robins. "We have unanimously recommended that you come as transitional pastor. We made a presentation to the church this evening, and there was not one single opposition. In fact, the church broke out in applause. When can you give us an answer?"

"Now. I'll come!"

So forty-one years later, I have made a full circle. I feel that I have done so with God's approval and Vonzeal's approval, as I give direction to Central Baptist Church.

A few weeks afterward I dropped by Jerry and Beth's house for the weekend. When I arrived Maggie had made several preparations for me. She grabbed my hand, ushered me into the den and seated me in the big overstuffed lounge chair in front of the television. Then she brought a pillow and plumped it up behind my head. Next, she delivered a big glass of iced tea and a box of Kleenex. When she had me all comfortable, she crawled onto my lap and said, "It's okay to cry, G'Daddy," and put her little head on my shoulders. It was a touching moment, but she was so cute that I was more inclined to smile. I almost felt obligated to cry.

Later that evening Maggie insisted I sleep in the extra single bed in her bedroom. We kissed good night, and I closed my eyes to sleep. Moments later I felt a gentle touch on my pajama sleeve. "G'Daddy," she whispered. "Here's the bunny rabbit that Grandmother kissed all over for me. You sleep with it tonight, and if you need a kiss from Grandmother, you can get one anytime during the night."

She placed the little rabbit in my arms and retreated to her own bed. I lay there, my heart breaking and shattering into a million pieces. I wept silently for hours, a grown man, clutching a stuffed animal covered with Vonzeal's kisses. The next morning, I returned the wet little bunny to Maggie's bed.

Remember one thing from the pages of this book . . . there is no laughter in hell. Jesus said, "Be of good cheer, for I have overcome the world. I came that you might have life and that you may have it more abundantly." Christians should be the happiest people on the face of the Earth.

I've always said if long-facedness constitutes Christianity, I know an old gray mule in Alabama with more Christianity than anyone else I've ever seen. I believe the Lord wants us to smile and be happy and enjoy the earth, the beauty of the earth and the things of the earth. There's nothing that God does not want us to enjoy within the frame-work of his direction and leadership.

The family doesn't know why, but even though Vonzeal's Bible had hundreds of notations in the margins and underlines throughout the pages, the only Bible scripture notated on the front white page of her Bible was Isaiah 58:11. "And the Lord shall guide thee continually, and satisfy thy soul in drought, and make fat thy bones: and thou shalt be like a watered garden, and like a spring of water, whose waters fail not."

"If it's in the Bible, it's true!"

In her role as a preacher's wife, Vonzeal lived by the famous declaration found in Ruth 1:16b, ". . . whither thou goest I will go." Now I must wait to reciprocate. Our love triangle has been temporarily broken, but one day we will be a trinity again.

Amen

APPENDIX

THE VALUE OF A MINUTE

Luke 4:1, "Jesus being full of the Holy Ghost returned from Jordan and was led by the spirit into the wilderness being 40 days tempted of the devil. And in those days, He did eat nothing. And when they were ended, He afterwards hungered. The devil said unto him, "If thou be the son of God, command this stone that it be made bread." Jesus answered him saying, "It is written that man shall not live by bread alone, but by every word of God." Then the devil took Him up into a high mountain, and showed unto Him all the kingdoms of the world in just a moment of time. A minute of time.

The devil said unto Him, "All this power will I give thee and the glory of them for that is delivered unto me and to whomsoever I will, I give it. If thou therefore will worship me all shall be thine." Jesus answered and said to him, "Get thee behind me, Satan, for it is written, thou shall worship the Lord thy God and Him only shalt thy serve."

Then the devil brought Jesus to Jerusalem and sat Him on a pinnacle of the temple and said unto Him, "If thou be the Son of God, cast thouself down for hence, for it is written that He shall give His angels charge over thee to keep thee . And in their hands they shall bear thee up, lest at any time thou dash thou foot against the stone." And Jesus answering said unto him, "Thou shall not tempt the Lord thy God."

It is my opinion that these three temptations of Jesus represents the three most important minutes in the life of the Lord Jesus Christ.

It was because of the sin of one man that death was

passed upon all men. When Adam disobeyed God and Eve took of the forbidden fruit, sin began. Death was passed on mankind. Therefore by the death of a single being God's plan said, "Salvation shall be put in reach of all people."

The only person that has ever lived a perfect life was Jesus. He was the sinless Saviour. No one else.

One night a preacher was foolish in asking his congregation, "Have you ever known anyone perfect other than Jesus?" And one little lady raised her hand timidly. The preacher was shocked and said, "You're known someone other than Jesus that was perfect." She nodded. He said, "Would you tell us who?" and she answered, "My husband's first wife."

She may have thought she was right but she was mistaken. There's been no perfect person, no perfect husband, no perfect wife, no perfect individual – except Jesus, the Saviour of the world He was the only one who was perfect. He never committed a sin.

If he had permitted Himself to sin, if he had given into the devil, if he had submitted to any one of these temptations; then He could not have been the Saviour of the world.

Notice how simple these three temptations were. Forty days fasting. And it is said afterwards, Jesus was hungry. No wonder.

You can look at me and tell I haven't been four hours fasting. Last year when I was having my physical I was instructed to eat nothing after midnight. The next morning I went to Emery and had my examination which lasted all morning and well past the noon hour. In the early afternoon, Dr. Paul Seavy was fluoroscoping my stomach and said, "Preacher, how would you like to have some country ham, red-eye gravy and hot biscuits?" And before I could answer he starting laughing and said, "I wish you could have seen your stomach. It was undulating, twisting and turning." I wasn't aware of that, but the suggestion of food did that automatically.

Take a look at this temptation. Forty days without food. "If thy be the son of God command this stone that it be made bread." Jesus saw a stone that may perhaps have reminded him of bread from Mary's oven.

Before my first visit to Israel I thought of the wilderness of Judea as being trees and forest. How shocked I was to learn that it's a barren land with rocks of every description on the ground everywhere. Just rocks, rocks, rocks.

But Jesus saw a stone and the devil was aware of what he saw. Don't forget, the devil is aware of every desire you have in your mind and he'll come to the very seat of that desire to tempt you at that moment. And when Jesus gazed upon the stone that reminded him of bread, knowing that he was hungry, the devil said, "If thou be the Son of God, command this stone that it be made bread."

Jesus could have said, "Stone, be bread!" and it would have been bread because He's the Son of God.

It was within His power to change the stone to bread, but had He done that, He would have been committing a sin. Jesus never performed a miracle for himself. He could raise the dead and multiply the fishes for the multitudes, but he did not do anything for himself. Everything he did was for others.

Therefore, He answered with the word of God, "Man shall not live by bread alone." We must live by this bread. We need to feed our souls on this bread. Foolish is the person who doesn't, for if you want to find the will of God for your life, you'll find it in the Word of God. No where else. So don't ever hesitate to know that this is important. We need to feed ourselves the Bread of Life.

Well, since that didn't work the devil tried again and showed Jesus all the kingdoms of the world. What a magnificent thing it would be to be the king of all the world to have dominion over everything. And the devil could have. He was the prince of the power of the air. This moment when he said to Jesus if you'll just worship me, all shall be thine. Jesus answered, "Get thee behind me Satan."

I heard about this preacher whose wife would spend money for clothes that they couldn't afford and she would say, "Oh, I forgot, honey. I didn't really mean to do that." He said, "Might I suggest that you do like Jesus. Next time you find something and you're tempted, just say Get thee behind me Satan. That'll be a reminder." He came in one night and she was wearing a new dress. He said, "I thought I reminded you to say 'Get thee behind me Satan,' She said, "I did say that and Satan said it looked as good from the rear and it did from the front."

Isn't it amazing how we can figure out a way to get around temptations saying it won't hurt us. I'll do this and I'll take that and I'll get along with this and get along with that, knowing that we are permitting a sin or progressing towards sin. Creeping away from the Lord. Before you realize it, you're too far gone.

Not the Lord Jesus for he answered immediately, "Get thee behind me satan. Thou shall worship the Lord thy God and Him only shalt thy serve."

We need to worship Him and serve Him. We don't serve the preacher. We don't serve the church. We serve the body of Christ, the Lord Jesus.

Keep your eyes upon Jesus.

Some forty-five years ago during a revival meeting, Brother Andy Miles would pace down in front as he preached, "Keep your eyes upon Jesus. Don't set your eyes upon Brother Andy. Brother Andy may disappoint you, but Jesus never will."

I like that thought. I may disappoint you, but Jesus never will. Keep your eyes upon Him. Look full in His wonderful face. The things of earth will grow strangely dim in the light of His glory and grace. We need to worship Him and only Him.

Then the Devil brought Jesus to the pinnacle of the temple and said, "How about it, just jump off. What a thrill. You don't have to worry about the ground, just jump! He'll give His angels charge over thee. They'll catch you before you hit the ground."

It's foolish for someone to say, I don't know what's right and what's wrong. This Book tells you what's right and what's wrong. You don't even need a preacher to find out what you need to do. You need The Word. More than anything else – The Bible. And if it's in the Bible – it's true!

Don't tempt the Lord. Don't think that you can make it on your own. Don't think that you're strong enough to stand. Jesus warned us in Corinthians 10:12, "Wherefore let him that thinketh he standeth take heed lest he fall."

If you ever get to the point that you feel that you are beyond sin, that you will not sin, that you cannot sin... you're probably on the verge of sinning. Run scared all the time.

Don't be tempted. These are the three most important minutes in the life of Jesus. How valuable is a minute of time. The Bible is so filled with examples, it would take days to point them all out.

Esau lost his birthright to Jacob in a moment of time. In Genesis 25:27 Esau was first born of the twins and the birthright was his. Esau grew to be a man of the field, Jacob became a man of the home. Esau enjoyed hunting in the fields, Jacob like to stay at home and cook. Esau returned from a hunting expedition and was faint with hunger. Jacob was cooking, the Bible mentions venison hash, perhaps with potatoes, onions, garlic, and the aromas caught the nostrils of Esau and Esau said to Jacob, "Give me a mess of pottage. I want something to eat." And Jacob said sure, just sell me this day thy birthright.

I don't think Esau intended to do that. I think he just kicked in the sand and said, "Oh, sure whatever. All I want is something to eat." In that moment he desired more than anything else a bowl of stew. Not really knowing that to take that stew, he lost his birthright in that minute of time .

Another example was David, a man after God's own heart. A man who loved the Lord and the Lord loved David. David was a great Christian. One evening he walked out onto the roof of the palace and saw on the next roof Bathsheba taking a bath and gave into his appetite and desired her for himself. And in that moment of time, he lost his fellowship with God.

Ask yourself, how valuable is one minute of time. There's enough time in one minute to lose, not only your fellowship with God as His child, but even enough time for you to lose your soul. You can lose so much in one moment of carelessness.

Psalms 119: 11, "Thy word have I hid in mine heart that I might not sin against thee." We need to memorize scripture and hide it in our hearts and read it and conserve it. Then when we need it, it will be there. And it will come to our rescue.

Or else in a moment of carelessness we will lose so much.

Luke 23: 39, The two thieves on the cross, convicted to death, ready to be crucified. "And one of the malefactors which were hanged railed on him, saying, If thou be Christ, save thyself and us. But the other, answering rebuked him, saying, Dost not thou fear God, seeing thou art in the same condemnation? And we indeed justly; for we receive the due reward of our deeds: but this man hath done nothing amiss. And he said unto Jesus, Lord, remember me when thou comest into they kingdom. And Jesus said unto him, Verily I say unto thee, To day shalt thou be with me in paradise." In that moment his eternal soul was saved forever. For he said, "Remember me when thou comest into they kingdom."

Luke 15: 11-32 tells the story of the prodigal son – yet another example. The younger son didn't want to stay at home anymore so he asked his father to give him his share of worldly goods. He went out and wasted everything in unrighteous living. He lived it up, he partied, he wasted his sustenance. When his money was gone, he had no friends. No one would have anything to do with him. He began begging and no one would even give him food. Then he attached himself to a herd of swine and the Bible says, "And he would fain have filled his belly with the husks that the swine did eat: and no man gave unto him. And when he came to himself, he said, How many hired servants of my father's have bread enough and to spare, and I perish with hunger! I will arise and go to my father, and will say unto him, Father, I have sinned against heaven, and before thee" While in the midst of that hog pen, covered with filth and dirt the Bible says, he thought within himself. How long does it take to have a mental image? Only a flash. How many servants of my father has food to spare? and here I am starving. I know what I'll do. I'll arise and go to my father. He got up and began to make his way back. His father saw him and said, "Bring forth the best robe and put on him, and put a ring on his hand, and shoes on his feet. And bring hither the fatted calf, and kill it; and let us eat and be merry: For this my son was dead, and is alive again; he was lost, and is found."

For all the time he was lost, in a minute of time he was found. His salvation came before he could get out of the hog pen, the moment that he decided to go to his father. He gained all of his future in that one minute.

Saul of Tarsus was on the Damascus Road with orders to find and persecute Christians and throw them in prison that they be eaten by the lions. On that journey, in a flash from heaven he was blinded by that light and heard his name. Acts 9:4 "And he fell to the earth, and heard a voice saying unto him, Saul, Saul, why persecutest thou me?" and he said, Who art thou, Lord? And the Lord said, I am Jesus whom thou persecutest: it is hard for thee to kick against the pricks. And he trembling and astonished said, Lord what wilt thou have me to do? And the Lord said unto him, Arise and go into the city, and it shall be told thee what thou must do....And he was three days without sight, and neither did eat nor drink." And he received instructions for the delivery of a great sermon. Instantly, in only a moment of time, he was totally changed and completely restored even to the point where he became Paul the Apostle who wrote so much of the new Testament and carried the gospel to Rome and was perhaps responsible for us receiving the Gospel in our nation today.

Another example is in Acts 24 when Paul was arrested and brought before Felix the governor. Paul witnessed to Felix and reasoned to him and Felix was so convinced in his heart that he told Paul that he was free to go. "And after certain days, when Felix came with his wife, Drusilla, which was a Jewess, he sent for Paul, and heard him concerning the faith in Christ. And as he reasoned of righteousness, temperance, and judgment to come, Felix trembled, and answered, Go thy way for this time; when I have a convenient season, I will call for thee."

It appears that Felix wanted to accept the decision that Paul had presented him, but he could not. The Bible never mentions him again, so we conclude that he never had another moment to accept Jesus and he lost his eternal soul.

We Baptist's don't have confessionals, but I've heard so many confessions. So have other pastors. Some men have lost their families in just a moment of passion, some have lost their homes in a careless moment. How valuable is one minute of time?

But let's reverse the whole procedure and ask , "how much can be gained in a moment? How valuable is a minute in what we can gain?"

Peter denied the Lord in a minute of time and the moment he did he remembered that Jesus had warned, Matthew 26: 34 "Jesus said unto him "Verily I say unto thee, That this night, before the cock crow, thou shalt deny me thrice. Peter said unto him, Though I should die with tree, yet will I not deny thee." And that night when Peter followed Jesus as far as he could then lingered in the courtyard with the enemies of Jesus, Matthew 26:69 "Now Peter sat without in the palace: and a damsel came unto him saying, thou also wast with Jesus of Galilee. But he denied before them all saying, I know not what thou sayest." Later another maid asked Peter again and more emphatically he denied it, "I do not know the man" That was number two. Just at the daylight hour they said again, " Surely thou also art one of them; for they speech betrayeth thee. Then began he to curse and to swear, saying, I know not the man. And immediately the cock crew." and he remembered the words of Jesus and he went out and wept bitterly. Tears of repentance. And in that one moment of repentance Peter's soul was saved.

Several years into my ministry while working in my den late one night, I received a telephone call. I answered the ring to find a young lady, I'll call her Judy, on the other end of the line. Although I didn't know her, I immediately could tell she was in much distress; she was weeping and almost incoherent. After telling me her name, she began this story. Since she had become a teenager she had constantly rebelled against her parents. Truancy and violent arguments had become a way of home life. No longer able to live this way, she had swallowed several bottles of pills, then unable to die alone, had randomly called a couple of pastors who unfortunately had not realized the severity of the situation. Then she found my name. Judy wanted me to be on the telephone line with her as her life ebbed away; even in her destitution, she didn't want to die alone.

It doesn't take much imagination to know how I reacted. My son, Jerry, was studying in the next room and in desperation, I removed my shoe and slammed it against the wall to get his attention. Quickly I scribbled a note to him. Go to the neighbors house and call the police! Trace this phone call! I have a suicide attempt on the line!

While Jerry ran to the neighbors, it was left to me to keep Judy on the line. Why are you rebelling against your parents? Surely you love your parents? Tell me about yourself. Judy, I love you and God loves you!

In those few moments of time in which I kept her talking, the police were able to trace the call, summon the ambulance and the paramedics were on the way to Judy's home. And her life was saved.

But, I determined that just saving her life wasn't enough and began visiting her in her hospital room, talking about Jesus, telling her about the salvation that would set her free. And she accepted Jesus Christ into her life and in a moment of time, her salvation was complete.

Judy is a mother of two now and has become a dear friend whom I've kept in contact with over the years.

I John 1:9 "If we confess our sins, He's faithful and just to forgive us our sins and to cleanse us from all unrighteousness."

How much can be gained in a moment of time. In one moment you can change your direction from hell to heaven. I did as a bare-foot fourteen year old boy when I made the decision to walk down that aisle. I didn't even have on my best overalls. But in that moment when Brother Glover said, "Son, do you want to give your life to Jesus and be saved?", I lifted my hand towards him, "Yes, sir I do" and changed the direction of my life – in a moment of time.

Much can be gained in one minute of time.

It takes thirty seconds to sing one stanza of "JUST AS I AM" and we're going to sing all six stanzas. This could be the three most important minutes in your life. You can be saved.